Victory in Spiritual Warfare

Tony Evans

Victory in Spiritual Warfare

Tony Evans

HARVEST HOUSE PUBLISHERS
EUGENE, OREGON

Cover by Koechel Peterson & Associates, Inc., Minneapolis, Minnesota

Backcover photo by Iam Second/Trey Hill

Cover illustration © iStockphoto/MandarinTree

VICTORY IN SPIRITUAL WARFARE
Copyright © 2011 by Tony Evans
Published by Harvest House Publishers
Eugene, Oregon 97402
www.harvesthousepublishers.com

Library of Congress Cataloging-in-Publication Data
 Evans, Tony
 Victory in spiritual warfare / Tony Evans.
     p. cm.
 ISBN 978-0-7369-3999-7 (pbk.)
 ISBN 978-0-7369-4278-2 (eBook)
 1. Spiritual warfare. 2. Christian life. 3. Success—Religious aspects—Christianity. I. Title.
 BV4509.5.E833 2011
 235'.4—dc22

                                                    2010050022

Printed in the United States of America

16 17 18 19 20 21 22 / LB-SK / 16 15 14 13 12

Dedicated to my oldest grandchild,
Kariss (Bear)—whom I love deeply.

Acknowledgments

I would like to thank my friends at Harvest House Publishers—Bob Hawkins Jr., LaRae Weikert, and Nick Harrison—for their partnership in this work. May this book be the beginning of something great together.

CONTENTS

Part 1

THE BATTLE

1

THE NATURE OF THE BATTLE

There's a story told about a painting titled *Checkmate*. As the story goes, on one side of a chessboard sits the devil, full of laughter. His hand is poised, ready to make his next move. On the other side of the chessboard sits a shaking, frightened young man. Sweat covers his forehead, dripping down and mixing with a solitary tear on his cheek. The game is obviously drawing to a close, and the winner appears to have already been decided.

One day, a chess champion from a far off country visited the gallery. Naturally, the painting caught his attention, inviting him to examine it for a very long time. In fact, while others had moved on throughout the gallery, the chess champion remained fixated on the game and especially on the devil, who sat eagerly waiting for his next turn, in which he planned to steal this man's soul.

Minutes turned into hours as the chess champion studied the board from every possible angle. The sweat on the young man's forehead urged him to continue. Finally, as the gallery was about to close, the chess champion found the proprietor of the gallery and asked him, "Sir, would you happen to have a chessboard here?"

After looking around in several of the offices, he located a chessboard and brought it to the man. The chess champion laid the board out at the base of the painting precisely as it was in the painting. He made a move and then countered that move in the only way that the devil could to avoid checkmate. He then made another move, and countered it again knowing that the devil would have to defend himself in his next move as well. The chess champion did this several more times, putting the devil on the defensive each and every time. Eventually, a loud yell was heard throughout the gallery as the chess champion cried out in relief, "I did it! I did it! I did it!"

Turning to the painting, the chess champion lowered his voice and said, "Young man, your enemy miscalculated a very important move. I uncovered it, and as a result, you don't have to lose! You win!"

This chess champion had discovered a way not only for the young man to escape but also to checkmate the devil himself.

Friend, if you have picked up this book, the chances are that you may have felt like the man in the painting. Fear or anxiety has crept up on you as you imagine the devil preparing to make the final move in your personal life, marriage, home, health, career, finances, or any number of other arenas. Satan's confident laughter and swift moves have tricked you into believing that he is running the show and calling the shots. He has been toying with your emotions as if you were a puppet on a string.

But as we journey through this study together, I encourage you to wipe the sweat from your forehead and dry the tears from your eyes. You can do this because you have a Champion who knows how to guide your every move. In fact, this Champion has already made the final move on the devil, securing your victory forever. If you will simply play out the remainder of the game according to His directions and underneath the overarching rule of His kingdom agenda, you will claim your victory. That is guaranteed.

The great thing is that you don't have to earn your victory, nor do you have to figure it out for yourself. God has already given you everything you need in order to make your next move on your path to triumph. As we begin, I want you to realize this key principle: You are not fighting *for* victory—you are fighting *from* victory. This battle has already been won!

The History of the Battle

To grasp the truth behind this principle, you first need to understand the history of the battle. It all began when God made the first move by creating the angels. Lucifer, the anointed angel, responded negatively to that move by rebelling against God and taking one-third of the angels with him in that rebellion. God countered that move by creating man, in His own image, a little lower than the angels. Satan rebelled against that move by enticing Adam and Eve to sin, thus turning earth over to his control.

God then countered Satan's move by providing a redemptive covering for Adam and Eve so they could return back to fellowship with God. Satan made his next move by inciting Cain to kill Abel in order to cut off the godly line.

But God responded to Satan's move through the birth of Seth, making a way for men to begin calling on the name of the Lord again. Satan countered that move by luring Nimrod at the Tower of Babel into thinking he could make himself and his people as high as the heavens.

For God's next move, He turned His gaze onto a man named Abraham, calling out a nation through him to be holy and set apart. Satan, however, countered that move by trapping this nation in Egypt under Pharaoh's rule. But then God grabbed Moses in Midian and placed him in position to knock Pharaoh out of the equation altogether.

Throughout the remainder of the Old Testament, the game went on like this—move, countermove, move, countermove. By the end of the Old Testament, we have reached a time of four hundred years where no move is recorded by either side as both sit staring at the board in silence.

But when the New Testament opens up, we see God reach for a special piece—His own son, Jesus Christ—and move Him into a new location, from heaven to earth. Satan attempts to counter God's move by tempting Jesus in the wilderness. Jesus overcomes his move through using the Word of God. So Satan then tries what he thinks is going to be his final move of checkmate by orchestrating the crucifixion of Jesus Christ. But Satan miscalculated something very important because he didn't realize that death on the cross was not a checkmate move. In fact, it was just a setup for the final move that God would make to checkmate Satan by raising Jesus from the dead.

The accomplishment of the cross, through the resurrection of

Christ, was God's final move and offered each one of us victory over an enemy who is seeking to intimidate, deceive, and destroy us. The ultimate winner of this game has been decided. Victory has been secured. While you and I are on earth and still in play, we need to live in light of the truth of the victory gained through that final move—the resurrection of Jesus Christ. Because of that decisive move by God, Satan no longer has authority over you to defeat you. His only means to overcome you is to deceive you—to make you believe that the winner of the battle is yet undecided.

How the Spiritual Impacts the Physical

By illustrating spiritual warfare though a simple game of chess, I don't mean to minimize the severity of the battle nor the enormous depth of pain and number of casualties that have resulted from it. It *is* a battle. We are in a war. In fact, the war we are in is like no other war that any of us have ever known or heard about or could even conceive. If I were to ask you to think of the absolute worst war in human history, it would pale in comparison to the spiritual battle waging all around us.

This war is different from all other wars not only because of its sheer magnitude and scope but also because this war is fought in a place we have never seen. Spiritual warfare is *the cosmic conflict waged in the invisible, spiritual realm but simultaneously fleshed out in the visible, physical realm.* To put it another way, the *root* of the war is something you cannot see, but the *effects* of the war are clearly seen and felt. This is because everything physical is either influenced or caused by something spiritual.

Behind every physical disturbance, setback, ailment, or issue we face lies a spiritual root. Unless we first identify and deal with the root spiritual cause, our attempts to fix the physical problem will provide only temporary relief at best. In other words, everything that your five senses experience physically is first generated by something that your five senses cannot detect.

In light of this truth, you and I need to engage a sixth sense—a spiritual sense—when doing battle in this war. We must employ that which goes beyond physiology and address the spiritual root before we can truly fix the physical fruit. Here is the key to experiencing and living out on earth the victory that God has already secured in heaven: to learn how to intentionally and effectively do battle in the spiritual realm.

Satan often tries to prevent you from taking the spiritual realm seriously. If he can divert your attention away from the spiritual realm, he can keep you away from the only place where your victory is found. If he can distract you with people or things you can see, taste, touch, hear, or smell, he can keep you from living a life of victory.

The Location of the Battle

This battle is so important and its spoils so costly, it is essential that we start at the beginning and lay a solid foundation for our strategy. The first thing you need to know is where this battle takes place. Paul gives us the answer in the sixth chapter of Ephesians, which is the passage we will be using as the basis for our study throughout this book.

> Finally, be strong in the Lord and in the strength of His might. Put on the full armor of God, so that you will be able to stand firm against the schemes of the devil. For our struggle is not against flesh and blood, but against the rulers, against the powers, against the world forces of this darkness, against the spiritual forces of wickedness *in the heavenly places* (Ephesians 6:10-12).

Paul tells us that our battle is not against flesh and blood. Our battle is not against our neighbor, spouse, coworker, child, or even our own propensities or weaknesses in our flesh. People are simply conduits of the spiritual battle taking place in another realm. Our battle, according to the Word of God, is against the rulers, powers, and world forces of wickedness located in heavenly places. "Heavenly places" simply means in the spiritual realm.

Here's a second principle I want you to take hold of: Whatever has gone on, is going on, or will go on in your visible, physical world is rooted in the invisible, spiritual realm. If you do not know how to navigate in the spiritual realm, you cannot hope to truly overcome in the physical realm.

This highlights a problem we often run into. We usually try to fix things in the physical realm by using methods of this world even though this world is not where our problems originate. We are like a police officer in his living room shooting his TV because he sees a criminal on a reality show pulling a gun. If the officer shoots at the television, he will have merely added to the mess that's going on. He might feel better for a moment because he did something, but in the end, nothing has been solved. In fact, things have only gotten worse.

Our battles originate in the spiritual realm—the heavenly places— so the only way to fight them is with weapons that work in that realm.

Heavenly Places

Paul uses the phrase "heavenly places" a number of times in the book of Ephesians, letting us know both the scope and occupants of the location. His first reference to this realm comes in chapter 1, verse 3: "Blessed be the God and Father of our Lord Jesus Christ, who has blessed us with *every spiritual blessing* in the heavenly places in Christ."

We learn from this verse that everything God is ever going to do for us, He has already done. Every spiritual blessing is already located in this unseen realm. Every promise God has ever made and plans to fulfill on your behalf, every gift you will ever receive, and every hope that will ever be satisfied has already been deposited in your account in the spiritual realm. God has "blessed us with *every* spiritual blessing in the heavenly places in Christ." Your blessings and victory are already located there with your name written on them, waiting for you to grab them, use them, and walk in them.

Many believers live defeated lives simply because they are unaware of this truth. Yet Paul makes it clear in this passage that we have already been blessed with *every* spiritual blessing in the spiritual realm.

In spiritual warfare, Satan tries to deceive you into believing that God is holding out on you and that it is up to you to get God to give you both blessings and victory. Satan wants you to think that if you pray more, give more, serve more, sin less, do better, or worship more, maybe God will give you more. This shifts the focus off of God and what He has already done in the spiritual realm and puts the focus on you and what you need to do in the physical realm. Doing those things in the physical realm is good and beneficial for spiritual growth and cultivating intimacy with God and others, but those things are not the keys to accessing what God already has for you in the spiritual realm.

The way to access the power of your blessings is through a biblical understanding and application of grace through faith. In grace, God has made every believer complete in Jesus Christ. Religious "works" that we do in an effort to get something from God actually nullify grace (Galatians 5:1-4) because grace and works can never be mixed (Romans 11:6). Grace is the point of access to God.

The way we enter this point of access is through faith. Faith is acting as if God is telling the truth. It is acting as if something is true even when it doesn't *appear* to be true in order that it might *be shown to be* true simply because God *said* it's true. The job of faith is to discover what the spiritual blessings in the heavenly places already are, ask God for them, and make life choices in light of that reality. We will look more deeply at grace and faith a little later.

The Occupants

So far we have seen that you are not fighting *for* victory—you are fighting *from* a position of victory. We have also seen that whatever has gone on, is going on, or will go on in your physical world is rooted in the spiritual realm. And every spiritual blessing is located in this spiritual realm. Paul tells us more about the spiritual realm when he writes, "These are in accordance with the working of the strength of His might which He brought about in Christ, when He raised Him from the dead and *seated Him* at His right hand in the heavenly places" (Ephesians 1:19-20).

Paul has already told us that our blessings are waiting for us to access them in heavenly places, and he now tells us that the One who is in charge, Jesus Christ, is seated in these same heavenly places. That means that if you want to get to the One who is in charge—Jesus—you will need to approach Him where He is—in the spiritual realm, the heavenly places. In the next chapter of Ephesians, Paul gives us more details about this.

> But God, being rich in mercy, because of His great love
> with which He loved us, even when we were dead in our
> transgressions, made us alive together with Christ (by grace
> you have been saved), and raised us up with Him, and
> *seated us with Him* in the heavenly places in Christ Jesus
> (Ephesians 2:4-6).

We've seen that our blessings are located in heavenly places and that Jesus Christ is seated in heavenly places. Now we learn that *we ourselves* are seated with Jesus in these same heavenly places. Right this very minute, you and I are spiritually seated with Christ in the spiritual realm.

This is an important truth to remember. If you are focusing only on where you are sitting right now physically, you are not viewing your location as being in the same place as where the solutions to your problems actually exist. Where you are physically is not the only place you are located. You are equally located in another realm. Paul tells us that at the moment you trusted in Christ for your salvation, you were transported to another realm. Even though your physical body is here on earth, your spirit—the part of you that has been designed with the capacity to control your physical body—is operating in another location.

Paul tells us more about this other location in the next chapter of Ephesians.

> To me, the very least of all saints, this grace was given, to
> preach to the Gentiles the unfathomable riches of Christ,
> and to bring to light what is the administration of the mys-
> tery which for ages has been hidden in God who created
> all things; so that the manifold wisdom of God might now
> be made known through the church *to the rulers and the
> authorities* in the heavenly places (Ephesians 3:8-10).

Not only are your spiritual blessings, Jesus Christ, and you yourself located in the spiritual realm at this point in time, the angels (rulers and authorities) are also operating in the spiritual realm. Why is this important to know? Because it is better to have an angel battling a demon than to battle a demon yourself in your flesh. If you are facing a demonic problem, you need an angelic solution.

The Bible calls God "the Lord of hosts." That name refers to His military charge over an angelic corps whose job is to go up against any demonic actions that are attacking you. You may be physically strong, you may lift weights, and you might be powerful in your body, but trust me—you are no competition for a demon. In order to call on angelic help, you need to have a heavenly mind-set because angels do battle in heavenly places.

What is critical to note in our look at angels is that every Christian has at least one angel who has been assigned to operate on his or her behalf in the spiritual realm. We read in Hebrews 1:14 (NIV), "Are not all angels ministering spirits sent to serve those who will inherit salvation?" You have someone who knows and understands the spiritual realm better than you and whose job is to function in that realm in a way that benefits you. That is a potent truth.

Yet while every Christian has an angel whose task is to minister to him or her from heavenly places, every Christian also has demonic opposition whose goal is to make all hell break loose in his or her life. We saw in our previous look at Ephesians 6:12 that "the spiritual forces of wickedness" (demons) are also located "in the heavenly places."

So Paul tells the church at Ephesus that our blessings are in the heavenly places, Jesus is in the heavenly places, we are in the heavenly places, angels are in the heavenly places, and the demonic realm is in the heavenly places. With so much going on in the heavenly places, it only makes sense that we should learn and apply as much as we can on how to function and operate effectively in heavenly places. After all, we are in a war where ground zero is located in the heavenly places.

The physical world simply manifests what is already happening in the spiritual realm. If you are unaware of the reality of the spiritual realm, you will be unaware of how that realm operates, causing you to be unprepared and ill equipped to live out your victory in your physical life.

I recently had the chance to see the blockbuster film *Inception*, which illustrated a similar truth cinematically. In the film, the main characters had discovered a way to enter into another realm—the realm of dreams. The dreams appeared to be as vivid and as authentic as the real world they were currently sleeping in, but the dream realm was not real.

Because the dream appeared to be real to all of their five senses, each character had to choose an item that would let them know whether they were in a dream or in reality. Without the item, the person in the dream might begin to believe that the dream was reality, and he or she might stay there—operating by the laws of reality within the realm of a dream.

The main character's item was a spinning top. If his top kept spinning endlessly, that meant he was in a dream. The knowledge that he was in a dream then affected the way he functioned within the dream. Essentially, he could take more risks and live differently in the dream because he knew that at any time, he could simply wake back up in reality.

I'm not suggesting that the physical world we live in is a dream or that physical realities do not carry with them both physical and spiritual consequences. But I want us to realize that our ultimate reality is taking place in the heavenly places—in the spiritual realm. Conversations, decisions, battles, and the like that occur in the spiritual realm unilaterally impact what takes place in our physical lives. Unless we realize that truth, we will continue to look for physical solutions to solve spiritual problems manifesting themselves in our physical lives.

Thankfully, God has given us an item to use—a guide—that we are to look at in order to remind us of our true spiritual location, and that is His Word. When we read God's Word, we are reminded that all spiritual warfare as well as our solutions for that warfare are located in the spiritual realm. This world is not our home. As believers we are citizens of and seated in the heavenly realm.

Physical solutions cannot fix physical problems that originate in the spiritual realm. So rather than spending all of our time, money, effort, strength, mental energy, conversations, and anything else we can come up with to help us fare better in the physical world, we ought to first be learning and applying spiritual warfare practices and techniques so we can defeat our enemy and access our blessings in the spiritual realm.

The demonic realm doesn't want you to know that. The demonic realm wants you to continue to live and do battle in the world of your five senses so that you will try to fix your situation with the limited weapons associated with your five senses. What ends up happening, though, is that a lot of time, money, and energy gets wasted trying to do away with bad fruit while not addressing the spiritual root. But remember this principle: *If all you see is what you see, you will never see all that there is to be seen.*

Since the invisible realm affects the visible realm, if you want to fix something in the physical realm, you must first address the invisible and spiritual root behind it. A failure to address the invisible, spiritual cause simply leads to a failure to experience a long-term and complete visible, physical cure.

Studying Satan's Game

Paul tells us that we wrestle not against flesh and blood, but against the powers and rulers in the spiritual realm. These powers seek to rob you of all that God has stored up for you in the heavenly places. But Paul encourages each of us to wrestle in a unique way—by standing firm against the enemy's schemes and strategies.

One way to stand firm is to learn what those strategies are. Beings in the demonic realm don't want you to know their methodology. They don't want you to figure out their approach. They want you to continue to picture them with horns and a pitchfork and wearing a red jumpsuit. If you continue to think of demonic beings in that way, you will not take them seriously. Nor will you battle them effectively.

Everyone who knows me knows I love football. When I was young, I played football every week. A leg injury sidelined me early on from pursuing the sport, but my passion for the game has never diminished.

Football is the consummate male sport. Well-trained athletes battle it out with precision moves and power-packed plays filling every second of 60 minutes with elevated levels of testosterone similar to those of the gladiators in previous centuries.

One of the highlights of my ministry has been getting to serve on the frontlines of these battles as a chaplain not only in football but also in basketball. I've been the chaplain for the NBA's Dallas Mavericks for more than 30 years. I also served as chaplain for the NFL's Dallas

Cowboys during the height of Coach Tom Landry's era, and I currently teach at the Dallas Cowboys' Bible study as well as provide personal counseling for any of the players who need it.

Football is a great life coach. It teaches us the value of self-discipline, determination, and hard work. It also teaches us how to not only outplay our opponents but also outsmart them.

Before an upcoming game, players watch what is called game film. Watching game film includes viewing clips from the upcoming opponent's previous games. The purpose of watching the film is to identify the opponent's weaknesses. Once those weaknesses are identified, a plan is put together on how to best go about exploiting those weaknesses.

If you are a football player, watching film is a good thing to do prior to a game because it gives you an edge you would not normally have over your opponent. The only problem is that your opponent also has film of your games and is studying it to exploit your weaknesses.

In the spiritual war, our opponent, the devil—along with his team of demons—has had thousands of years watching humanity's film. He's an expert on exploiting personality weaknesses, traumas, racial and gender divisions, our flesh and its desires, and many other areas of our human nature. And the demonic realm has been watching your own game film and mine since our conception.

Satan and his demons know what happened to you when you were a child that messed up your thinking, lowered your self-esteem, or led to sin patterns that now seem unbreakable in your life. They know about the issues and abuse (either to you or from you) that operate within your physical world. They know what frustrates you or wears you down, thus giving them an opportunity to move in on you. And they have one purpose for watching your film and gathering this knowledge: to exploit your weaknesses to their advantage in order to defeat you.

This may sound bleak, but the good news is that we also have access to game film. Not only that, but we have a Coach who knows our opponent's weaknesses, and He has told us what those weaknesses are in His Word. He has given us a step-by-step summary of the game film—the Bible. In it, we discover everything we need to know in order to experience victory in this spiritual battle.

Any NFL team that takes to the field on any given Sunday that has not done its homework by first studying its opponent is setting itself up for defeat. In fact, any player who would run out into the game unprepared like that would not find himself being a player for much longer.

The same is true in the Christian life. God has given each of us everything we need to defeat our enemy, but it is up to us to watch the film and to play according to His rules and strategies. Our enemy is a crafty opponent, and unless we do battle against him correctly, he will outwit us. After all, he has our game film. He knows just what button to push to get you to go somewhere you never thought you would go—both in your emotions and your actions. Satan has your game film. It's time for you to study his.

The story is told about a farmer who was perpetually having his melons stolen by thieves. He had to come up with something to do about this theft, or he was going to end up losing a large amount of his profits. So the farmer came up with a brilliant idea. He decided to post a sign on his farm that read, "One of these melons is poisonous."

The next day, the farmer went out to view his melons, and he discovered what he thought would be the case all along—none of his melons had been stolen. Satisfied that he had outsmarted the thieves, the farmer went about the rest of his day smugly filled with gratification. However, the following day, when the farmer went back to work in his field, he saw that the word "One" had been scratched out on his sign. Scribbled next to it was the word "Two." The sign now read, "Two of these melons are poisonous." The farmer lost his entire crop because he didn't know which other melon had been poisoned.

That story is a lot like dealing with the devil. No matter what you or I come up with, Satan is going to try to come up with something better. No matter what New Year's resolution or positive-thinking ten-step plan you or I make, Satan is going to try to knock us off course by the time we take step number one. The only way to live in the victory that has been secured for us in spiritual warfare is to study Satan's game film, learn his strategies and weaknesses, and stand firm in God's strength and according to God's prescribed plays in the heavenly realm.

We cannot outwit or outsmart the father of lies and master of deception. To try to do so on our own would be foolish. If winning this spiritual chess game were left up to us, we would be sweating and crying like the young man in the painting I mentioned at the beginning of the chapter. In fact, many of us take it upon ourselves to battle this war in our own strength and with our own wisdom, so we *are* sweating and crying more than we ought.

However, we have a Champion who has already studied every move on the game board. He knows what we need to do to finish this game well. It's time to put God's strategies for victory in spiritual warfare into practice and make the devil and his demons the ones who sweat and cry instead.

What do you say? Are you ready to view some game film? Let's take a look and advance in victory.

2

THE OPPOSITION IN THE BATTLE

The apostle Paul shows us a clip of Satan's game plan when he writes in a passage we referenced in chapter 1: "Finally, be strong in the Lord and in the strength of His might. Put on the full armor of God, so that you will be able to stand firm against the *schemes* of the devil" (Ephesians 6:10-11). The word "schemes" simply means "deceptive strategies." Satan's overarching strategy, which he carries out in many ways, is to deceive. He is the ultimate magician, operating not only with smoke and mirrors but also by sleight of hand.

In fact, we read in Genesis chapter 3 that when Adam and Eve were in the garden, Satan came to them in the form of a snake. The snake was the most deceptive of all the animals that God had created (verse 1).

The reason Satan took on the form of a snake is because he and his demons operate best when there is a physical presence through which to work. Remember this principle: While spiritual warfare is being waged in heavenly places, our enemy is very skilled at locating available vehicles in the physical realm through which to influence, manipulate, and deceive.

Satan even comes to you in a form that you would not suspect. Paul tells us in 2 Corinthians 11:14, "Satan disguises himself as an angel of light." This adds another dimension to the problems we face and fight in the spiritual realm because our problems do not exist only in the invisible spiritual realm; they also exist in the often unsuspecting vehicle Satan uses to get to you in the physical realm, which includes you—your mind, will, emotions, and body.

Satan's Agenda

Just as God has a kingdom agenda that involves His comprehensive rule over every area of life, Satan has an agenda as well.* Satan uses deception in order to accomplish his agenda of bringing the world under his influence and control. He also seeks to make Christians ineffective in the spiritual battles waging all around us, thus reducing the glory believers give to God. Satan pursues his agenda by intentionally penetrating the same four realms that God works through to manifest His glory: the individual, family, church, and society.

The Individual

Scripture makes it clear whom Satan is targeting in his schemes. First Peter 5:8 tells us, "Be of sober spirit, be on the alert. Your adversary, the devil, prowls around like a roaring lion, seeking someone to devour." To put it another way: Satan is after *you*. No matter who you are, what your status is, what your income is, how successful you are, or how well known you happen to be, Satan seeks to overpower you. What's worse is that he has become very successful at carrying out his schemes in an effort to do just that.

In fact, if we look closely enough in Christian circles today, we will find many brothers and sisters who are POWs in camps run by demons. Satan has overpowered them in the areas of drugs, alcohol, relationships, sex, bitterness, hopelessness, discouragement, low self-esteem, depression, arrogance, and codependency. Psychologists have fancy names for all of these and more, but essentially what Satan has done is turned an overcoming, blood-bought child of the King into a POW held hostage to mental instabilities and inaccuracies. If Satan can cripple or destroy an individual, he is that much further along in crippling families, churches, and societies.

---

* See my book *The Kingdom Agenda* (Moody, 2006) for a complete discussion on this subject.

The Family

The second realm that Satan seeks to penetrate is the family. We saw this initially when Satan tempted Eve and Eve then tempted Adam, thus bringing the entire family under the authority of hell. We also saw it when demonized men had relationships with the women on earth, producing a generation of rebels (see Genesis 6). There have been countless ways that Satan attacked the family in the Bible and over the course of history.

Why is the family so important to Satan? Because in Genesis 3:15 we learn that God will use the seed of mankind to bruise Satan in battle. The spiritual battle will be waged by the offspring. This is one reason God has issued the command in Genesis 1:28 to Christians to "be fruitful and multiply, and fill the earth, and subdue it."

Satan wants to destroy you as an individual, but he wants to destroy your family even more. If he can destroy your family, he can do more damage than simply destroying the present generation. By destroying your family, he increases the potential to destroy future generations. This is because if he can get to your children before you have a chance to mold, shape, direct, and guide them correctly, he not only has influence over your home but also has influence over their future homes. If they are given over to strongholds in their lives, they will be less equipped to raise their children in such a way that will teach them to live in obedience to Christ. If their children cannot raise their own children according to God's principles, then those children will also be ill-equipped to raise their children well. A cycle will repeat itself down through several generations.

The tragedy today is that many Christians think they are fighting flesh and blood in their marital and parenting issues, rather than realizing that Satan has an agenda to destroy their home. Whoever controls the family controls the future.

The Church

The third realm Satan attacks is the church. He does this by manipulating and exploiting personality weaknesses and preferences in order to promote division, denominationalism, legalism, and other things.

Satan wants to split the family of God because he understands something that many Christians do not: God's work and involvement is greatly reduced in a context of disunity. There must be harmony brought about through a genuine and authentic humility and a biblically defined love in order to witness the fullest manifestation of God's presence and power.

If Satan can divide the body of Christ along class, racial, gender, and personality lines, he can deceive entire churches into making governmental and functioning decisions based on personal partiality rather than on God's viewpoint.

Fellowship in the body of Christ is based on our allegiance to Christ. He is our standard. We may have different preferences of music, worship, or teaching, or we may even have idiosyncratic differences between various branches of the faith, but our one unifying factor is Jesus Christ—His death, burial, and resurrection. This is why God tells us in Ephesians 4:3 that we are to "preserve the unity" within the body of Christ. Satan seeks to divide us because in doing so he lessens our effect in advancing the kingdom of God.*

The Society

The fourth realm Satan targets is the society. In Daniel chapter 10, we see how Satan is behind the rulers of nations. He is behind the Hitlers, Mussolinis, Idi Amins, and countless other rulers who have wrought havoc on innocent people around them. Satan frequently strives to provoke, empower, and enable them to destroy entire nations and groups of people.

When sin entered the world, it corrupted not only individuals but also human institutions that comprise societies as well. Satan seeks to capitalize on this corruption to such a degree as to make societies into entities that oppress personal freedom and opportunity rather than serve as instruments, as they have been designed by God, to promote biblical justice. The Bible is clear that God has made distinct

---

* For more in-depth teaching on the issue of unity and the kingdom, see my book *Oneness Embraced* (Moody, 2011).

arrangements, or covenants, through which He works. He works with the individual, family, church, and the government. All have been created by God and are to be influenced by God.

When you understand Satan's agenda to overpower individuals, families, churches, and ultimately societies as a whole, you can understand the complex nature of the spiritual battle we're in. Until we trace the origin of personal POW status, family POW status, church POW status, and societal POW status, Satan has us defeated in the body of Christ because he has us wrestling against flesh and blood rather than against principalities, powers, and world forces located in the heavenly places.

Satan's Strategy

Just like any excellent military commander or athletic coach, Satan has a strategy—a game plan—for accomplishing his agenda. His strategy has many parts, and before we dig deeper into what we need to do to suit up for battle, I want to look at Satan's strategic approach.

One of the devil's main tricks is to cause you to miss the goodness of God. As he did with Eve in the garden, Satan wants to get you to question the value of all of the trees that God has provided by getting you to focus on the one tree He has said to avoid. Satan wants you to complain about what you don't have so you will lose sight of what God has given you. However, God instructs us how to counteract this scheme in Philippians 4:6-8.

> Be anxious for nothing, but in everything by prayer and supplication *with thanksgiving* let your requests be made known to God. And the peace of God, which surpasses all comprehension, will guard your hearts and your minds in Christ Jesus.
>
> Finally, brethren, whatever is true, whatever is honorable, whatever is right, whatever is pure, whatever is lovely, whatever is of good repute, if there is any excellence and if anything worthy of praise, dwell on these things.

God tells us to start by praising and thanking Him for all the things He has provided. He wants us to begin by giving thanks for all He has done and by thinking about His goodness—not only in our own lives but also in the world around us.

Satan tries to pull our focus away from the goodness of God because he knows that the only way he can defeat us is through deception. Truth exists within the goodness of God, and wherever the truth of God is present, Satan's ability to deceive is diminished.

Keep in mind as you face Satan's tricks of deception that you cannot fight him on your own, with your own methods, or even with your own thoughts. God's Word—His truth—trumps Satan. *You don't.* Satan has constitutional superiority over every man and woman because he is a spirit being. He is not bound by the limitations of flesh and blood. Therefore, you cannot compete with him on the level of his deception. He is the master chameleon.

In fact, Satan is such a masterful chameleon that rarely will you find him strutting his stuff in a red jumpsuit carrying a pitchfork. That's too obvious. His scheme is to trick you. He doesn't want you to see him for who he truly is. He's not merely hanging out at the First Church of Satan. Rather, he's also concerned with finding a way to infiltrate First Baptist, First Methodist, or First Bible Church of Anytown, USA.

Not long ago, I sat down after a long day to spend some time relaxing in front of the television. A popular old show called *The Outer Limits* was playing on one of the stations. I had seen this show before, but this time something stood out. There was a clear similarity between what was playing on the television and what Satan often does in our own lives.

The Cliff Notes version of this show is that a ship had crashed in an alien environment. One of the human prisoners was taken captive and fiercely interrogated. When he wouldn't give up any information, the aliens tried another approach. They sent a beautiful young woman into the room with him to be incarcerated as a prisoner as well. As the two prisoners talked and as days drifted into weeks, they shared secrets with each other.

Over a period of time, scales began to appear on the woman after she would be taken away for questioning and then returned to the cell.

The man was concerned for her and asked her what they were doing to her when they took her. She told him that they were injecting her with something that was turning her into them.

Eventually, she became completely scaled and looked like the alien creatures questioning her every day. It was at this point that they came to take her away for good. But this was only after she had successfully retrieved all of the information that there was to get out of the man. As she was leaving, the man said, "You have completely changed."

She stopped, turned around to face him, and replied, "No, I have completely changed *back*. I was always this way. I was just made to look like you so I could get your information. Now that I've got it, I can go back to being who I really am."

The devil is no different. He comes to us as an angel of light in forms we rarely recognize because he wants to steal from each of us what God has in store for us. However, once he achieves his goal, we end up seeing him for who he truly is.

Four Stages in the Strategy

Desire

There are four stages in Satan's strategy of spiritual warfare. The first stage begins with desire. A common term we often associate with desire is the word "lust." Lust is not necessarily a bad word, nor is desire a negative thing to have. Legitimate desire motivates us in our lives and provides an avenue for obtaining satisfaction and delight. However, when desire or lust manifests itself through illegitimate means, it turns into temptation, giving the potential for sin.

Desire for food is good; gluttony is a sin. Desire for sex is good; immorality is a sin. Desire for sleep is good; laziness is a sin. Satan's initial strategic point in our lives is to play on a legitimate God-given desire within us and twist it into something illegitimate. He knows the desire cannot be avoided or ignored—God has planted it within us. So Satan tries to warp that desire by influencing how it is directed and used. Essentially, he wants the desire to be the master over you rather than you being the master over your desire.

Deception

The second stage in Satan's strategy is the use of deception. A great illustration of this is how a fisherman sets out to catch a fish. If a fisherman were to put a hook into the water all by itself, he would be waiting a long time before anything ever took a bite. In fact, it's doubtful that anything would ever bite his hook. Instead, what the fisherman does is put a worm on the hook to deceive the fish into thinking it's getting a tasty meal.

Satan doesn't simply throw unbaited hooks out to us either. He doesn't advertise the local tavern by saying, "Come here and get drunk, become addicted to drugs or alcohol, lose your family, lead your kids into alcoholism, and throw away your future." Rather, what Satan does can be called the "foot in the door" technique. This was a common technique for traveling salesmen. They understood that if they could get potential customers to allow them to put their foot inside the door and talk about something unrelated to the sale, they would more than likely also have the sale. To do this, they diverted the potential customer's attention to something else.

Satan tries to get believers to let him into their lives little by little just like that. First, it's just a foot in the door—maybe a movie you shouldn't have watched, a conversation you shouldn't have had, or a relationship that shouldn't have been redefined in such a way. At first, it seemed harmless. But as Satan makes his way in, it becomes easier to graduate to the next level and buy what he is selling.

The primary way Satan does this is by planting an illegitimate or sinful idea in our minds, just as he did with David: "Then Satan stood up against Israel and *moved* David to number Israel" (1 Chronicles 21:1). David got the idea that he didn't need God at that point and that he was able to take care of his army himself. As a result, he disobeyed God's instructions, and 70,000 people ended up losing their lives. Whatever controls our minds controls our actions.

Disobedience

The third stage in Satan's strategy is disobedience. Desire leads to deception, which then leads to disobedience. The first half of James

1:15 tells us, "When lust has conceived, it gives birth to sin." Desire is not sin. Sin is the illegitimate application and placement of desire. For example, when a young child makes a decision, it's often based on feelings and desires. The child feels like playing, watching TV, eating, running, or anything of that sort. The child says, "I want that" or "I don't want that." If the desire is not managed, it can end up dominating the child's actions in forms of disobedience. However, as the child matures into adulthood, the process of maturity leads him or her to begin to operate based on the will. He or she may not feel like getting up and going to work, but because it is a responsibility, he or she gets up and goes to work.

Victorious Christian living occurs when the Holy Spirit's presence is free to manage—through our spirit—our feelings, emotions, and desires. That's not to say we need to negate our feelings. We are human beings, and emotions are very real. But the placement of their expression must be brought underneath the Spirit's control, or we run the risk of letting our volatile emotions be used by Satan to lead us straight into sin.

Philippians 2:13 says, "It is God who is at work in you, both to will and to work for His good pleasure." Victory in spiritual warfare involves intimacy and identification with Jesus Christ to such a degree that His will reveals itself as the dominant force in our own will. That is the difference between victory and defeat. Only when God's will directs our lives are we then also equipped with the power to do what He wills us to do. God promises to give us this power if and when our will aligns with His. But to do this requires faith that God knows what He is talking about. The opposite of faith is not doubt. The opposite of faith is disobedience.

Death

Satan's intention in spiritual warfare is to cause us to miss out on the goodness of God, leading us onto a path of destruction. We learned from James 1:15 that lust gives birth to sin. Here's the second half of that verse: "And when sin is accomplished, it brings forth death." Sin produces death in a variety of ways, all of which diminish our ability to experience God's promise of the abundant life. This death can show up as the death of a dream, relationship, career, virtue, or any number of other things. Primarily, sin produces a death within the fullness of our spirits as our fellowship is broken with God.

Breaking fellowship with God makes us ineffective as believers who have been designed to experience God and to glorify Him in all we do. As we saw earlier, Satan's goal is to make us ineffective. He does this through a strategy of taking a legitimate desire and guiding it down a path toward sin. Oftentimes, the death in our relationships, hopes, careers, families, or in other areas will lead to depressing thoughts and discouragement. Depression and discouragement are Satan's aim because he seeks to make our lives void of the abundance Jesus has promised us. As a result, we often question God and His promises. Not only that, but when our lives feel miserable, we are frequently too dejected to give God any glory or to tell others about Him. In fact, many of us even end up blaming God for the misery we're experiencing.

In time, Satan tries to work himself out of a job by training the deceived to become deceivers themselves (see 2 Timothy 3:13). He turns people into "evangelists of deception" who quickly and effectively spread his lies among us.

Because Satan does not have the power of creation, he has to maximize the potential of deception. He has turned deception into an art form. In fact, his skill at deceiving mankind will one day be so powerful that his antichrist will sit in the temple as god, and people will truly believe that he *is* god.

Yielding to Hell

Satan's agenda and his strategy are all-encompassing, but there's something you and I need to know about both: *They have already been defeated.* In fact, Satan and his minions have already lost this battle. Any advancement they make in your life or on this earth is because they have been given permission to do so. The only power they have is the power that is granted to them. Satan was able to get access to ruling planet earth only because Adam and Eve gave him permission to do it. Essentially, demons need permission from us to bring hell to us.

If hell is happening in your life, it is because hell has been given permission to do so. Hell was told—either through sin or circumstance—that you were willing to yield. You communicated something like this:

- "Hell, it's okay for you to rule my mind. It's okay for you to rule my emotions. It's okay for you to rule my will or my body."
- "I give you permission to tell me that I'm not really a man even though I was born a male."
- "I give you permission to tell me I'm not really a woman even though I was born a female."
- "I give you permission to tell me that I want drugs, I need drugs, and I can't stop using drugs."
- "I give you permission to tell me I need a drink, can't live without a drink, and can't go to sleep without a drink."
- "I give you permission to tell me that I should wake up depressed, stay depressed, and go to bed depressed."
- "I give you permission to tell me that I can't control my anger, my spending, or my desires; that I am not loved or that I will never amount to anything of significance."

The list of things we allow Satan to tell us can go on forever. Some of it may certainly be related to chemicals or biological malfunctions, but much of what we even call "mental illness" today is actually caused by demons who have been given permission to make someone mentally unstable.

After more than 35 years of working with individuals through struggles in their lives as a pastor and counselor, I'm convinced that much of what we label or try to drug away is simply a result of Satan having his way. I'm not saying that the physical components aren't real, but they are often incited and encouraged by demons who have been allowed to roam free.

Satan operates by consent and cooperation. He operates by subtly changing the worldview, beliefs, and thought patterns of the individual, family, church, or society that he's targeting. Once those schemes are adopted, he is given greater permission to make himself at home. Much like roaches that have been allowed to stay in a filthy kitchen, demons that have set up camp are difficult to drive off.

I've often heard it said that some people are just too demon conscious. Maybe you feel that way. Perhaps this is the first book you've picked up on spiritual warfare because you think people sometimes make too big a deal about demons and the spiritual realm. But that's exactly what Satan would like you to believe. As long as he can keep your focus on the physical manifestations instead of the spiritual root, you will forever be fighting the wrong battle. It's hard to win a war when you don't even know where to show up to do battle.

The foundational principle for a life of total victory is this: *We do not wrestle against flesh and blood.* When we think people are our problem, we will continually be addressing people and miss the root of the problem altogether. If one of us were to set our minds on the spiritual world and less on other people, more of us might still be in our right minds. But when people's minds are divided—fighting this person, that challenge, or some other issue—they don't seem to have much of a mind left at all.

The people are real. The problems are real. The health issues are real. The challenges are real. The conflicts are real. The strongholds are real. They are just not the root of the problem.

The job of Satan and his demons is to keep you and me from experiencing the abundant life God has in store for us, and they do that by distracting us from focusing on the root. Doing that is their full-time occupation. And we are not their first job assignment. They have had plenty of years to study, practice, and perfect what they do.

But God, who is not bound by time or space, has already won this battle. Learning His strategy is our key to overcoming Satan and his demons and living a life of victory.

3

THE STRATEGY FOR THE BATTLE

A father and his son were traveling across the Wild West in a wagon one day when a prairie fire broke out. The father and his son tried to outrun the wildfire in their wagon, but they quickly realized that it wasn't going to work. The fire was coming too fast, and unless they tried something else, it would catch up to them and consume them.

Much to the confusion of the son, the father turned the horse and wagon around and rushed directly back toward the fire. He took them to a spot that had already been burned and yelled to his son, "Jump out and stand here. Don't move!"

They both jumped out, but the boy became afraid as he saw the fire raging and moving toward them. He wanted to run, but his father grabbed his hand and said, "Don't move, son. Stand firm!"

"But the fire is almost here," the son cried, his voice shaking with fear. "I don't understand!"

"This spot has already been burned," his dad replied. "There is nothing left for the fire to grab. The fire will come near, but it cannot burn again what has already been burned once before." The boy was safe because he stayed with his father in a place that the fire could not reach.

As Satan battles you in spiritual warfare, he wants you to step away from the ground that has already been burned in the spiritual realm, which is Jesus Christ. Jesus has already been crucified, and His resurrection has already secured the victory. Satan can't touch you when you stay close to Christ. If you stand firm in the center of the safest location—the cross, where the victory has been accomplished—you will stand victoriously because Satan can't reach you there.

But that raises a question. How do you stand firm? As Paul said in Ephesians 6:10, we are to "be strong in the Lord and in the strength of His might." You stand firm by appropriating God's strength, not your own determination, positive thinking, or even self-discipline. While those things are good, they are not good enough to overcome an enemy battling you from another realm. Instead, you are to be *strong in the Lord Jesus Christ and in His might*.

In order to know how to be strong in Jesus Christ, we need to understand a few things about His power and His authority to exercise that power. For us to fully experience the power of Christ, we need to look at how things began.

When God created man, He made a very significant decision. He created Adam out of the dust of the ground, and then He said, "Let them rule" (Genesis 1:26). By letting mankind rule on earth, God willingly imposed a limitation on His own involvement in human affairs. He erected precise boundaries where He would respond, either for good or for bad, based on the decisions of men.

It was up to Adam, therefore, to use his God-given capacity to cultivate and rule his world. But in order to do that, Adam had to withstand the attacks of a sly serpent in the garden.

The problem was that Adam *did not* withstand the deceptive attack of the serpent. In fact, he allowed that serpent a strong presence in the garden, forcing Adam out. As a result, Adam allowed the serpent to rule in his place. In football language, we would say Adam fumbled the ball in the devil's red zone, and the serpent recovered it.

What caused the fumble? Eve had gotten out of alignment under Adam, and Adam had gotten out of alignment under God. This stripped the ball called "rule" from Adam's hands and gave it to Satan. He took possession of the garden from that point on.

So cataclysmic was Adam's fumble that Satan and his team sprinted down the field all of the way to mankind's red zone. Now they have the ball, they call the plays, and they are running out the clock. Because of the fumble, the Adamites—the human race—have been scrambling ever since.

And that's what we're doing, even to this day. I hear it all of the time. Maybe you hear it too. People talk about trying to stop the devil. If you are trying to stop the devil, he's obviously coming after you. He has the ball. He's calling the shots. He's running the show. He's setting the agenda. And the reason you're trying to stop him is that you are now in a defensive mode.

Jesus recognized this change of position by referring to Satan three times as the ruler of this world (John 12:31; 14:30; 16:11). Because of Adam's fumble, Satan is the one who now calls the plays in this world. Of course Satan can only govern the world within the sovereign boundaries set up by God, the ultimate Governor, but he still rules through deception, intimidation, and a myriad of other means.

Not only that, but when Satan took over the rule of this world, a curse came with it. This curse affected Adam's career, family, finances, children, security, and even his life. And unless you and I understand the theology of authority, we will never overcome the curse handed off to us by Adam, and we will never be completely victorious in spiritual warfare.

The bad news is that Satan recovered Adam's fumble. The good news is that you can get the ball back. You can live in both hope and victory when you stand firm in the strength of Christ. You can force another fumble—this time, by Satan—and in so doing recover the authority that has already been secured for you.

If you have come to Jesus Christ for the forgiveness of your sins and for the gift of eternal life that He freely offers, you have already forced that fumble. Now all you need to do is pick up the ball and run with it. Through Christ's sacrificial atonement, you have already been repositioned for victory in your life. Remember, you are not fighting *for* victory—you are fighting *from* victory. Let's find out how.

Headship and Authority

When God pronounced the curse to the serpent for luring Adam out from underneath his designated alignment, He coupled it with a prophecy: "I will put enmity between you and the woman, and between your seed and her seed; He shall bruise you on the head, and you shall bruise him on the heel" (Genesis 3:15).

In these words, God said, "Adam, you have fumbled the ball. You have turned over the rule of your life, and others' lives, to the evil one by moving out from underneath My alignment. Adam, you blew it— big-time. But I've got some good news for you because a woman is going to have a child. And that child will have his heel hurt by the serpent, but that same child—the seed of the woman—will crush the serpent's head."

He will crush the serpent's head. Don't read that too quickly. God said that the seed of the woman will crush the serpent's head. Let me help you grasp the significance of that statement by adding something onto the end of a word. Look at it this way:

The seed of the woman will crush the serpent's head*ship*.

"Headship" means rule and authority. With the coming of the seed of the woman—Jesus Christ—the headship (the rule and authority of Satan) has been crushed. Eliminated. *Gone!* The heel of the seed was wounded in the process, along with His humanity, on the cross, but when all was said and done, Satan's headship was crushed, and Jesus Christ negated the devil's authoritative rule.

That truth alone is enough for you to know that you can get back on the offense in this life. On the cross and through the resurrection, Jesus Christ has already crushed Satan's authority. It's a done deal. The whistle has blown. The play is dead. The ball is now yours once again. In fact, when Jesus spoke about His future death on the cross, He declared Satan's ultimate removal of authority: "Now judgment is upon this world; now the ruler of this world will be cast out. And I, if I am lifted up from the earth, will draw all men to Myself" (John 12:31-32).

This is so vitally important that I want to put it another way just to make sure we're on the same page. *When you come to Jesus Christ and accept His sacrifice for your life, you are putting yourself under the new Head of State.* The head of state is the one who has final authority for the matters in that land. In America, the head of state is our president.

Our president, by virtue of his office, holds the final and ultimate say on what goes on in our nation. It is what we call "veto power."

When the opposition to the president passes a law that he does not approve of, he doesn't have to accept it. He can disarm it with his veto power. With one stroke of his pen, he can literally undo what took hours, days, and even months for Congress to enact.

Jesus Christ, through the power of the cross and resurrection, has the ultimate veto power in our world. Satan no longer holds final authority over your life. Sure, he may spend hours, days, months, years, and even decades persuading you to believe his lies and pressuring you into feeling that he has the final authority over you, but once you realize that Jesus Christ has already defeated him, you will be set free to live your life in victory. Satan got pummeled at Calvary. He dropped the ball. He knows that. God knows that too.

The problems come, though, when *we* don't know that truth and stand firm in it. Knowledge—what you know and what you believe about a matter—is vital. It's one thing for someone to point a gun at you that has bullets in it. But it's entirely something else for someone to point a gun at you that is empty. Both people do not have the same power over you. One of them has been disarmed. His firepower has been removed.

It's just that we don't always know that. We don't always have adequate knowledge for a situation like that. If a gun were pointed at us, we wouldn't have any way of knowing whether it was loaded. To be safe, most likely we would walk, talk, and act as if the gun is loaded.

But let me ask you something: What would you do if somebody let you know that the gun was empty? Or what if you saw the gun fired six times, and all six times, nothing came out? What then? Would you still be making your decisions based on that gun? Probably not. And neither would I because that empty gun no longer holds any authority. We have no need to fear an empty gun.

Of course, the devil doesn't want us to know that his gun has been emptied at the cross of Jesus Christ. So he keeps pointing it at us and putting it in our face as if it were loaded. And we don't realize it's empty, so we keep bowing under its presence. We don't realize that at the cross,

Jesus Christ took the bullets out of Satan's gun. We don't realize that the most the devil can do is pretend that his gun is still loaded.

If you don't know that Satan's guns are not loaded, you're going to act as if you're defeated because you will erroneously believe he has power over you.

And that's how many of us live our lives. We forget that at the cross, Jesus Christ deactivated, dismantled, and disarmed Satan's headship.

Satan has lost his authority. Or, to make it more personal: Satan no longer has any authority over *you*.

Authority Versus Power

"Hey that's nice, Tony," you say. "It sounds very heavenly minded and ethereal, and it even looks good on paper. But what about me living down here in the real world with real battles—financial wars, career wars, family wars, and emotional wars? What about those? I don't seem to be living in victory in my wars. Rather, my enemies are being victorious over me. Yet you're telling me that Jesus Christ is the head. You're telling me that Jesus Christ is calling the plays now and that I'm underneath His authority. So what gives? That's not what's going on in my life."

Those are good questions that we all face. To answer them, we need to keep in mind this essential truth: *Satan lost his authority, but he didn't lose his power.* Satan still dominates our world in many ways because he has retained his power. Satan is as powerful now as he has ever been. The things he does are real, damaging, and destructive. He is and will always be a liar, thief, and murderer with intentions to kill, steal, and destroy. It only takes a glance around our globe, around our communities and homes, or even in our own souls to see that Satan still operates with power.

The truth we need to realize, and the truth that will set us free, is that Satan no longer has authority. That is the key.

Authority is the right to use the power that you possess.

In order for Satan to use his power in your life, he now has to keep you from functioning underneath your authority because his power is only effective when he has the right to use it. Satan does not have the authority to use his power when you are living underneath your legitimate authority as a Christian. Therefore, he seeks to lure you out from underneath God's authority and rule in your life because he knows that you are secure underneath Him. Colossians 1:13 tells us that God has "rescued us from the domain of darkness, and transferred us to the kingdom of His beloved Son." God rescued us out of the wrong kingdom and brought us into the right one. By rescuing us, He brought us under the rule of a new King. You used to be under Satan's rule before you met Christ, but now you are part of a new kingdom of which Jesus Christ is the King. Satan, in order to rule your world, must entice you to leave your kingdom and come back over to his.

The reason we don't experience more victory in spiritual warfare is that we've been duped into believing that attending church on Sunday and simply getting more information about the real kingdom is enough. Or maybe we think that adding a Wednesday night Bible study will be sufficient to affirm our allegiance to our King. Or maybe we'll toss in some serving and praise songs and think we've got it covered.

But then we go back to work on Monday, or back to our routine at home with our mate or with our children, and we flip back over into our old way of thinking. We slide back into the other kingdom and operate under its authority. We align our thoughts with the wisdom Satan has set up in this world. We base our decisions on how we feel or what our friends are telling us or even what our fears are telling us. We transfer our allegiance from the conclusive and authoritative Word of God through Jesus Christ back to Satan's worldly schemes.

We wind up not being victorious in spiritual warfare because we keep flipping sides. We come to church under one kingdom, but we operate on the job in another kingdom. We have our devotions in one kingdom, but we operate among our friends in another kingdom. We keep flip-flopping kingdoms and wonder why the victory is not there. We wonder why we can't get over the hump. We wonder why the enemy keeps calling the plays. We wonder why our prayers go unanswered, our battles end in defeat, and our power over our own lives runs out. The opposition keeps intercepting the ball and returning it for a touchdown.

But the answer is simple: The enemy is victorious in our lives because we are yielding the power to him by not standing firm in our identity in Jesus Christ. We are failing to firmly remain in the union we were designed to have with Christ, under His headship.

Our Union with Christ

Our union with Christ is essential to our victory over Satan's rule in our lives. The book of Colossians goes into great detail about this.

> See to it that no one takes you captive through hollow and deceptive philosophy, which depends on human tradition and the basic principles of this world rather than on Christ. For in Christ all the fullness of the Deity lives in bodily form, and *you have been given fullness in Christ, who is the head over every power and authority.* In him you were also circumcised, in the putting off of the sinful nature, not with a circumcision done by the hands of men but with the circumcision done by Christ, having been buried with him in baptism and raised with him through your faith in the power of God, who raised him from the dead (Colossians 2:8-12 NIV).

Everything that makes up God—His essence and totality—is in Christ, fully. The only difference is that it's in a human body. "For in Christ *all* the fullness of the Deity lives in bodily form."

All of the fullness of God is in Jesus Christ. Not some, not a bit, but *all*.

That's why Jesus is the Son of Man *and* the Son of God. That's why He can get thirsty one minute, and the next minute He can go out and walk on water. That's why He can get hungry one day, and the next day He turns sardines and crackers into a Moby Dick sandwich to feed more than 5000 people. That's why Jesus can die—and then *get up*! He can do all of these things because He is the God-man; fully God and fully man in one person. "For *in* Christ all the fullness of the Deity lives in bodily form."

In fact, if we were to backtrack a few paragraphs, we discover even more.

He [Jesus] is the image of the invisible God, the firstborn over all creation. For by him all things were created: things in heaven and on earth, visible and invisible, whether thrones or powers or rulers or authorities; all things were created by him and for him. He is before all things, and in him all things hold together (Colossians 1:15-17 NIV).

Jesus Christ holds all things together. Therefore, if you find yourself falling apart, it is a result of you not having stood firm with Jesus in union with Him. We are told that *in* Him, all things hold together and maintain their equilibrium. Take a look at these very important phrases in Colossians 2:

"in Him" (verse 9)
"in Him" (verse 10)
"in Him" (verse 11)
"with Him…with Him" (verse 12)
"with Him" (verse 13)

Do you see the pattern? Our victory in spiritual warfare is intimately connected to Jesus Christ. *In* Him. *With* Him. If we miss this truth, we miss the key to our victory: our union with Jesus Christ. Let me illustrate a little bit about that union.

Our church in Oak Cliff becomes a vibrant place of worship, fellowship, outreach, and teaching each and every Sunday morning for thousands of people. If you ever find yourself in the Dallas area on a Sunday, I invite you to come. I would love to meet you personally and let you experience the unique atmosphere in the sanctuary we call Oak Cliff Bible Fellowship. Sundays are a highlight of my week. I enjoy gathering with the saints.

But by Sunday afternoon, I admit, after having sung, sat, and preached through two two-hour-long services, I'm tired.

Knowing this is going to happen, I usually start my Sunday morning with a cup of coffee. Now, some people like their coffee black, and that's fine if that's how you like your coffee. But I always like to have some cream in my coffee.

So every Sunday, before I drink my coffee, I get the white cream and pour it into my black coffee. Then I take the stick and stir it so that a *union* occurs between my black coffee and my white cream. When that happens, there is no longer any black coffee or white cream. Instead, I now have brown coffee. It is brown because a union has occurred.

If I want to take my formerly black coffee with me into my office before the service, the cream must come along as well. If I want to take my cream into the prayer room, my once-black coffee will be coming with it as well. Once they are mixed, wherever one goes, the other must go as well simply by virtue of the union that has occurred.

This is how our relationship with Christ has been designed, as we saw earlier in Ephesians: "Even when we were dead in our transgressions, [God] made us alive *together* with Christ (by grace you have been saved), and raised us up *with* Him, and seated us *with* Him in the heavenly places *in* Christ Jesus" (Ephesians 2:5-6).

When Christ died, we died with him. When Christ arose, we arose with him. When Christ was seated at the right hand of the Father, we were seated with him. In other words, we were made to function in union with Christ.

Jesus Christ *is* over all things; He is sovereign over everything. He has recovered the fumbled ball and has legal authority and victory in the spiritual realm. For us to access that victory, we must stand firm under His headship in our thoughts, in our actions, in our hearts, in our decisions, on our job, in our homes, and throughout our lives.

Only when we stand firm under His Word and authority will we be able to live victoriously in spiritual warfare. Friend, you can go to all of the meetings you want. You can read all of the self-help books and magazines you want. You can name and claim whatever you want. But until you stand firm under the comprehensive rule of God in your life and in union with your identity in Jesus Christ, you will only find a temporary reprieve. Only in Christ will you find the authority to live in victory.

I often hear people quoting the Scripture, "If the Son makes you free, you will be free indeed." But when I look around me, I see very few people who are free *indeed*. And the reason is that we have settled for the temporary rather than aligning ourselves with eternity. Satan has already been beaten. He has already been disarmed. The bullets have already been removed. The fumble has already been recovered. Jesus has already defeated Satan. He is already victorious. And you are in union with Him.

Stand firm in His authority by the rules of His kingdom, and you will see His victory manifested in your own life. He has already given you everything you need to do so each and every day—through putting on the armor of God. And just as God wouldn't have you get partially dressed when you woke up this morning before you headed out the door, He doesn't want you to get partially dressed when it comes to war.

The six pieces of armor that we will study in the next several chapters are divided into two categories. The first category includes the first three pieces of the armor and begins with the word "having," taken from the verb "to be." This means that the first three pieces of the armor are pieces you should wear all the time. You put them on every day. They are like a uniform that a baseball player wears when he goes out to play ball.

The last three pieces of the armor are given to you to pick up as the situation demands. We are told to "take" them up. This is like that same baseball player grabbing either his glove or his bat, depending on what is going on in the game.

With this armor, God has supplied everything you and I need to live a life of complete victory in spiritual warfare. It is our job, through faith, to use each piece of the armor He has given us. God is not going to dress us, but He has given us what we need to be armed for victory.

It's time to suit up. Game on.

Part 2

THE ARMOR

4

THE BELT OF TRUTH

My wife, Lois, and I recently celebrated our fortieth wedding anniversary. Forty years of sharing a life together through both good and challenging times is worth honoring in a special way. I wanted to take Lois to just the right place, where we could spend some quality time together and where she would feel the depth of how much she means to me.

Knowing my wife, I sought to pick someplace peaceful where we could relax and enjoy each other's company away from the demands of everyday life and ministry. So I took Lois to a resort getaway with a view of the ocean. We had a wonderful time remembering what God has done in and through our marriage.

But before we went on our trip, we had to do something—we had to pack. We couldn't just show up at the airport with what we had on and expect it to last us the several days we had planned to be there. Instead, we filled suitcases with clothes and belongings to take with us.

Looking at the weather forecast, we knew that we would be experiencing pleasant weather, so we packed comfortable clothes. Some were dressy (for an intimate night of dining), and some were casual (for when we wanted to relax outside together during the day). We didn't pack our coats, boots, mittens, and scarves. Neither did I pack any long-sleeve shirts or thick, wool socks.

In other words, what we packed in our suitcases to spend a few days at a beachside resort in the summer was entirely different from what we would have packed if we were going to my parents' home for a family vacation in Baltimore at Christmas. Where you are going should determine what you pack for the trip.

Prior to going anywhere, for example, you assess the occasion to determine what attire is appropriate for your destination. If you're going to a formal event, you'll put on a formal outfit. Ladies will probably spend extra time choosing just the right pair of shoes. Men may even reach for their cuff links. But if you are going to spend an evening at a ballpark, you will probably leave your formal clothes hanging in the closet. Most people wouldn't wear shorts to a wedding or suits to an outdoor barbeque because the attire does not fit the occasion.

The apostle Paul wrote to the church at Ephesus and to Christians everywhere about what we are to wear when we're engaged in spiritual warfare.

> Therefore, take up the full armor of God, so that you will be able to resist in the evil day, and having done everything, to stand firm. Stand firm therefore, having girded your loins with truth, and having put on the breastplate of righteousness, and having shod your feet with the preparation of the gospel of peace; in addition to all, taking up the shield of faith with which you will be able to extinguish all of the flaming arrows of the evil one. And take the helmet of salvation, and the sword of the Spirit, which is the word of God (Ephesians 6:13-17).

Within these verses, Paul has given clear instructions about a specific wardrobe that is necessary for us, not only to wear but also to have packed and ready to put on if we are going to have victory in spiritual warfare. This list of armor can be compared to a travel guide that's given to you when you're going somewhere you've never been before. For example, before people go on a safari in some remote region of the world, they usually go online and find a travel guide that recommends all of the articles of clothing and items to bring with them. In the same way, in Ephesians 6, Paul has given us our travel guide so we will know what to suit up in and take with us as we conduct ourselves in spiritual warfare.

Let's take a brief refresher before we begin our look at the various pieces of our armor. Why is Paul so concerned that we know what we need to wear? He realizes something we often don't: *We are in a battle.* Not only that, but this battle is fundamentally not against flesh and blood. People are not your ultimate problem. People are merely conduits for something else that's operating in the invisible realm. People, and even your own flesh, are merely hosts for the invisible conflict to manifest itself in the physical, visible realm.

Everything visible and physical is preceded by something invisible and spiritual. Therefore, if your goal is to address some form of a stronghold, conflict, or trial in your visible, physical world, you will first need to address its invisible, spiritual antecedent. You must investigate that which has come before it as its root cause. What we see, hear, taste, touch, and smell is simply the fruit and not the root behind our battle. We cannot ignore the fruit, but our problem is that we too often focus so heavily on managing or attempting to overcome problems with the fruit, we ignore the root altogether.

Many of the issues we must deal with in our lives come to us as flesh-and-blood situations, so we use up a considerable amount of our energy trying to overcome them through flesh-and-blood solutions. We spend a large amount of our time attempting to use physical means to fix physical problems because we have forgotten or have never realized that a spiritual cause is behind the circumstances we're facing. The primary focal point of our battle is not down here—it's up there, in the spiritual realm. When we fail to realize this, the spiritual realm does not get the same attention we give to the physical realm. As a result, we often end up frustrated, hopeless, and defeated.

As Christians, our major problem is that we are in a wrestling match against principalities and world forces in the spiritual realm, but far too often we do not take that into consideration. Until we discover that our journey on this earth is right in the heart of spiritual warfare, which originates in another realm, we will never learn to pack or dress accordingly. And we will remain defeated.

Trust me, sitting outside in a wool outfit with a knitted scarf near the ocean recently with my wife would not have been the best way to celebrate our fortieth wedding anniversary together. Similarly, going through this life as a believer wrongly dressed for spiritual warfare will inhibit us from walking in the purpose and God-appointed destiny that He has designed for us.

Only when we shift our attention to the invisible realm and start addressing our issues from the root first will we walk in a more potent, powerful, and permanent victory. Jesus has already accomplished this victory for us. Paul admonishes us to "stand firm" in the truths God has given us in order to actualize this victory in our own lives.

Have you ever been to an amusement park or a public place where there are a lot of children? Occasionally when I go to one of these places, I will see a mother or a father with a leash around his or her wrist. Naturally my mind thinks that the leash is going to be attached to a dog. But then I look and notice that the leash is actually attached to a child. Apparently some children today need more than their parents' words to keep them nearby.

Unfortunately, the same is true for many Christians as well. God has already told us in His Word how to find our greatest source of strength and victory—by recognizing how very close to Him we actually are. "[God] raised us up with Him, and seated us with Him in the heavenly places in Christ Jesus, so that in the ages to come He might show the surpassing riches of His grace in kindness toward us in Christ Jesus" (Ephesians 2:6-7).

It is in this location where we receive the "surpassing riches of His grace in kindness." It is in the authority attached to this location that we are to "stand firm." It is here where we are to remain, not wandering away like the child at the amusement park.

God longs for us to believe and live in obedience to His words because we *choose* to, not because He has to put us on a leash to abide with Him "in the heavenly places," where the spiritual war is taking place. If you run away from your location near Jesus Christ, you will be running away from your victory. But when you stand firm in your heavenly location, you will then be able to utilize the full armor down here in order to live out the complete revelation of your victory.

Putting on the Belt

The first piece of the wardrobe God has given us to wear as we wage victorious spiritual warfare is a belt. We read in Ephesians 6:14, "…having girded your loins with truth." In biblical times, Roman soldiers "girded their loins" by fastening a belt around their midsection.

Now I, probably like you, have a number of belts hanging in my closet. When I'm getting dressed, I choose which belt I wear based on its color. If you are a lady, you probably also consider a belt's design. However, when Paul instructed us to gird our loins with truth, he was not talking about ordinary belts, colors, or designs.

A Roman soldier's belt was a useful tool—a place where some of his other armor could hang. He might hang his sword on his belt. He might also hang a dagger there or any number of needed items. When the soldier was ready to head into battle, he could reach down and pick up the part of his tunic that was draping near his feet and tuck it in this belt. If you've ever seen a movie that takes place in the Roman era, you've seen that the men frequently dressed in long robes. You've probably also noticed when it got time to get serious with work or move into battle, the Roman soldier would lift his robe and tuck it underneath his belt. By doing this, he was given greater freedom to move his feet.

The belt not only held additional pieces of armor and provided soldiers with increased mobility, it also produced stability by holding things in place. When you or I wear a belt today, we put it on to fulfill a few fundamental purposes. The first purpose is that we want it to hold up our pants. The second purpose is that it needs to keep our shirts tucked in. Maybe a third purpose is that it offers some decorative appeal, but most importantly, belts stabilize whatever else we are wearing.

What Paul is telling us in Ephesians is that the belt of truth is designed to stabilize things by keeping them in their proper order.

Satan is the ultimate truth twister. Like a magician at a stage show, Satan distorts reality, altering it into any number of shapes and forms. John 8:44 reveals what we are up against when we face him. "[Satan] was a murderer from the beginning, and does not stand in the truth because there is no truth in him. Whenever he speaks a lie, he speaks from his own nature, for he is a liar and the father of lies."

Everything about Satan is a lie, and he uses his lies to create chaos and disorder—moving things out of alignment in our lives. However, everything about God is true.

- "[God] interposed with an oath, so that by two unchange-able things in which it is *impossible for God to lie*, we who have taken refuge would have strong encouragement to take hold of the hope set before us " (Hebrews 6:17-18).

- "…in the hope of eternal life, which God, *who cannot lie*, promised long ages ago…" (Titus 1:2).

- "God is not a man, *that He should lie*, nor a son of man, that He should repent: Has He said, and will He not do it? Or has He spoken, and will He not make it good?" (Numbers 23:19).

- "Also the Glory of Israel *will not lie* or change His mind; for He is not a man that He should change His mind" (1 Samuel 15:29).

When a believer understands the objective nature of God's truth—and operates in that understanding—all other areas in that believer's life are automatically stabilized. Jesus said in John 8:32, "You will know the truth, and the truth will make you free." I often hear Christians quoting this verse, frequently emphasizing that the "truth will make you free." However, the factual reality of truth doesn't free anyone. If it did, we would all be free because truth exists whether we want it to or not. Truth is truth whether we recognize it or not.

Rather, it is the truth that you "know" that will make you free. "You will *know* the truth…" is the part of the verse that should be empha-sized because the truth that you know is the truth that frees you. And since God is the only one who cannot lie, He is the only one who lives and exists in a state of absolute truth. He is the Source of our freedom, our stability, and our victory.

Feelings cannot be the standard by which we measure reality. Feelings are important, but they aren't always true. Our feelings must always be brought in line with God's truth, or they can guide us down an unstable path. In fact, Christ goes so far as to say we are to be sanctified in the truth. To be sanctified means to be set apart and holy. We are to be unique in our responses, thoughts, decisions, relationships… and also in the way we do battle in spiritual warfare.

What Is Truth?

"What is truth?" Pilate asked 2000 years ago. People everywhere today are still asking the same question. We live in an age where relativism permeates our culture, with the result being that my truth may not be your truth, and your truth may not be your neighbor's truth. This leaves us in a state of constant flux because there is no overarching and guiding truth to which we all subscribe. It's similar to the situation we read about in Judges 21:25: "In those days there was no king in Israel; everyone did what was right in his own eyes."

Yet doing what was right in their own eyes got the Israelites into a world of hurt and defeat as their culture entered into a number of destructive behaviors, including rape, violence, and bloodshed. Truth cannot be defined by the individuals who have been created because individuals are finite beings with limited knowledge and deceitful hearts (see Jeremiah 17:9). Only the Creator of truth Himself can define truth because He is the only one who knows and understands all truth. Truth is fundamentally God-based knowledge.

Truth, at its core, is God's view of a matter. Truth is powerful enough to stabilize lives both in history and for eternity. The presence of truth brings clarity and victory, but the absence of truth leads to confusion and defeat.

Truth Includes God's Original Intent

The first principle of truth is that though it is comprised of information and facts, it also includes God's original intent, making it the absolute, objective standard by which reality is measured.

This reminds me of a story about a man who went fishing and brought home 20 catfish for his wife. He said, "Honey, I caught twenty catfish today." That was a fact. He had actually done what he said—he had brought home the 20 catfish he had caught.

His wife, however, knew that he wasn't a very good fisherman, so she asked him, "How did *you* catch twenty catfish?"

He answered, "Well, I went to the fish market and asked the guy to toss me twenty catfish. And I caught them all."

Originally this man had given the facts, but it wasn't the truth. He had cast the facts in such a way so as to hide the truth. Truth always involves more than just facts; it also includes the intention behind the facts. That's why Scripture tells us that God desires truth within us and not just outwardly in what we do. We read in Psalm 51:6, "Behold, You desire truth in the innermost being, and in the hidden part You will make me know wisdom." God wants truth to resonate in our "innermost being" because that's the core out of which our intentions flow into our actions.

Truth Is Predetermined by God

The second principle of truth is that truth has already been predetermined by God. Truth is not on trial.

An accountant, a psychologist, and a lawyer got together one day to discuss the nature of truth. The psychologist said, "Working with people, I've learned that truth is what you *feel* it to be." The accountant said, "Working with accounts, I've learned that truth is what you *need* it to be." And of course, the lawyer offered, "Working in the justice system, I've learned that truth is what you *want* it to be."

Our world today is in a constant shifting of its analysis of truth. Truth is comprised of opinions, perceptions, and ideas. What was true yesterday is rarely true today. One week we are told that coffee is bad for us. The next week a new study comes out that says coffee might save our lives. One year we're told we should avoid eating eggs. The next year a new study comes out telling us we should eat two eggs every day. New studies offering supposed truth pop up all around us all the time. But truth is objective, predetermined, and fixed. It cannot change with the latest fad or find. Truth is the standard to which all other things must conform because truth is reality in its original form.

One plus one equals two. One plus one has always equaled two. One plus one will always equal two. Even when I don't feel like one plus one should equal two, and I really feel like I want it to equal three, one plus one will still equal two. Even if I hope, believe, and name and claim that one plus one should equal three, one plus one will never equal three because the laws of mathematics are not adjustable. I must adjust to the laws of mathematics rather than suppose that mathematics will adjust to me. When I pay the bills each month, I use an objective standard in counting the numbers I will be subtracting. If I didn't, I would have confusion and chaos in my finances.

Truth cannot change simply because we want it to. Truth never adjusts itself to our feelings, hopes, or desires. God is the originator of all things true, and He does not lie, so He and His Word comprise the point of reference by which all else must comply.

Lois and I were recently walking in London near Westminster Palace when I noticed a number of people looking down at their watches and then looking back up again. This pattern continued for some time. They would look down at their watch, make a small adjustment, and then look back up.

They were setting their timepieces according to England's timepiece, Big Ben. While I was there, I never saw anyone approach a guard and tell him he needed to get whoever was in charge of Big Ben to change its time because it was five minutes off. To do that would have been ridiculous because everyone in England knows that all timepieces must be adjusted to match the true time as declared by Big Ben.

Big Ben doesn't care about anyone else's watch. Big Ben doesn't care how anyone else feels about his or her watch. Big Ben doesn't even care if a lot of people prefer a certain kind of watch or have the same time that's on each other's watches. Big Ben is not impressed by how much money someone spent buying his watch. Big Ben doesn't take polls to find out what everyone's watch has to say. Big Ben simply tells the time, and everyone else is supposed to adjust to Big Ben.

Or suppose you go to a doctor for chest pain, but instead of examining you, he tells you he wants to put you on some great new pills he had just read about. He tells you he isn't exactly sure what they're for, but he says a fancy flier described how good they tasted. Would you take the pills? No. Instead, you'd probably get yourself out of that office immediately and never go back.

When it comes to things like time and health, we want to function by a standard of truth. How much more important is it to function by a standard of truth when it comes to facing and battling the enemy, whose mission it is to destroy you with his lies? The devil doesn't want you to know the truth because the truth is the one thing that can set you free. Truth is a powerful reality predetermined by God. It sets the standard under which our thoughts and decisions must align.

Truth Is an Internal Reality

A third principle of truth is that it must resonate internally in order to have any validity externally. What is true outside of us in our actions, decisions, conversations, and choices ought to be true inside our spirit because it is within our spirit that God relates to us. When Jesus is speaking to the Samaritan woman about knowing God, He says, "God is spirit, and those who worship Him must worship in spirit and truth" (John 4:24). Cultivating internal truth—being honest with who we are and our motives, sins, mistakes, beliefs, desires, longings, and issues— is one of the essential steps to strapping on the belt of truth. God is not a God of pretense, but He is a God of great mercy.

In 2 Corinthians 3:18, Paul tells us, "But we all, with unveiled face, beholding as in a mirror the glory of the Lord, are being transformed into the same image from glory to glory."

One of the primary places Satan seeks to distort truth is within our relationship with God. His goal is to keep us veiled before God. He wants our relationship with God to be a charade rather than a spiritual reality. But let me tell you a secret—God already knows everything about you. He even knows the things you think you are hiding from

Him. You can't shock God. You can't surprise God. He already knows it all. This is the God who says of Himself, "I make known the end from the beginning, from ancient times, what is still to come" (Isaiah 46:10 NIV). God knows the past, present, and future of all things—your thoughts, your actions, and even what you want to do that you don't do. He knows all of it. You're not hiding anything from Him by praying in superfluous, spiritual-sounding holy words. Wearing the belt of truth means being real with God, being raw and unveiled before Him. When you get real with God, you will find it much easier to get real with yourself.

People can look fine on the outside. They can even do good and moral actions. But God views more than the outside. He views us holistically. He views us intimately, internally. What's more, He knows what we're up against within us, let alone what we have to face with others. "He knows how we are formed, he remembers that we are dust" (Psalm 103:14 NIV).

He knows that we're struggling, hurting, desiring, and failing, and He knows that at times we doubt Him. Since He already knows all this, why should we go to Him camouflaged and veiled? Why should we simply look the way religion says a Christian ought to look or pray the way religion says a Christian ought to pray. If a person cannot be truthful with God, who already knows the truth, then Satan has stripped that person of the foundational piece of armor before the battle even begins.

The Battle Between Our Ears

Here is the question I want you to ask yourself regarding truth: What will you use to determine what you believe to be true? Will it be your emotions? Emotions fluctuate, respond, and change. If I tell you I'm going to give you $1 million, your emotions might fly high. But then if I tell you that the $1 million is in play money, your emotions would undoubtedly sink back down. We need to acknowledge our emotions because they are real, but they should never be the final arbiter for determining truth.

Will you use your intelligence? Yes, I hear you—you're smart. You have your degrees, experience, and your common sense. Others admire you for that. But are you infinite in your brilliance? No, of course not. None of us are. How many times have you learned something, only to later find out new information and have to change your opinion? There is always new information and new data to influence what you believe. God is the only one who has all of the information. The rest of us are still gathering information as we go through life.

Will you use your moral instincts to determine what you believe to be true? Everyone has some form of a moral compass within them, but even that can change with emotions, new information, outside influences, or maturity.

What will your standard be? Will it be feelings (which are constantly changing) or intelligence (which is finite) or moral instincts (which differ)? Or will it be divine revelation? Only God is the author and originator of truth. Knowing Him and His Word is the only way to know how to function with the belt of truth because only God can define what is entirely true.

Much of our battle takes place right between our ears. The things you are struggling with, the things that make you feel defeated, the things you think you cannot face for yet another day...none of these is the real problem. The real problem is waged in your mind—what do you believe to be true? Your problems may show up in your feet, hands, eyes, heart, mouth, bedroom, bar, workplace, hospital, computer, and anyplace else, but the root of the problem is in what you believe to be true.

I'm sorry to have to tell you this, but it is important to know: *You can't trust yourself.* I'm disappointed to have to admit it, but I can't trust myself either. Why? Because our souls—our mind, will, and emotions—have been distorted. They have been contorted since birth. Have you ever been to an amusement park and seen the mirrors that make you look fat, tall, short, or skinny? Our souls have become distorted like these mirrors. The penetrating effects of sin have reached into our souls and twisted them so that they are no longer recognizable as what they were created to be.

A person looking into a carnival mirror could not accurately describe the true person who is being reflected in the mirror. Neither can you accurately define truth when looking through the distorted mirror of your soul. The soul within you, your viewpoint on a matter, needs to be restored. You need to exchange your thoughts with God's truth.

How does this process take place? It happens through the help of the third person of the Trinity, the Holy Spirit. Paul writes in 1 Corinthians 2:10, "The Spirit searches all things, even the depths of God." The Greek word Paul uses for "searches" (*ereuna*) means to "continually examine" something. In this case, the Holy Spirit is continually examining everything—even the depths of God.

Paul goes on to explain, "Now we have received, not the spirit of the world, but the Spirit who is from God, so that we may know the things freely given to us by God" (verse 12). It is through the work of the Spirit that we gain the ability to know God and the truth that can give us the capacity to walk in victory in our day-to-day lives. Please note that we *gain the ability* to know God. The Holy Spirit never forces us to know God or be restored by His truth. But it is through the work of the Spirit that we are given the opportunity to exchange our viewpoint on a matter with God's.

This exchange is a key aspect of wearing the belt of truth. We read in 2 Corinthians 10:3-5 how critical it is.

> For though we walk in the flesh, we do not war according to the flesh, for the weapons of our warfare are not of the flesh, but divinely powerful for the destruction of fortresses. We are destroying speculations and every lofty thing raised up against the knowledge of God, and we are taking every thought captive to the obedience of Christ.

In this passage, God reveals one of Satan's key strategies. Satan seeks to set up speculations (wrong thoughts) that contradict God's truth. In fact, anything that inhibits, distorts, or alters God's viewpoint on a matter is used by the enemy in his bid to defeat you. It could be something that seems as harmless as your mother's or father's opinion about what you should do or think. It could be what your friends or the media are persuading you to do or believe. It could even be the thoughts generated in your own distorted soul.

Satan doesn't care if you mix some of God's truth with the rest of the "truth" you're gathering from all of your other sources because he knows if he can twist what you believe to be true, that will be enough for him to set up speculations and raise lofty things against the knowledge of God. It can be compared to a woman who decides to prepare a pan of lasagna. She slices up the tomatoes, boils the noodles, fries the meat, adds some chopped onions and garlic along with cheese and sauce. Then, just as she's about to put the pan in the oven, she sprinkles arsenic all over the top.

Would you eat the lasagna? Neither would I. But that's what Satan seeks to do in order to strip us of the belt of truth. He says, "Go to church. Read your Bible. Memorize your verses. As a matter of fact, even I quote those verses—*out of their contextual truth*. But at the end of the day, sprinkle in a little bit about what the world says, what your parents say, how your friends think, what the television portrays, or whatever else you feel, desire, or want to believe." Satan knows that when you have done that, you have taken off your own belt of truth.

He didn't even have to take it off for you.

Wearing the belt of truth involves realizing that truth is fundamentally God-based knowledge—His viewpoint on a matter, containing three principles:

- Truth is comprised of information and facts, but it also includes God's original intent, making it the absolute, objective standard by which reality is measured.

- Truth has already been predetermined by God.

- Truth must resonate internally in order to have any validity externally.

When you wear the belt of truth and operate with it by aligning your mind, will, and emotions underneath God's view on a matter— His truth—He will then empower you to fight your spiritual battles with the freedom of greater mobility and increased stability. By knowing and functioning according to the truth of God, you will be on your way to experiencing victory over anything or anyone seeking to overcome or defeat you.

5

THE BREASTPLATE
OF RIGHTEOUSNESS

Satan cannot take away your salvation, but he can ruin your life. He attempts to do just that by waging war in a way that keeps you from experiencing all that God has planned for you. His aim is to prevent you from realizing the full potential of your life and salvation.

As we have seen earlier, one way Satan does this is by trying to shift your gaze off of the spiritual realm and onto the physical realm. That way he keeps you focused on what you can see, taste, touch, smell, or hear rather than on him and the demons he has working with him. This keeps you from dealing with the root behind the fruit manifesting itself as a negative reality in your life.

Satan's scheme reminds me of something that happened on a recent trip Lois and I took for our annual vacation. Once a year, Lois and I take some time away from our busy schedules to refresh ourselves, plan the next year, and enjoy each other. For this particular getaway, we had decided to spend some time on a Mediterranean cruise. The thing I enjoy most about cruises is visiting a number of places without having to pack and unpack our bags or change where we are staying. They also give me a significant amount of "away" time to recoup from a busy preaching and traveling schedule, allowing me the luxury of throwing myself into the Word and study books that I use in preparation for my sermons when I return.

A few days after Lois and I boarded the ship, however, the upper left side of my mouth began to hurt. At first it was just a slight, irritating pain that I tried my best to ignore. But every hour the pain continued to get worse. Not too long into the pain, I took some aspirin to see if that would help, but it didn't. So then I tried some ibuprofen to see if that would do the trick, but it didn't do much to alleviate it either. In fact, the pain just seemed to be getting worse.

After four or five days of using different over-the-counter remedies, I found myself in such excruciating pain that I couldn't even get out of bed, let alone enjoy the different sites we were supposed to be visiting. Now, anyone who knows me at all knows that it takes an awful lot to keep me down, but that's exactly the kind of knockout punch this pain had turned into.

Eventually I drug my joyless self down to the ship doctor's office and told him, "This is killing me. My mouth is killing me. I can't move. I can't think. I can't eat. I can't read. I can't do anything but focus on this agonizing pain!"

The doctor, knowing that not being able to eat on a cruise was nothing short of cruel and unusual punishment, quickly came to my aid and gave me some codeine to address the pain. He then sent me on my way, assuring me that I should be fine for the remainder of the trip. What he had said sounded good. The only problem was that the codeine didn't work either. In fact, even when I increased the amount the doctor had instructed me to take, I felt no relief.

So making my way to an onboard telephone, I finally called my dentist halfway around the world in Dallas. I explained to him what I was feeling and that nothing was taking away the pain, and I even told him that I would fly back to Texas if he would just do something—anything!—to make it stop. My dentist calmly told me that flying back to Texas wouldn't be necessary. He said, "Tony, you've been treating the wrong problem. You've been addressing the pain, but your pain is simply symptomatic of a much deeper problem. From what you've described to me, it sounds like you have an abscess. All of the aspirin or codeine in the world won't solve the problem of an abscess. Only an antibiotic will get to the root of what you are experiencing."

My attempts to fix what I could see and feel had only masked what really needed to be addressed all along. In fact, had the aspir profen, or codeine worked, it would have only led to a larger problem because I would have thought that my issue had been solved. This would have enabled the infection to deepen and eventually spread into other parts of my body.

Sure enough, after only a day on antibiotics, I no longer needed to turn to anything else to reduce my pain. This is because the prescribed antibiotics dealt with the root behind the fruit that I was feeling.

We often do a similar thing when addressing the results of spiritual warfare waging in our lives. We miss the source behind what we're facing when we direct our efforts and attention solely toward managing the mess. Oftentimes we will wait, as I did on the ship, until we have exhausted all of our human efforts before we will turn to the Expert. But when we delay like that, we waste valuable days, weeks, months, years, and sometimes even decades living within the limitations of a life dictated to us by circumstances or emotions rather than living the abundant life that God has promised every believer. Had I taken the antibiotic sooner, I would have enjoyed several more days of my vacation that were instead wasted as I dealt with the fruit and not the root of my problem.

It's common to think that a "carnal" Christian is an individual who is steeped heavily in a life of obvious sin. While this can be the case, what we sometimes fail to realize is that to operate carnally does not always mean engaging in specific, recognizable sins. The word "carnal" simply refers to "relating to physical needs." A carnal Christian can also be someone who is living a life fixated in the physical realm. A carnal Christian makes his or her decisions based entirely on what can be seen, touched, tasted, smelled, or heard.

When Christians choose to depend on the five senses as the deciding factors for addressing life's choices, they set themselves up as easy targets of the enemy. Satan knows if he can just get you to believe that your battle is being waged in your flesh, or within the fleshy world around you, he has you beat. He will keep you down as you try human remedy after human remedy to deal with what can only be cured with a spiritual solution.

Imputed Righteousness

So far we've looked at the first piece in the armor of God—the belt of truth. After the belt of truth, Paul gives us the next item in our wardrobe. He says in Ephesians 6:14, "Put on the breastplate of righteousness." Righteousness simply means being or doing what is right. The belt of truth comes before righteousness because there can't be righteousness apart from truth. Truth is the standard. Righteousness reveals how to work that standard out.

There are two sides to righteousness—the *being* side and the *doing* side. Righteousness has been imputed to everyone who has trusted in Jesus Christ for the forgiveness of their sins. When we talk about salvation, we often think of this idea of the forgiveness of sins. While this is one thing that happens at the moment of salvation, it is not the only thing. In fact, forgiveness on its own is not enough to get a person into heaven.

God did more than forgive our sins through Jesus Christ. He also imputed, or credited to our account, the righteousness of Jesus Christ. We read in 2 Corinthians 5:21, "He made Him who knew no sin to be sin on our behalf, so that we might *become the righteousness* of God in Him."

God not only removed the stain of your sin when you trusted in Jesus Christ but also replaced that stain with the righteous standard of Christ. So now when God looks at you, He sees you as equal to His son. He doesn't just see someone who has been forgiven of his or her sins; He sees someone who has kept the full standard of righteousness.

Imputing righteousness can be compared to God crediting your account, or putting money in your bank. The money now belongs to you. No one can take that money away from you. Even Satan cannot take that money away. Once you are saved, Satan can do nothing to change your righteous standing—your justification—before God.

However, because Satan cannot take away your imputed righteousness, what he tries to do is restrict your personal practice of righteousness. He knows he can't take away your standing before God, so he looks for a way to break your fellowship with God by causing a breach between your *position* of righteousness and your *practice* of righteousness.

Coming Clean

Now, granted—none of us are without sin. There isn't a person on this planet who can live his or her life absent of sin. Sin manifests itself in many different varieties. There are overt sins, which are done outwardly through our actions. But then there are also covert sins, which take place in our minds, hearts, and emotions. Beyond that, there are also sins of commission (doing things the Bible says we should not do) and sins of omission (not doing things the Bible says we ought to do). We read in James 4:17, "Therefore, to one who knows the right thing to do and does not do it, to him it is sin."

One of the major problems in identifying and addressing sin is the standard we measure it against. Like truth—which includes not only information and facts but also the intention behind the information and facts—righteousness includes more than right behavior. Righteousness includes the motivation behind doing right behavior or not doing wrong behavior. In fact, a person can literally do the right thing and yet contaminate it with wrong motivation. Maybe the motivation is pride, a form of self-righteousness. Or maybe the motivation is fear, knowing that doing the wrong thing will lead to severe consequences.

It's like the young boy who was told by his teacher to sit down. He didn't want to sit down, but he knew what he would suffer if he didn't. So he sat down. Yet in his heart he said, "I'm sitting down on the outside, but I'm standing up on the inside." Unlike the teacher, who cannot see the boy's heart, God sees deep within us and measures the motivation of all that we do or don't do.

A lot of us would be surprised if we learned to view sin the way God views sin. For example, we read in 1 John 3:15 that God equates hatred with murder: "Everyone who hates his brother is a murderer." Apparently, we have a lot of convicted felons coming to church every week—many not even aware of the gravity of their sin. Keeping us unaware of our own sin is one of Satan's strategies in spiritual warfare because he knows we will not confess that which we do not recognize.

However, when we do confess the sin in our lives, God removes that stain and stench of sin from us. We read in 1 John 1:9, "If we confess our sins, He is faithful and righteous to forgive us our sins and to cleanse us from all unrighteousness." Because of your positional righteousness in Jesus Christ, you are able to maintain relational righteousness before God at all times by confessing your sin to God.

In Zechariah 3, we read about a similar thing taking place. A preacher named Joshua came before the Lord with dirty clothes on. He came before God in unrighteousness. He didn't do like many of us and try to hide his dirty clothes from God, or try to persuade God to believe that his clothes really weren't as dirty as they appeared. He simply stood before God in his unrighteousness.

> Then he showed me Joshua the high priest standing before the angel of the LORD, and Satan standing at his right hand to accuse him. The LORD said to Satan, "The LORD rebuke you, Satan! Indeed, the LORD who has chosen Jerusalem rebuke you! Is this not a brand plucked from the fire?" Now Joshua was clothed with filthy garments and standing before the angel. He spoke and said to those who were standing before him, saying, "Remove the filthy garments from him." Again he said to him, "See, I have taken your iniquity away from you and will clothe you with festal robes." Then I said, "Let them put a clean turban on his head." So they put a clean turban on his head and clothed him with garments, while the angel of the LORD was standing by (Zechariah 3:1-5).

God responded to Joshua's dirty clothes and Satan's accusation by removing Joshua's iniquity and covering him instead with clothes designed for a unique and special purpose—with festal robes. Joshua hadn't done anything to deserve the festal robes. God gave him these robes out of His mercy.

In like manner, Satan accuses each of us when we stand before God. The book of Revelation tells us that Satan accuses us day and night.

> Then I heard a loud voice in heaven, saying, "Now the salvation, and the power, and the kingdom of our God and the authority of His Christ have come, for *the accuser of our brethren* has been thrown down, he who accuses them before our God day and night" (Revelation 12:10).

Satan's number one hobby is to accuse you and me of all of the wrong things we have ever done or thought. Yet confessing our sin to God and receiving His forgiveness will restore our *practice* of righteousness back into alignment with our *position* of righteousness. We underestimate the power of coming clean with God. Too often our prayers focus on how God can bless us, take care of us, protect us, and deliver us, but God has given us the key to victory through one critical move—confession.

Doing wrong is wrong—sin is sin. However, unconfessed sin breeds an even greater environment for it to continue. Not only that, but it breeds an environment that demons will want to hang out in. Let me explain it this way: Having trash in your house is a bad thing when it's not kept in a container and then taken out and emptied regularly. Trash or food left out on the counters or on the floor will breed an environment for roaches to come and live in. It's almost like putting down a welcome mat for your new guests. The roaches will invite their cousins and make themselves at home in your trash. Similarly, demons make themselves at home in sin—whether that sin is being committed or just remains around residually having not been addressed through confession and repentance.

Unrighteousness and disobedience unlock a door that allows Satan and his demons to enter in and influence the environment or even take control of it. In 2 Thessalonians 2:7, Paul calls this "access principle" the mystery of lawlessness. This hidden principle further underscores the truth that we wrestle with the invisible realm even though our battle may be manifested in the visible realm.

Instead of confessing and removing the sin or unrighteousness from our lives, we often end up settling for trash management. This can also be called soul management.

We want to manage things—move stuff here, adjust things here, and hide stuff here—so we don't appear to have much trash. This is like getting an unexpected guest when you don't have the time to clean up your house all of the way. So you stuff things in a closet or in an empty room and maybe push a few things under the bed. The house looks clean to your guest, but the mess is still there to attract the roaches because you haven't removed the root attraction that brings them there in the first place.

Or you might do what I sometimes do in our home. Since I'm responsible for taking out the trash in our home, I purchased a machine called a trash masher. Maybe you have one too. I love my trash masher. My trash masher will give me at least one extra day before I have to empty the kitchen trash. Depending on how many people are in the house, it might even give me two days.

The problem with my trash masher is that it's no match for my wife's standards. Lois can smell day-old trash even before it's a day old. She doesn't want any of that smell permeating the home that she spends so much time making comfortable for all of us, so she'll ask me, "Tony, did you forget about the trash?" Lois knows that even smashed trash is smelly trash. Similarly, hidden sin leaves its stench in and through-out our lives, giving Satan and his demons a warm welcome to make themselves at home in it.

Two things happen in spiritual warfare when the breastplate of righteousness is not worn. First, an invitation is sent out to allow demons to hang out in your life. Second, the movement of God is hindered within and through you because there is a break in your fellowship with God. God does not abide with darkness.

Feeding Your Spirit

An important point to note about the breastplate of righteousness is what it is designed to protect—the heart. Why should we want to protect our hearts? Because the only reason the rest of us works is due to the heart. Once the heart stops, everything else stops. This is true not only in the physical realm but also in the spiritual realm. The book of Proverbs tells us, "Above all else, guard your heart, for it is the well-spring of life" (Proverbs 4:23 NIV).

As the heart is the physical pump controlling the flow of blood throughout our body, so the heart, our essence and our core, is the spiritual pump that God uses to infuse life into us. As I mentioned earlier, once you trust Christ for your salvation, you are made new with His righteousness. Second Corinthians 5:17 says, "Therefore if anyone is in Christ, he is a new creature; the old things passed away; behold, new things have come." Keep in mind that you're made up of three distinct parts: body, soul, and spirit. Sometimes we talk as if our soul is the part of us that is made new at salvation. We say things like "Jesus saved my soul."

However, the thing that was immediately made new when you became a Christian was your spirit. Your soul is in the process of being sanctified and made new over time. That's why you can be a Christian but still have an addiction, or be angry all of the time, or be depressed. Your soul (your mind, will, and emotions) is still distorted, and it is telling your body what to do.

Satan wants you to think that your soul is what was made new so that you'll believe that in order to gain victory in the spiritual realm, you just need to focus on managing your mind, will, and emotions so you can then get your body in line. He wants you to think that way because he knows you'll never be able to fix what your body does on your own. Your real problem is an unsanctified soul.

The work of the new spirit within you is to pump life into the soul so that eventually your new spirit becomes the dominant influencer in what you feel, think, and do. What religion often does is try to change a person from the outside. Religion tells us we will be victorious if we go to church more, be better people, give more, serve more, worship more, deny ourselves more, sing louder, or try harder. But those things simply produce more and more weary and defeated Christians.

Authentic victory happens on the inside when the new spirit within us pumps God's truth into the different areas of our life. Just as our hearts pump blood to the different parts of our bodies, our spirits pump the truth of God into our souls—our mind, will, and emotions. Then our souls tell our bodies to adjust to God's standard instead of their own.

Don't misunderstand me, soul management—managing our sin and propensity toward sin—is not a bad thing. I wouldn't want a murderer walking around doing whatever he wanted to do. I think we would all want him to manage his impulses. But soul management alone won't bring about the freedom and abundant life that God promises. For that, we need soul *restoration*. We need God to restore our mind, will, and emotions so they function the way He intended them to when He first created mankind in the garden. Soul management may stop you from doing something you shouldn't be doing, but it hasn't dealt with your tendency to do it or the effect it has had on you. And so the battle continues even though it has already been won. Far too many of us have settled for behavior modification, which can lead to hypocrisy. We look spiritually "well-done" on the outside, but we are "raw" on the inside.

Because our souls are distorted, we need to access the perfect righteousness placed within us in our new spirit. We have to receive the truth of God's Word deep within us, or we will continue to live defeated lives and focus on outward attempts at transformation. Our soul cannot fix our soul. It cannot be righteous on its own. As we allow the new life of the spirit to dominate and permeate our soul, we will find true and lasting victory.

The book of James refers to this process. "Therefore, putting aside all filthiness and all that remains of wickedness, in humility receive the word implanted, which is able to save your souls" (James 1:21). The first point we need to recognize from this passage is that James is writing to believers. A few verses earlier he has called them "beloved brethren." Yet even though they are already "saved," James says their souls need to be saved. This is because he is referring to the saving process called sanctification.

Yet in order for the soul to be sanctified in righteousness, it needs to receive the word implanted. The New International Version says, "Humbly accept the word planted in you." This occurs through the enablement of the Holy Spirit's presence and power in our lives.

One of the reasons we are not experiencing victory in spiritual warfare is that we are trying to force on ourselves a man-made breastplate of righteousness rather than submitting to, accepting, or receiving God's truth as the standard of righteousness He wants us to wear.

Receiving this implanted word within our spirit is best illustrated by a fertilized egg in a woman's womb. The fertilized egg has been planted inside the uterus of this woman. It receives nourishment from the woman. As the woman nourishes this egg, the egg receives the necessary nutrients it needs to produce growth. The more nourishment the egg receives, the more dominant of a presence this baby makes in the mother's womb. This continues until eventually, during delivery, the baby dictates the mother's mind, will, emotions, and even her physical body.

Likewise, the righteousness of God made known through His Word must reach from His Spirit into our spirit, feeding it as it grows to dominate our soul. The Bible is to the spirit what food is to the body. As the Word of God feeds your spirit and begins to influence your soul, your actions will begin to naturally reflect God's viewpoint on a matter. They won't just be reactions that you do for a time based on a good sermon, book, or encouragement you read or heard. Your desires and your propensities will organically change as they become influenced by the Spirit's presence of truth and righteousness within you. As Paul tells us in Galatians 5:16, "But I say, walk by the Spirit, and you will not carry out the desire of the flesh." True righteousness is *released*, not manufactured.

Feeding the righteousness planted within you will take more than a minute. It means meditating on, rehearsing, and considering over and over again the truths found in God's Word. Fantasize about God's truth. You read that right—fantasize about what God says in His Word. Let it become as real to you in your thoughts as whatever you see all around you. Worrying about something can actually make it seem worse over time, but fantasizing about the righteous truth and promises of God revealed in His Word will make them more real to you. Memorize and then meditate on God's Word. Allow it to resonate in your heart to such a degree that it becomes your breastplate of righteousness.

This principle is so important that I've taken the time to compile specific promises and truths from God's Word for you in part 4 of this book so you don't even have to look them up yourself. I want you to live in the victory that has been bought for you, but living in that victory requires replacing the deceptions of Satan and the distortions in your soul with the truth and righteousness of God found in His Word.

When truth flows freely from your spirit because it has been received, accepted, and submitted to, it releases righteousness into your soul, thereby restoring it. As the soul breathes in the righteousness being released into it, it then tells the body, "You have to walk differently. You have to think differently. You have to talk differently. You have to dress differently. You have to choose your friends differently. You have to spend your money differently. You have to live differently. Because you *are* different."

Using the Breastplate of Righteousness

The breastplate of righteousness has been deposited within us. It's our job to feed it and nourish it with the truth of God so that it expands to surround us with the protection in warfare that we desperately need.

If I told you that I had buried $10 million in your backyard, you would put this book down right now and make every effort to get a shovel and get to your backyard. You would leave wherever you are and quickly go tear up your yard. You would dig as deep as you needed to dig because the thing you were digging for would have life-impacting value. That $10 million would be worth all the effort required to find it.

When you got saved, God deposited deep down within you all of the righteousness that belongs to Jesus Christ. But you can't benefit from its restoring abilities unless you're willing to dig down deep with the shovel of truth so that God will release a brand-new you surrounded by the secure protection of a breastplate of His righteousness.

Wearing the breastplate of righteousness involves walking securely in your imputed righteousness by virtue of the cross, coming clean with God in your practice of righteousness, and feeding your spirit with the Word of God so that the Spirit will produce the natural outgrowth of right living from within you.

6

THE SHOES OF PEACE

You have probably either seen or heard about the 1994 Academy Award–winning mega-blockbuster *Forrest Gump*. The film captivated audiences with its ability to capture the nuances of a unique character named Forrest. Several times during the film, we see Forrest sitting on a bench next to a local nurse.

At one point, Forrest begins a conversation with the nurse, and after admiring her comfortable shoes for a while, he says, "My momma always said you can tell a lot about a person by their shoes. Where they're going. Where they've been."

Shoes play an important role in our lives whether they are simply the latest trend, the most scientifically proven athletic shoe, or an expensive name brand. They can be symbols of something more than what they actually are, as we've seen with Dorothy's ruby slippers or Cinderella's glass one. Many women (and a few men) have obsessions with shoes, as in the notable cases of Imelda Marcos, Eva Peron, or former Romanian president Nicolae Ceausescu. When God addressed Moses in the desert and Joshua at the border of the promised land, He told them to remove their shoes.

Not surprisingly, then, the next piece of armor necessary for experiencing victory in spiritual warfare involves shoes. After all, you can tell a lot about a person by their shoes.

In Ephesians 6:15, Paul reveals that taking up the full armor of God includes "having shod your feet with the preparation of the gospel of peace." The term "shod" used in this statement refers to what you have on your feet. Paul says that not only do you need to wear the belt of truth and the breastplate of righteousness, but you also need to put on the right shoes.

A Roman soldier's shoes were called *caliga*—sandals studded heavily with nails. These nails, known as hobnails, were firmly placed directly through the sole of the shoe for increased durability and stability. Similar to cleats worn on football and soccer fields today, hobnails provided traction when needed. This traction kept the soldier from slipping and sliding, much like cleats help a football or soccer player today. It gave him sure footing, making mobility in battle easier while also making it more difficult to be knocked down.

So when Paul instructs you to have your feet shod, he is talking about placing yourself in a stationary position to stand firm. This creates traction so that when Satan comes, he can't knock you off your feet. In fact, you are able to "stand firm" because the nails coming out of your "peace shoes" have dug deep into the solid ground beneath you.

You know what it means to be knocked over from time to time. You know what it's like when your circumstances, situations, friends, finances, career, or any number of other things have removed you from your position of stability. Things happen that make you feel unstable, shaky, and defeated. In fact, the economic downturn in our nation has no doubt led to a large degree of instability in many people's lives.

What Paul is telling us in this passage is that it doesn't have to be that way. You don't have to slide or move with every hit or trial. Having your feet shod with the preparation of the gospel of peace creates a stability that even Satan cannot undo.

As I mentioned earlier, the goal of Satan and his demons in spiritual warfare is to keep you defeated. It is to keep you on the defense. That is how Satan keeps you from experiencing God's purpose, provision, forward movement, and blessings in your life. Satan knows he can't take away your salvation, so he attempts to make you a miserable Christian. He can't keep you out of heaven, so he tries to make you experience hell on earth.

However, one way to move from defense to offense in spiritual warfare and bring a little bit of heaven right down to earth is to have your feet shod with the preparation of the gospel of peace.

The Greek word for "preparation" in this verse is *hetoimasia*, which means readiness, promptness, and speediness. It's similar to the instruction given us in 1 Peter 3:15: "Always be prepared to give an answer to everyone who asks you to give the reason for the hope that you have" (NIV). Putting on your peace shoes involves making yourself ready to deal with whatever comes your way.

But what is this "gospel of peace" that we are to wear on our feet?

The Gospel of Peace

It seems like today we see the word "peace" thrown around all over the place. The popular peace symbol can be found on jewelry, bumper stickers, clothing, notebooks, tattoos, and television advertisements. Peace means different things to different people. In the Middle East, it can mean the absence of war. To a stay-at-home mother of three small children, it can mean nap time. The concept of peace is popular in our culture, but in order for you to put on this third piece of the armor and experience victory in spiritual warfare, you need to understand and wear God's peace.

The Greek word translated "peace" in the Scripture is *eirene*. This word is equivalent to the Hebrew word *shalom*. Essentially, *eirene* embodies completeness, wholeness, and an inner resting of the soul that does not fluctuate based on outside influences. A person who is at peace is someone who is stable, calm, orderly, and at rest within. The opposite of peace, of course, is inner chaos, anxiety, and worry.

This reminds me of a story about two painters who were asked one day to paint a picture of peace. Whichever painter could paint the best picture of peace was going to win $250,000. As you can imagine, both painters were highly motivated to paint the absolute best picture of peace that had ever been painted.

The first painter set to work on his painting and began by creating a serene portrait of a lake with the sun glistening off of it at just the right angle so that it sparkled across the top of the water. A shepherd walked near the lake with sheep following him at a distance. Trees stood off to one side of the lake with birds gathered in their tallest branches.

After finishing his painting, the painter leaned back and took a deep breath of satisfaction. In his mind, he had portrayed peace.

The second painter had a different idea in mind when he painted his portrait. In his painting, the sky was pitch black. Lightning shot through the air in zigzagged movements. This painter also had water, but the waves in his painting thrashed as if they were somehow awakened from a terrible dream. Trees bent and bowed down in the wind. The painting looked like a portrait of chaos.

But when you looked closely at the second artist's painting, all the way down to the bottom on the left-hand side, just near the very edge of this horrific scene, you could see a little bird standing on a rock. The little bird had its mouth open, as if singing a beautiful song. One faint light shone down from the darkness of the clouds onto the bird as it sung in spite of the situation all around it.

The second painter won the competition. The judges chose him as the winner because he showed the truest manifestation of peace— a peace that resonates from within despite what's going on all around. Peace doesn't refer to an inner calm when all around you is calm. When you are surrounded by tranquility, you are supposed to be calm. When you experience godly peace, you are at rest even when everything else is all wrong.

Thunder and lightning might be chasing each other all around you. The wind could be blowing unexpected and unpleasant circumstances into your life. Nothing looks right. Nothing looks promising. All is dark. But it's exactly in those moments when true peace wins the battle. This is because even when you are experiencing chaos on the outside, the tranquility on the inside eases your mind.

In fact, the Bible says that the peace of God is so opposite to the natural way of responding to life's trials that we often cannot even understand it. This peace then goes to work for you in spiritual warfare by guarding you from the enemy's tactics. We read about this in Philippians 4:7: "And the peace of God, which surpasses all comprehension, will guard your hearts and your minds in Christ Jesus." Peace protects you.

God offers us a peace that reaches beyond what we can comprehend. When we receive and walk in that peace, it settles in as a guard over our hearts and our minds. This is the peace that cradles people who lost their jobs so that they don't also lose their minds. This is the peace that produces praise when there is no paper in the bank. This is the peace that restores hope in the face of failing health. This peace is so powerful that we're instructed to let it control us. We are taught to let it call the shots, make the decisions, and dictate our emotions.

Paul writes in Colossians 3:15, "Let the peace of Christ rule in your hearts." The Greek word used for "rule" in this verse essentially means "to umpire." Peace is to be our umpire. What is the main job of a baseball umpire? The umpire ultimately declares the way things are. If he calls a pitch a ball, it is a ball. If he calls a runner out, the runner is out. The game is centered around what the umpire calls. Likewise, the peace of Christ is to make the call in your life. The reason this is so important is that life serves up so many choices and opportunities for decisions. We wonder which job to take, which conversation to have, and which person to marry. Do I go on this trip, should I spend this money, what church do I attend, where should I live...?

However, God says that when you allow peace to be the umpire in your life, He will call the shots. If you align your thoughts and your desires underneath His comprehensive rule over every area of your life, you will walk in peace. He will calm your heart and your mind by giving you peace.

Have you ever been in a situation where all of the facts seemed to line up one way, but inside you're thinking, "I just don't feel right about this—there just isn't any peace attached to this decision." Oftentimes, in a situation like that, a person should wait to make a decision because the confirmation of peace is not there. If the peace of Christ is ruling, that automatically means the peace of Christ is present. When it is not present, something else is in charge. That something else could be worry, or it could be anxiety. Whatever it is, if there is no inner peace ruling your heart and your mind, you have taken off the peace-shoes God made especially for you.

Jesus provided a powerful example of peace in the midst of chaos the night He was about to be crucified. Jesus was about to go into a very non-peaceful situation. Yet in the middle of the storm, He said, "Peace I leave with you; My peace I give to you; not as the world gives do I give to you. Do not let your heart be troubled, nor let it be fearful" (John 14:27). Jesus was saying that His peace is different from the world's peace. The world might offer you peace in a pill, peace in a song, peace in a drink, peace in entertainment, peace in an injection, peace in a relationship, peace in a Louis Vuitton bag…The world serves up peace in a variety of ways. The problem with the world's peace is that it only lasts as long as the thing that it comes in. The effects of the pill or alcohol wear off. The entertainment ends, and so does the peace.

But the peace that God gives produces rest on the inside. It *remains*. No matter what's going on around you—even if it's a cross—you can still have peace. You can handle it. You may not like it, but you can handle it. Jesus says *that* is the kind of peace He wants you to have. In fact, He told the disciples they were to have that kind of peace later when He said, "These things I have spoken to you, so that in Me you may have peace. In the world you have tribulation, but take courage; I have overcome the world" (John 16:33).

In order to overcome something, you have to have something to overcome. Peace is always tied to overcoming something. You won't truly know that you have peace until something goes wrong because everyone can feel peaceful when everything is right. But in the midst of a struggle, battle, war, addiction, conflict, or any number of things— that's when you discover the need to cover your feet with peace.

So how do you cover your feet with peace? The secret is in the gospel. We have been instructed to put on "the preparation of the gospel of peace." The Greek word for "gospel" is *euangelion*, which simply translated means "good news."

The word *euangelion* was frequently used in the New Testament but rarely used in either Classical or Koine Greek. The reason it wasn't used in either formal or informal Greek is that it referred to news that was so good, it was too good to be true. It was a word reserved for special usage. That's why its importance is felt so heavily when it's used in the Bible. To the natural eye, what comes packaged in the gospel is so good, it's too good to be true.

At the heart of the gospel is the death and resurrection of Jesus Christ as the substitute for our sins, but there is more to it than that. Most people apply the gospel only to what it takes to get to heaven; however, the gospel also has an awful lot to do with earth. We read about this in Romans 5:6-10.

> For while we were still helpless, at the right time Christ died for the ungodly. For one will hardly die for a righteous man; though perhaps for the good man someone would dare even to die. But God demonstrates His own love toward us, in that while we were yet sinners, Christ died for us. Much more then, having now been justified by His blood, we shall be saved from the wrath of God through Him. For if while we were enemies we were reconciled to God through the death of His Son, much more, having been reconciled, we shall be saved by His life.

In other words, we are saved for heaven through Christ's death, but Jesus is also delivering our lives in the here and now through His life. In Christian circles today, we are familiar with the gospel of Jesus' death. What we have often missed is the gospel of Jesus' life. When you accepted Jesus, you were justified. However, the rest of your time on earth, you are being sanctified. And God is the One who will do this.

This is revealed in greater depth in 1 Thessalonians 5:23: "Now may the God of peace Himself sanctify you entirely; and may your spirit and soul and body be preserved complete, without blame at the coming of our Lord Jesus Christ." When Paul writes, "the God of peace Himself," the word "Himself" is a reflective pronoun, indicating that God will sanctify you apart from anyone else's help.

Also notice the order that God sanctifies…from spirit to soul to body. God does not start with the body and then go to the soul, only to wind up at the spirit. As we saw in the last chapter, God starts at the spirit to nourish and grow its influence over the soul, which then brings about a change in the body.

This is an important truth because it lets us know why so many of us are unable to find true and lasting peace. We're marching to the tune of "Backward Christian Soldiers." We're trying to whip our bodies into shape without the help of the only One who can sanctify and restore us from within. That is the wrong direction.

At salvation, God deposited within each of us a new nature—that is our spirit. The spirit contains all of God's power, presence, joy, peace, righteousness, holiness, and much more. Everything God has in store for you is resident in the new spirit within you, and it is perfect. Your new spirit, which hosts the divine nature of God planted in you, is the only place that the spiritual realm of darkness does not have access to. The problem is that your perfect spirit is lodged within your imperfect soul.

Remember, your soul has become distorted through the consequences of your own sin and also the effect that others' sin has had on you. Your soul was affected by the way you were raised. Your soul has been affected by what your peers have said or done to you. Your soul has been affected by the media and culture. It has even been affected by the things you learned in school.

Your soul—mind, will, and emotions—is affected by so many different and changing variables, you can find yourself acting one way one year and another way another year. Your personality can be up one day and down the next because your soul is telling your body what to do. Have you ever noticed that sometimes when you worry for a long time, your body starts twitching? If you stay nervous long enough, your eye can start twitching, your voice might crack, or your breathing can become shallow.

A large number of our health-related issues are what psychologists call psychosomatic illnesses. These are real, felt, and negative health effects taking place in people's bodies even though doctors can't find any cause for the symptoms. In such cases, the damaged soul is rubbing off on the body, and the body is simply acting as an expression of that damage.

That's exactly what Satan wants in spiritual warfare. He wants us to take off our shoes and lose our peace. When you lose your peace, you can't sleep as well anymore. You can't think as clearly anymore.

You can't function as well anymore. You say things you regret. You do things you know you shouldn't. You become someone you don't even recognize at times.

Every one of us has a distorted soul. You are not unique in that regard. Some people's souls are more distorted than others, but everyone is viewing life through the lens of a distorted soul. Our bodies do wrong things because they're following the direction of our distorted souls. This is an important point to realize: *You can't fix you.* At the most, all you can do is try to manage you.

That's why New Year's resolutions rarely last. They are simply attempts to manage the mess through external means. God doesn't work that way. God works from the spirit first, then to the soul, and finally to the body. So if you want your body to be victorious in spiritual warfare, begin by getting your soul to be victorious in spiritual warfare. And if you want your soul to be victorious in spiritual warfare, begin by feeding and nourishing the spirit implanted within you.

Instead of nourishing our spirit, many of us go to a counselor and try to understand what we need to do to change our souls. But I can save you $200 an hour right now if you will simply grasp this one fundamental truth: *God gives peace all by Himself, and He starts the process right inside your spirit.*

Here is how it works. The Holy Spirit releases the truths, the essence, the presence of God—what you might call the DNA of God—into your human spirit. Your spirit then delivers it to your soul. Yet we're not experiencing this release in our lives to a greater degree because in order for the soul to grab onto and receive the things of the spirit, it must agree with the spirit. However, most of our souls are so filled with deception and distortion, the spirit isn't free to release its power into us. Therefore, you must start by replacing the distortions within you with the truth—placing the truth of God into you—because the truth is the only thing that the spirit and the soul can agree upon.

The only way to experience true and authentic peace is to submit your mind, will, and emotions—your soul—to the overarching truth of God. For example, let's say that you recently lost your job and you have no money in the bank. Those are the facts. Those facts would cause you to worry. But the truth of God says, "My God shall supply all your needs." Which one are you going to believe? The facts you see or the truth that may not be so readily visible to the natural eye? Which one are you going to operate by?

Your soul is telling you, "Hey, you're broke. They're going to turn off your lights and kick you out of your house."

Your spirit is telling you, "God will provide."

Putting on peace-shoes means aligning your soul under the rule of your spirit. When you choose to do that, God will release peace into your life because the peace of Christ is now ruling your thoughts and actions. When worry creeps back in, you remind it that it's lying to you, because God has promised that He will provide.

That's why knowing and living by the principles we have already seen in Philippians 4:6-7 are vital to your victory: "Be anxious for nothing, but in everything by prayer and supplication with thanksgiving let your requests be made known to God. And the peace of God, which surpasses all comprehension, will guard your hearts and your minds in Christ Jesus."

Why does Scripture tell us to go to God with thanksgiving? When God deposited the spiritual seed of new life in your spirit, that implanted seed included everything you need in order to experience complete and total victory. It can be compared to an acorn. A small, seemingly insignificant acorn has everything within it to become a big, tall, mighty oak tree. All it needs is nourishment, and then it will grow.

Similarly, you don't have to add anything to your spirit. Everything you need is already in there. Instead, you need to do thank God when you face a trial, battle, or need of any kind. You need to thank Him that He has already given you everything you need to overcome. Your goal isn't to add something new to your spirit; your goal is to draw out what God has already deposited.

Sailors on a submarine don't have to get nervous when they head into a storm, because they can go deep underneath the storm. So too, you don't need to get nervous when the waves of life appear to be crashing in on you. Instead, you can go deep within the new spirit placed within you—past your mind, will, and emotions—and tap into God's presence. That's the place where you will discover true joy, true rest, and the peace you need to wear on your feet in battle.

Peace in the Fire

The book of Isaiah gives us the perfect prescription for how to strap on our peace-shoes. Isaiah 26:3 says, "The steadfast of mind You will keep in perfect peace, because he trusts in You." Pay close attention to this principle because it has the power to literally restore all aspects of your life: When your mind agrees with God's mind—His truth and His standard—you will access God's power for victory in spiritual warfare. He will give you your peace-shoes. Trusting God produces peace.

One of my favorite stories in the Bible illustrates the power of peace in spite of the presence of realized or potential pain. When Shadrach, Meshach, and Abed-nego were faced with the command to bow down and worship their king as god or be thrown into a fiery furnace, the three boys stood by their principles and refused to bow. This was their response to King Nebuchadnezzar's threat to throw them into the furnace:

> O Nebuchadnezzar, we do not need to give you an answer concerning this matter. If it be so, our God whom we serve is able to deliver us from the furnace of blazing fire; and He will deliver us out of your hand, O king. But even if He does not, let it be known to you, O king, that we are not going to serve your gods or worship the golden image that you have set up (Daniel 3:16-18).

God didn't keep these boys from the fire—they were thrown in. In fact, God allowed Nebuchadnezzar to heat the furnace seven times hotter than it normally was. But what God *did* do is meet Shadrach, Meshach, and Abed-nego in the fire. The passage tells us that three men were thrown into the furnace, but when the king went to look at them burning up, he saw four men unbound and walking around in the midst of the fire.

God didn't change their world. He joined them in it.

Likewise, God doesn't always change our situations and circumstances—although sometimes He does. When He does, that's one reason to praise Him. But when He doesn't, if you are properly clothed with the armor of God—which includes having your feet shod with the preparation of the gospel of peace—God will join you in your situation or circumstance, and He will give you the peace you need to overcome it, not letting your circumstances overcome you. God promises in Isaiah 26:3 to keep those in "perfect peace" whose minds are steadfast because they trust Him.

If you feel as if you've been tossed into the furnace of spiritual warfare, I want to remind you to put your peace-shoes on and keep them on. If you've lost your job and don't know how you are going to buy food for your family, don't panic. Meditate on the truth of God's promise in Psalm 37:25, trust in it, and let it sink down deep within you: "I have been young and now I am old, yet I have not seen the righteous forsaken or his descendants begging bread." Hold on to that truth. Grab it. Own it. Walk in that truth instead of walking in worry, and see what God does.

While you're meditating on these truths, exchange your soul's perspective on your situation with what your spirit knows to be true. Scripture tells us in 2 Thessalonians 3:10, "If anyone is not willing to work, then he is not to eat, either." Instead of fretting or turning to something to ease your emotional pain, go to God and say, "God, You said that if a person doesn't work, that person shouldn't eat. I'm willing to work so that I can eat, so I'm thanking You now for the job that You are already preparing for me that hasn't made itself known just yet."

Every attack on peace in your life needs to be taken straight back to the spiritual realm and replaced with what God has to say on the matter. When you do that, you will wear shoes unlike many others'. You will wear shoes that let the demonic realm, yourself, and others know that you are covered by God's armor. You will walk without becoming weary, and in those shoes you will find the calming power of peace.

A young boy was a passenger flying on an airplane through a terrible storm. The turbulence was causing the passengers to panic. However, the young boy was not afraid. One of the passengers next to the boy turned to him and asked, "How can you be so calm in the middle of all of this?"

The young boy replied, "My father is the pilot."

When you know who is at the controls, you have peace even in the middle of life's storms.

7

THE SHIELD OF FAITH

Have you ever taken a spoon, fork, or knife and put it in a glass of water? If you set the glass just right on the counter with the light from the window shining through it, the silverware will look like it's bent. Even though nothing has happened to the silverware—it is as solid and straight as it was designed to be—the light hitting the water has created a distortion.

This distortion is caused by *refraction*. The object appears bent simply because of its environment.

We live in a world where refractions occur in almost every area of life. What we see, touch, hear, smell, or taste is often distorted by the atmosphere around it. Things that are straight appear to be crooked. Things that are crooked appear to be straight. An upside-down world leads to an increase in upside-down people. After a while, people can lose the ability to discern which way is up and which way is down. They may think they know the right way to go about something, but they end up choosing the wrong way because their reality has been distorted by an environment filled with sin and its effects.

As we've seen in the previous chapters, "Our struggle is not against flesh and blood, but against the rulers, against the authorities, against the powers of this dark world and against the spiritual forces of evil in the heavenly realms" (Ephesians 6:12 NIV). The physical world gives us the fruit—the distorted manifestations of the battles in our everyday lives—but the spiritual world is the root—the source of the battles causing those manifestations.

When we address the fruit of our battles without thoroughly addressing their root in the spiritual world, we merely perform patchwork in the physical realm. It's like trying to straighten a fork that only appears to be crooked—you will end up making the straight fork bent.

Don't misunderstand me, the five senses are real, relevant, and important—they are just not the starting point in our battle of spiritual warfare. If we make them the starting point, our perspective is refracted because we're not seeing things as they truly are. We're only seeing things as they appear to be.

So far we have looked at three pieces of the armor of God that you need to wear in order to be well-dressed for warfare. The first three pieces are what you wear all of the time. The "to be" verb—translated "having"—indicates "at all times." We are to *have* the belt of truth, *have* the breastplate of righteousness, and *have* the shoes of the gospel of peace.

The next three are what you are to have at hand, ready to pick up and use when you need them. Paul switches verbs for the next three pieces of the armor, telling us to "take up" the shield of faith, the helmet of salvation, and the sword of the spirit.

As I mentioned earlier, this can be compared to a baseball player who suits up in his baseball uniform during a ball game. He never removes his uniform, but he picks up his bat or his glove as needed. The bat and the glove are provided by the team and made available to him at all times, but it's the ballplayer's responsibility to grab them and use them at the appropriate time. No one forces him to do that, just as God doesn't force the shield of faith, helmet of salvation, or sword of the spirit into our hands when we need them the most. God makes them available to us, instructing us to use them when the situation calls for it.

The Shield of Faith

The first of these next three pieces of armor is the shield of faith. We read in Ephesians 6:16, "In addition to all, taking up the shield of faith with which you will be able to extinguish all the flaming arrows of the evil one."

A Roman soldier's shield typically measured two and a half feet wide and four feet long. In the battle, the soldier could crouch down and hide behind it when being targeted by arrows.

The best visual example I've ever seen of the importance of a shield in battle came in the film *300*. In this movie, 300 brave Spartan warriors went into battle against a million soldiers fighting on behalf of the Persian Empire. In one scene, a Persian leader says, "A thousand nations of the Persian empire descend upon you. Our arrows will blot out the sun!"

To this, Stelios—a young Spartan foot soldier—replies, "Then we will fight in the shade."

A few scenes later, thousands of arrows darken the sky with their all-encompassing presence. The command is given to raise the shields. All of the Spartans raise their shields simultaneously, giving them complete safety against the attack of arrows falling like a torrent. Hidden underneath the shade of the shields, one of the soldiers begins laughing hysterically. Stelios asks him what he is laughing about.

He replies, "Well, you had to say it!"

"Say what?" Stelios asks.

"Fight in the shade!"

When positioned correctly underneath the protection of a shield, the soldiers were completely covered. In fact, they were so well covered that they were even able to laugh and make light of their dark situation. At times like these, soldiers would link their shields together so that the entire army could hide behind whatever was thrown at them—arrows, javelins, or anything else meant to annihilate them.

So when does a Christian need to take up his shield? We've been given this answer before: "Therefore, take up the full armor of God, so that you will be able to resist *in the evil day*" (Ephesians 6:13). But when exactly is the evil day?

The evil day is the day that all hell breaks loose in your life—when you are under attack. It's when the finances are so low, you don't know how you are going to make it through the end of the week. It's when you've lost your job, and there is no new job in sight. It's when you are breaking down emotionally and have lost your passion for life. It's when your marriage seems hopeless, your kids have turned away, your health deteriorates, or your future looks bleak. It's when your friend has betrayed you, you're overcome by an addiction or impulse, or life seems to deliver any other piercing stab.

It is on this day—what Scripture calls "the evil day"—that you especially need to be covered. You need a shield. You need protection because on this day you are most vulnerable to the targeted attacks of the evil one.

To understand the importance of the protective powers of the shield of faith, consider a space capsule reentering earth's atmosphere. When a space capsule returns to the earth after having accomplished its mission, it would not be able to reach the earth if it were not surrounded by a shield. The heat generated upon reentry into the earth's atmosphere would burn up the capsule and everyone inside it in just a matter of seconds if it were not completely protected. With the shield, flames and smoke can engulf the entire capsule, but nothing inside is damaged at all. Similarly, taking up the shield of faith enables a believer to live a life of victory in an atmosphere that has the potential to bring harm.

The Shield That *Is* Faith

The shield of faith can also be called the shield that *is* faith because the shield is actually faith itself. So in order to know what we are to shield ourselves behind, we need to fully understand both the content and scope of faith. *Faith is critical to achieving victory in spiritual warfare.*

Hebrews 12:2 tells us that Jesus is both the "author and perfecter of faith." We read in Galatians 2:20, "I have been crucified with Christ; and it is no longer I who live, but Christ lives in me; and the life which I now live in the flesh I live by faith in the Son of God, who loved me and gave Himself up for me." First John 5:4 says, "For whatever is born of God overcomes the world; and this is the victory that has overcome the world—our faith."

From these verses we learn some very important truths. First, Jesus Christ embodies all the ingredients of faith, from its creation to its perfection. Second, we learn that we who are saved by trusting in Christ are positioned for victory because He lives in us. And last, the key to victory in overcoming—strongholds, addictions, battles in spiritual warfare, and more—is faith.

So what is faith? The simple, most direct definition I can give you for faith is that faith is acting as if God is telling the truth. Another way of saying it is that faith is acting as if something is so even when it appears not to be so in order that it might be shown to be so simply because God said so. Faith is directly tied to an action done in response to a revealed truth.

This brings us back to truth again. It's no surprise that the belt of truth was the first piece of armor listed because many of the other pieces are interconnected with truth in some way. If you don't know the truth, or if you don't act on the truth, the shield of faith is impotent. In order to have faith, you have to know and respond to truth. And as we saw earlier, truth is fundamentally God's viewpoint on a matter.

Over the years, I have heard a number of people talk about faith who showed no outward connection to God's truth, and yet they still wondered why faith didn't seem to be working for them. Maybe you know people like that. They go through life thinking, "Well, if I can just get a little bit more faith, then what I am trying to do or get will happen." But even a large amount of faith—if it is not tied to the truth—will not be able to accomplish anything. Faith is only as valuable as the thing to which it is tied.

For example, if faith is tied to your feelings—that is, if you have only as much faith as you feel—that faith will be empty faith. You might feel entirely full of faith but take no actions in response to that faith because you really don't believe in what you say you feel. A person can actually feel very faith-filled but have absolutely no faith. Likewise, a person can actually feel faith-less but be very full of faith. That person may be willing to take a step of faith—or do an action in faith—simply because he or she believes that what God says is true. Faith is never based on how much faith you feel. Faith is always based on your feet—what you do in response to what you believe.

Faith is acting on the truth whether I feel the truth or not. It's acting on the truth whether I like the truth or not. It's also acting on the truth whether I agree with the truth or not. Simply put, *faith is a function of the mind that shows up in the feet.*

Let me give you an example of how our feelings cannot be trusted in connection with truth. Say you went to the movies and you saw the most recent slasher horror film. Now, you know that those monsters roaming around on the screen aren't real. You know that the zombies coming out of the graves aren't real. You know that the chainsaws are actually harmless. But even so, you sit through the movie and squirm, cover your eyes, and maybe even scream.

When you finally get home at night and try to go to sleep, you end up tossing and turning. Your mind is racing with the scenes from the horror film. You *know* it's not real. In fact, when you bought your ticket before it even began, you knew it wasn't real. When you drove home after it was all over, you knew it wasn't real. Yet your feelings are still responding as if you thought it might be real. This is because the film-makers made you *feel* as if it were real. They manipulated the lighting, sound, and effects to make the story seem real so they could manipulate your feelings.

You will never overcome the movie's effect on your emotions until your mind overcomes your emotions because your emotions are continuing to perpetuate the lie you have experienced. As long as that lie remains lodged within you, that movie can keep you up at night—even though you know it isn't true.

When we allow our faith to be defined by our feelings, we will be confused. Faith must have an objective standard by which it is defined—truth. In fact, when faith operates by an objective standard of truth, it will eventually dictate our emotions rather than the reverse. Oftentimes, what is required on our part is taking a step, making the move, doing the thing that God has asked us to do without the accompanying emotions to go along with it. However, as you continue to walk by faith in the direction God has called you, your emotions are soon to follow.

For example, the Bible tells us we are to love our enemies and pray for those who persecute us. If you choose by faith to do a kind action to someone you perceive to be your enemy, the emotion of kindness toward that person will one day override the emotions of hate, anger, or bitterness that you feel. Your emotions will eventually catch up with your action if you continue doing it by faith.

One of my favorite biblical illustrations of faith carried out regardless of emotions is found in the book of Luke. Jesus was teaching a group that had gathered to listen to Him near the lake of Gennesaret. Because the crowd started pressing in closer to Him, He called out to the owners of a couple of nearby boats. Borrowing their boats, Jesus continued to teach the crowd a short distance away from the shore. "When He had finished speaking, He said to Simon, 'Put out into the deep water and let down your nets for a catch.' Simon answered and said, 'Master, we worked hard all night and caught nothing'" (Luke 5:4-5).

I can hear the sigh in Peter's words as he carefully tries to answer while also letting Jesus know that this is not His area of expertise. In my Tony Evans translation, he's saying, "Master, no offense, but maybe You should stick with preaching. You're good at it. I've been fishing all of my life—as far back as I can remember. In fact, these boats are part of the Zebedee Corporation—we've even got a fancy logo. And beyond that, just so You're clear, we've been fishing all night—twelve hours straight. The fish aren't biting. And if they're not biting at night, they're definitely not going to be biting during the day. Throwing our nets down for a catch at this time of day is not only ridiculous, it's a waste of time and energy. It's an inefficient use of our equipment, okay?"

"Oh, by the way," Peter continues, "we're also in shallow water right now—which, if You knew anything about fishing, You would realize is not the place to catch fish."

To which Jesus responds, "Just cast the net on the other side. Do what I say, Simon."

Simon doesn't feel as if Jesus' command makes any sense. Simon's expertise in fishing—his perspective—fuels his feeling that this doesn't make sense. But, maybe even with a sigh or a huff, Peter does what Jesus says. He puts down his nets just because Jesus said to.

If you're familiar with this story, you know what happened next. Peter and the other fishermen got the biggest catch of their lives. "When they had done this, they enclosed a great quantity of fish, and their nets began to break; so they signaled to their partners in the other boat for them to come and help them. And they came and filled both of the boats, so that they began to sink" (verses 6-7).

What Peter and the other fishermen discovered on that day, and what you and I can discover through their experience, is the principle of faith. Faith means acting on what God says in spite of what you know, your background, your experience, or even your education. Faith is a recognition of your own finiteness in relation to God's infiniteness.

One of the greatest hindrances to living a life of faith is that many of us simply know too much. We have our masters degrees in our various subjects, but we fail to know what the Master of all subjects has to say. If we were half as educated in the Word as we are in the world, we would be further along in living a life of victory. Faith begins by knowing the truth and then acting on the truth so we can see God move.

The Point of Access

Before we go further into our look at this powerful shield, I want to point out that faith does not make God move. All faith does is access what God has already done. If you think that faith makes God move, you are going to be searching for a way to get more faith. However, as a Christian, you already have all of the faith you're ever going to need to access anything God is going to do for you. Jesus said that faith the size of a mustard seed could move a tree or a mountain (Matthew 17:20; Luke 17:6). In other words, as the saying goes, "A little dab'll do ya."

You don't need more faith. You need to know more truth. This is because *faith is the point of access, not the source of power.* The power is in what God has already declared and done in grace when He deposited the seed of His divine life within you. As the knowledge and presence of God nourishes that seed, it expands and grows, offering you access to all God has in store for you. All faith is doing is drawing on the grace that God has already put on deposit.

So I want to encourage you to *stop looking for more faith.* You've got it all upside down and contorted like the fork in a cup of water if you think victory is going to come by somehow getting more faith. Faith accesses the grace that God has already deposited for you. Faith is only as valuable as the object of that faith. When the object of that faith is God's revealed truth, even the tiniest amount can move mountains.

Oftentimes, we believe we need to do good works to access what God has in store for us in His grace. But our works actually just exhibit our faith. They prove the existence of faith. Faith accesses grace. Works don't access grace because once you attach works to grace, it's no longer grace. Paul reminds us of this in Romans 11:6: "But if it is by grace, it is no longer on the basis of works, otherwise grace is no longer grace." Works exhibit faith, and faith accesses grace (see Romans 5:1-2).

Hebrews 11 is frequently referred to as the Hall of Faith. In this chapter we read about men and women who were approved by God because of their faith. The list includes David, Samson, Rahab, Noah, Abraham, Moses, and others. The principle that's illustrated through their lives is that in each and every situation, their faith showed up in their feet. None of these individuals simply said that they believed in God or that they believed God would do what He promised. Instead, we read that their actions revealed their responses of faith.

"By faith Abel offered…"

"By faith Noah…prepared…"

"By faith Abraham…obeyed…"

"By faith Isaac blessed…"

"By faith Rahab…welcomed…"

By faith, each one reached down and picked up the shield instead of letting it sit leaning up against a wall. What would happen to a Roman soldier if he said that he believed his shield would protect him, but he never grabbed it? He would soon be dead.

Habakkuk 2:4 says, "The righteous shall live by his faith." To live by faith means that faith becomes our regular way of thinking, doing, and being. Faith becomes more than merely acknowledging that the shield is there and that it's an effective form of protection. Faith means grabbing it and using it to its fullest potential. This is the kind of faith that shows up in the way you walk, move, talk, and make decisions. Living by faith means that faith becomes your groove—your zone. It's what Paul is referring to when he says, "Walk by faith" (2 Corinthians 5:7).

Have you ever seen someone who has a distinct way of walking? When she walks toward you, you recognize her walk before you even see her face. The same should be true about believers. We should have a "faith walk" that sets us apart from everyone else. It ought to be so distinct that others will recognize it before we even get close enough for them to see who we are.

The only way we can have that kind of faith is to recognize that faith is not a feeling or a discussion. Faith is an action taken based on the authorization of Somebody who knows what He's talking about. Likewise, faith is only as valuable as the object in which it is placed. You can have all of the faith in the world that your car can fly, but unless God—who not only wrote the laws of physics but can overcome them—makes your car fly, it will never get off the ground. Faith has to be tied to truth, and truth is tied to God.

Faith needs an object worthy of it. For example, my wife Lois won't fly on small airplanes. Her faith is small because the plane is small. Lois' faith grows when the size of the plane grows. Your view of God—how big you think He is—will determine the size of your faith.

Not only that, but an authentic, genuine expression of faith cannot be limited to your five senses. This is true because faith accesses what is already true in the invisible, spiritual realm, where the spiritual battle is taking place. Faith is a conviction about the reality of what you cannot see. There is no empirical evidence. It's your positive response to God's Word. The writer of Hebrews tells us, "Now faith is the assurance of things hoped for, the conviction of things not seen" (Hebrews 11:1). In other words, if you can see it, you're not exercising faith. If it is a tangible reality in the physical realm, you're not practicing the faith that God is describing. Everyone can believe in something they can see. God is talking about a faith that spots and grabs something out of the unseen realm and brings it down into the physical realm.

Faith and Fiery Darts

Faith that's rooted in the reality of God can extinguish all of the fiery darts of the evil one. When a Roman soldier went into battle, he wrapped his shield in leather or in some kind of animal skin. Then he dipped it in water so that if a fiery arrow came at him, it would be instantly snuffed out.

In Western films, cowboys circled their wagon trains so they could hide behind them and shoot at the Indians. In the early days, it wasn't a very fair fight because the cowboys were the only ones who had the guns and the cover. The Indians' arrows were no match for the cowboys' bullets...until the Indians lit the tips of their arrows and aimed them at the wagons. The fiery arrows burned the canvas off the wagons, exposing the cowboys behind them. The cowboys had no place to hide.

Fiery darts are meant to dismantle things in your life so that you become open for any other form of attack Satan wants to send your way. However, the shield of faith is there to protect you from the attack and put out the fire.

As we saw earlier, 1 John 5:4 tells us the effectiveness of this faith. "This is the victory that has overcome the world—our faith." Faith is so powerful that this passage declares it to be the secret to victory in whatever we are facing in this natural world. This secret is hidden in the cross because on the cross, Jesus Christ accomplished the ultimate victory. On the cross, all of the sin (past, present, and future) of the entire world, and its consequences, were nailed to Jesus Christ. If Jesus was able to overcome those sins and rise up in victory over them, He can surely overcome any destructive force you're facing right now in spiritual warfare.

If a weight lifter can lift 500 pounds, will he have a problem carrying 25 pounds of groceries home for you? No, if he can handle the 500 pounds, he can handle your groceries. If Jesus Christ was able to overcome all the sin of the entire world on the cross, He can certainly take care of any situation you are in right now. Your part is to believe that Jesus can enable you to overcome, and to act on that belief. You already have enough power to do battle in your circumstance. You already have enough strength to fight. Your victory over the trial you're facing is already at hand. The only thing that's missing is the kind of faith that God defines.

The shield of faith has been given to us to protect us from the deceptive strategies of the enemy. When you use it properly, this shield will enable you to advance against the enemy because you will be confident that what God has said about your situation—in His Word and through His promises—is true.

Listen to the Coach

I enjoy watching the Olympics because they bring out the best in athletes. In the Olympics, athletes push harder, go farther, and aim higher than they ever have before.

One scene in particular from the 1996 Olympics is forever etched in my mind. It occurred on the final night of the women's gymnastics team event. The United States was in second place behind the Russians and needed a decent score on the vault in order to pass them.

Kerri Strug stood on the mat as the final gymnast in the lineup to vault for the Americans. The gymnast who had gone before Kerri had fallen on both of her vaults, so the Americans had to throw out her score. Being allowed to only throw out one score per round meant that Kerri's score would have to count. Whether the Americans went home with gold, silver, or bronze was now up to Kerri. The weight of a nation rested on her 88-pound frame.

Kerri didn't have a reputation for being all that tough in the clutch. In fact, she was known for buckling under the pressure. She had earned the term "baby" of the seven-member group over the years because the coaches often had to handle her with kid gloves. But the vault was her specialty, and the Americans had not anticipated the race being so close at this point, so she had been slated as the last girl to run.

Kerri needed to score higher than a 9.4 on her final vault in order to secure the gold, and she had two chances to do this. On Keri's first vault, she held true to her reputation of crumbling under the pressure. She fell. Kerri's fall sprained her ankle and tore ligaments as well. A hush came over the crowd, as the spectators began to doubt that America could get the gold. How could Kerri vault again? She could barely walk.

Kerri felt the urgings of her teammates to try again as she limped back to the starting point. Tears filled her eyes as she did her best to fight them back. She knew that all of her teammates' hopes and dreams were in her last vault. But, as she would say later on, she didn't even know if she could run, let alone vault. She considered walking away.

But the voice of her coach, Bela Karolyi, sealed her decision to stay. He yelled, "You can do it, Kerri. You can do it!" She looked at him, and she believed. We know this because her feet demonstrated that belief.

After saluting the judges, Kerri ran toward the vault—propelling herself one last time into the air. Hardly able to hold her foot down long enough through the pain to secure the score, she managed to do so for a moment, having nailed her landing. Then Kerri immediately collapsed on the mat in tears and agony. As she was carried down the stairs, Kerri's score went up. It was more than enough. The Americans had won. Kerri had grabbed the gold.

Later on, Kerri revealed what pushed her to try one last time. She said, "When Bela looks at you and says you can do it, you know you can."

Faith. Kerri got the gold because her faith showed up in her feet.

Perhaps Satan and his demons have knocked you down. Maybe you're limping from disappointment, pain, broken dreams, and other losses in your life. You might be questioning whether you will ever run again, and you might wonder if you should stop trying altogether.

But God reminds you that He has never asked you to do anything that He is not absolutely certain you can do through Him. If you'll listen closely, you might be able to hear His voice. He is saying, "You can do it. You can do it!"

Trust Him.

Pick up the shield of faith, and with it, grab the victory that has already been gained.

8

THE HELMET OF SALVATION

A man who operated a tattoo parlor was asked, "Why do you think so many people come in here to get tattoos?"

The man replied without any hesitation, "Because before there is ever a tattoo on the body, there is a tattoo on the mind."

In other words, he was saying that people display on their bodies what they have already pictured in their minds. What we think often shows up in our five senses as something we can see, touch, taste, hear, or smell. That's why the next piece of armor we need to strap on in this spiritual battle is a helmet. We read in Ephesians 6:17, "Take the helmet of salvation." This is because a helmet not only covers the head but also protects the mind.

The main purpose of a helmet—in battle, sports, or work situations like construction sites—is to protect the brain from injury. A football player's helmet is padded on the inside to help it absorb the shock when he gets pounded to the ground. The brain must be fiercely protected because once the brain becomes damaged, body function also becomes damaged. A football player suffering from too many concussions can no longer play at the level he once could. In fact, he may not even be able to play at all.

With the helmet, Paul has once again used a physical example to illustrate a spiritual truth. He demonstrates that just as the brain is the control center for the rest of the body, the mind is the control center for the will and emotions. The mind must be protected with a helmet that's able to absorb the shocks of being hit by the enemy and even knocked to the ground in the spiritual realm.

The Influence of the Mind

You may have a relative who has suffered from Alzheimer's disease. If you do, you are acutely aware that Alzheimer's is one of the leading debilitating diseases of our day. Notable people who have suffered from the effects of this disease include former president Ronald Reagan, boxer Sugar Ray Robinson, and actor Charlton Heston.

With Alzheimer's, the brain is no longer able to function as it should, so it deteriorates over time. As Alzheimer's sets in, patients become less able to control or care for themselves. The worse Alzheimer's becomes, the less control the person has over his or her life.

Likewise, when spiritual Alzheimer's sets in, we gradually lose control of our own lives. When our mind no longer functions as it was designed to, it impedes our will and emotions from doing what they should. This, then, influences the body as it responds to the will and emotions. So it's no surprise that one of Satan's primary strategies is to attack our mind. In fact, this is such a critical area that each of the different pieces of spiritual armor relates to our mind.

Satan doesn't care how he accomplishes his goal. He will use a fiery arrow of spiritual Alzheimer's, a conflict leading to a concussion, a poison dart of paranoia, or a battery of mental disorders and strongholds. Any damage to the mind that keeps us from knowing and operating the way God intends can lead to defeat. Satan will use any of these weapons to attack our minds.

But God has told us to put on the helmet of salvation as protection. In fact, He has even provided an illustration of the essential nature of putting on this helmet—the game of football. (Sometimes I think God created football just so preachers like me would have plenty of illustrations.) You see, in football, the quarterback is the leader on the field. He calls the plays so the rest of the team can hear them and then respond.

Because the quarterback runs the plays, he is constantly under attack from the opposing team. The defense is constantly trying to sack him, knock him down, block him, move him out of the pocket, intercept his pass, or strip the ball from his hands. The defense wants to make the quarterback eat dirt on each and every play. That is their objective. If they can do that, none of the plays will be effective. The quarterback's team will be unable to score, and they will eventually lose the game.

However, sitting in a booth high above the quarterback is a man who holds the title of offensive coordinator. The offensive coordinator's job, among other things, is to communicate with the quarterback during the game, warning him about what might be coming at him. The offensive coordinator has already spent hours studying the strategy of the opposition, and his job is to accurately predict and relay their moves to the quarterback.

Talking directly into the quarterback's helmet through the use of sophisticated technology, the offensive coordinator tells the quarterback how he is to move, what play he is to call, how he is to function, what he is to avoid, where he is to put up his guard, and where the weak points in the defense are that he is to try to exploit. One reason the offensive coordinator can do that so well, besides having studied the game film, is that he is sitting high enough to view the entire scenario below him. He is seated up above—in football's "heavenly places"—with a perfect view of what the enemy is doing down below. He analyzes every movement of the opposition in order to inform his quarterback which strategy to employ to overcome their attack.

Have you ever seen a quarterback in the middle of a very important game start waving his arms up and down to the crowd? He is signaling to his fans that they are being too loud and that he can no longer hear what is being spoken to him through his helmet. The quarterback wants the crowd to quiet down.

Similarly, people's voices—their opinions, thoughts, accusations, or even attempts at being helpful—will often drown out what God is trying to speak to a believer in his or her helmet of salvation. People may have excellent intentions, and they might even be trying to cheer you on, but in the middle of the battle, you must hear God's voice. If a believer cannot hear God clearly, just like if a quarterback cannot hear the offensive coordinator clearly, the result will be defeat.

One reason God wants us to wear a helmet is that the enemy is trying to stop us from accomplishing the things God has for us to do. God wants to speak truth into our minds. He sits up high—in the heavenly places—and views the scene below. He can see the field of life much better than we ever could. He can examine the opposition's strategy much better than we can. He has studied the game film much longer than we have. And because of this, God has a few secrets He wants us to hear. They are *secrets* because often what God has to say to you is meant only for you.

Have you ever seen a football coach during a game speak something into his headset microphone that he doesn't want the television cameras to pick up and broadcast to anyone else who might see it—especially the opposition? What does that coach do? He covers his mouth. He places his hand or a clipboard in front of his mouth. By doing this, he keeps the information—the truth that he wants to apply to this specific situation—a secret.

It isn't that the truth itself is a secret—every football coaching staff and player has access to game film and plays, and they all understand the rules and fundamentals of football. The secret is the implementation of that truth. We'll talk more about this in the next chapter, but that is what theologians call the *rhema*—the spoken word of God.

The deciding factor in victory or defeat is the mind. If the mind, the spiritual expression of the brain, operates on a false grid of reality and truth, then the body will also function according to that false reality. In other words, if a person's perspective is errant and his or her mindset is flawed, that person's function will also be flawed.

If a person says, "My name is Alec, and I'm an alcoholic," he is identifying himself wrongly. He runs a higher risk of giving in to another drink because what he is thinking tells him that he is inclined to give in anyway. The truth for a believer would be stated differently. It would be, "My name is Alec, and I am an overcomer. I have struggled with alcohol, but I am a blood-bought child of the King who can do all things through Christ who strengthens me." Those are two very different ways of summing up the same situation.

Proverbs 23:7 strongly warns us to guard our minds: "As he thinks within himself, so he is." In our football illustration, that would be translated to say, "As he hears from the coaching staff, so he executes the play."

Essentially, we do what we think. The Emancipation Proclamation is a perfect example of this. We all know from history that the Emancipation Proclamation was a document issued by President Lincoln proclaiming the freedom of slaves. But we also know from history that being *legally* free might be an entirely different thing from being *functionally* free.

News of the slaves' freedom didn't reach Florida until several months after the Proclamation was drafted. News didn't reach Texas until Union soldiers marched into Galveston a full two years after the document proclaimed their freedom. For years, legally freed slaves remained in bondage simply because of what they thought was true. Even though they were technically free, they had remained virtual slaves—trapped in a false reality because they did not possess knowledge of the truth by which they could escape their bondage.

Have you seen any of the newest virtual reality games? They are nothing short of astounding in their depiction of reality. In these games, you can be sitting as still as a rock in the comfort of your own living room and think you're on a roller coaster because that's what you're seeing through your headset. Your stomach starts to feel ready to come up through your mouth just as if you were on a real roller coaster. You're not actually on the ride, but the game makes you think you're on it. And because of that, you start moving, shifting, screaming, and responding just as if you were really on the ride.

What Satan wants to do is to keep us from wearing the helmet of salvation so that what he shows us through his own headset becomes the reality through which we interpret and respond to life.

Salvation: The Valuable Weapon

Jed Clampett was a hillbilly who lived in Tennessee. One day, as he was out hunting for some food, he saw something black bubbling up from underneath the ground. "Oil, that is—black gold, Texas tea." Selling his land, Jed moved with his family out to Beverly Hills, where they lived the life of millionaires.

The question is, when did Jed become a millionaire? Was it when he discovered the oil? Or was it when he acquired the land?

Jed became a millionaire when he acquired the land. However, because he didn't know the value of what he had in his possession, he lived for years as a hillbilly, struggling to simply find his next meal. In fact, Jed had gotten so used to the life of a hillbilly that even when he moved to Beverly Hills, he didn't know how to live up to what he had acquired.

Many of us are living today without the full knowledge of what we have been given in salvation. We are living hillbilly lives—struggling to get by—when all that we could ever use or need has been made available to us through the gift of salvation in Jesus Christ. One reason we have failed to recognize the magnitude and relevancy of this gift is that we too frequently limit our understanding of salvation to going to heaven. Salvation does include eternity, but it also includes much more.

Salvation

When a soldier goes into battle, any old helmet won't do. Paul knew that when he wrote about the weapons of warfare. That is why he specifically said to take up the "helmet of *salvation*." But what's interesting about Paul's use of the word "salvation" is that he was writing to people who were already saved. The book of Ephesians is written to people whom Paul refers to as "saints," "faithful in Christ Jesus," and to those who have already been blessed with "every spiritual blessing in the heavenly places in Christ" (1:1,3). Paul is implying that a person can be an "unsaved-saved" person. Thus in chapter 6 we find him telling the Ephesian believers to pick up and put on the helmet of salvation.

Pay close attention to the remainder of this chapter because at the core of most of our problems—and we all have them to varying degrees—is our lack of understanding of *salvation*. Many people think that salvation simply means to be born again. And it *does* mean being born again. When people trust in Christ for the forgiveness of their sins, an instantaneous change occurs. This change is called justification. Justification is the removal of the *penalty* of sin along with a declaration of legal righteousness.

However, the important truth to note is that while salvation refers to justification and the implanting of the new life in the form of an imperishable seed within our spirit, it does not refer to that *alone*. "Salvation" is an all-inclusive word that summarizes *all* that Christ has provided for us: past, present and future.

Justification is what occurred at the point of salvation—it is salvation in the past tense for any believer. The present tense of the word "salvation" signifies the ongoing renewal of a person through the work of the indwelling Holy Spirit. This removes the power of sin over a believer and is called *sanctification. Glorification* is the future sense of salvation—the removal of the presence of sin. Thus, when the Bible speaks about salvation, it can be referring to justification, sanctification, or glorification.

Sanctification is our focus as we look at the helmet of salvation. We briefly touched on this earlier where we read, "In humility receive the word implanted, which is able to *save* your souls" (James 1:21). James, like Paul, was writing to fellow believers who were already saved in the sense of justification. Salvation, in this passage, is sanctification—the process of a person becoming more like Christ.

Paul uses the same meaning of salvation when he writes in Romans 1:16, "For I am not ashamed of the gospel, for it is the power of God for *salvation* to everyone who believes, to the Jew first and also to the Greek." The word "salvation" in this verse means "to be delivered." It is the power of God to deliver from hell in the future and also from hell in the present.

There are a number of things that God may need to deliver you from in your daily life—an addiction, a wrong relationship, an unhealthy mind-set, a stronghold, emotional bondage, or any number of other things. If something is ruling you, if the enemy knows that all he has to do is push this or that button to get you to do or think something that you shouldn't, don't despair—the gospel has the power to deliver you.

A great verse that illustrates the multidimensional nature of salvation is one that we often quote.

> For *by grace* you have been saved *through faith*; and that not
> of yourselves, it is the gift of God not as a result of works, so

that no one may boast. For we are His workmanship, created
in Christ Jesus *for good works*, which God prepared beforehand so that we would walk in them (Ephesians 2:8-10).

Paul tells us in this passage that salvation is *by* grace, *through* faith,
and *for* good works. All of these components are included in the pack-
age we call salvation. Paul's letter to the church in Colossae emphasizes
this truth when he writes, "Therefore as you have received Christ Jesus
the Lord, so walk in Him" (Colossians 2:6). Paul is telling the believers
in Colossae that the way they were saved—by grace, through faith, and
for good works—is the same way they are to function. Recognizing
this critical truth is essential to living a life of victory because it emphasizes the holistic nature of the gospel. Unless we truly comprehend the
multifaceted nature of salvation the way that God has defined it—*by*
grace, *through* faith, and *for* good works—we will be grabbing any old
hat and trying it on for size, attempting to pass it off as a helmet. I don't
know about you, but when I'm in battle, I want more than a ball cap
covering my head. I want something strong and hard. I want a helmet.

God's Provision Through Grace

The first concept we need to dig deeper into while we examine our
salvation is *grace*. For starters, I want to remind you that grace has absolutely nothing to do with you. Grace is all about what God has done
for you, independent of you. You have no part to play in grace. Grace
includes all that God has already supplied for you. There is nothing
God can do for you that He hasn't already done. In fact, there is nothing God can provide for you that He hasn't already provided.

Everything God is ever going to do for you has already been done.
Every healing He will ever give you in your physical body has already
been provided. Every opportunity He is ever going to open up for you
has already been opened. Every stronghold God is ever going to break
in you has already been broken. Every victory you are ever going to
experience has already been won. The joy you're desperately seeking
already exists. The peace that you stay up at night praying and wishing
that you could enjoy is already present. Even the power you need to live

the life God has created you to live, you already have. This is because God has already deposited in the heavenly realm "every spiritual blessing" you will ever need.

Even so, I can hear your question from miles away. You are saying, "Tony, Tony, Tony—that all sounds good, spiritual, and even encouraging. But if you're saying that I already have it, how come I don't have it? If I've already got it, why can't I seem to get it?"

The problem is not that you are lacking in grace or the things that grace supplies. The problem has to do with the way you access grace—through faith. There is only one way to access what has already been given to you, and most of our problems arise out of a misunderstanding about faith. You don't access grace by doing good things or being a good person. The only access point to the grace that salvation supplies is faith.

Missing this fundamental distinction concerning grace is what has most of us wearing a soft cap with our own initials stitched into it instead of the helmet of salvation. That cap may have your name on it, it might be your color, and it might look good on you, but it will provide you with no protection. You cannot access grace through works. In fact, the very moment you try to access grace by works, you actually nullify grace. Grace, by its very definition, has nothing to do with you or what you do. It is what God does for you because of His unmerited favor.

What religion often tries to teach us and get us to do is to access grace—God's favor and blessings—by works. Religion says if you come to church more often, God will bless you more. If you give more money, you will get more money. If you treat your neighbor nice, God will be nice to you. Lists are made about "seven ways you can get all that you want from God" or "ten things you can do to make God like you more." The truth is, there is no such list.

The problem is not those good things we do in themselves. The problem is in the motivation behind doing them. If you are doing good works to try to earn God's favor so you can access His grace, you have disqualified yourself from grace simply because your actions have shown that you don't believe in what grace truly is. Religion will defeat you because it keeps you in a posture of trying to earn what has already been freely given.

Some of us are working so hard to do better. We go to church more, read more, and do more, only to discover that we're still not delivered. That is because we're turning to religion to try to be better rather than letting grace do the work both in and through us.

When I was in seminary, I was determined to get A's in all my classes. In one particular class, I remember spending an inordinate amount of time on a certain paper. Confident that I was going to get an A on my paper, I was shocked when I got it back only to discover that written on top of it was a big zero. Scribbled underneath the zero were these words: "Great work. Wrong assignment."

A lot of saints are trying to be delivered on earth by working hard, serving hard, and giving more…all the while not realizing they're working on the wrong assignment. We're saved by grace, through faith, and for good works which God prepared beforehand that we should walk in them. Our good works must flow out of God's work of grace in our lives rather than out of a heart that's trying to earn His favor or reduce His wrath. It's a subtle difference in the physical realm, but it makes all the difference in the spiritual realm. God knows our hearts.

It's like a child trying to earn her parent's love. In a healthy home that functions the way God designed it, the parent loves that child already unconditionally. There is nothing the child can do to make her parent love her. She is already loved simply by virtue of her relationship to the one whose love she is trying to gain.

Friend, I want to let you in on a secret that in all of my years of ministry and counseling I have discovered that few people really know: *God loves you.* In fact, He demonstrated it. God cannot love you any more than He already does—He showed that by sending His own son, Jesus Christ, to die for *you.* When God sacrificed His own son and turned His back on Him at the point of His death, He gave you all the love He could ever give you. You don't need to try to make God love you more. You can't do it. What you can do, though, is access His love through faith. Faith is your positive response to what God has already done. The good works you do express your faith; they don't earn God's grace. So when you give your tithe—and yes, the Bible teaches that believers are to give to the Lord—you do it not so you can earn God's favor, but as an expression of your faith in Him as your Source and a demonstration of your trust in Him.

Your home is connected to a local power company. This power company supplies your home with everything you need to run everything you have that requires electricity. Let's say you turned off all the lights in your home and were sitting in the dark. It would be foolish of you to call the electric company and ask them to give you more power. All the power you need has already been made available to you.

Instead, what you need to do is access that power. You need to flip on the switch, which opens up the flow of the power. Now, what would happen if you called the electric company and told them that all of your lights were off and that you needed them to come over to your house and turn them on for you? Do you think they would come? Most likely they would not come because their job is to supply the power, not to turn your lights on and off. It's your responsibility to access the power.

In the spiritual realm, it's the act of faith that accesses all that's supplied to us by grace. It's faith that flips the switch, releasing the flow of grace into our lives. In fact, there's only one way to access grace, and that's through faith so that no one can boast—not only about how we got into heaven but also about how we got delivered on earth.

Faith must always begin with a God-based understanding of truth. It cannot simply begin with facts because facts don't always reveal truth. If a person has a headache, the fact is that the person has a headache. However, the truth may be that the person has a tumor. Yet if all we looked at was the fact of a headache, that person may settle for some aspirin when he or she really needed surgery.

The key to accessing grace is faith—faith that's grounded in truth.

A New You

God gives grace only in response to faith. Your good works merely reflect the fact that you believe what God says about grace. You do them in response to grace, not to try to get grace.

When you fully embrace the truth that there's nothing you can do to get God to love you more, you'll discover the power for living a life of victory. When that truth takes root deep within you, you will have more confidence to overcome strongholds or resist temptations than you have ever known. In fact, you will become a whole new you!

The United States government has what is called a Federal Witness Protection Program. It is for individuals who are at high risk because they have testified against someone who wants to see them killed. What the government does for these individuals is literally change their identities. It changes their names, looks, social security numbers, and locations. If the people in the program don't accept these changes, the government will not guarantee their protection. But when they do accept the changes, the government protects them.

Let me let you in on a secret—Satan is very upset that when you trusted in Christ, you testified against him. In fact, your life is a testimony against him every day that you operate under the authority of Christ. Because of this, Satan is after you to destroy you. But God has put you in His own protection program. He can change the way you look at yourself by showing you how He looks at you. When you see yourself the way God sees you, you will begin to walk differently, talk differently, act differently, and live differently. You will live in the victory that He has already given you. And one way He wants to change you is by getting you to understand that grace comes through faith and not in response to anything you could do.

The apostle Paul spent years of his life sacrificing, laboring, and serving God, even to the detriment of his own health and comfort. He said in 1 Corinthians 15:10, "By the grace of God I am what I am." In fact, Paul's response to that grace is what produced the good works in his life. He continues the same statement by saying, "And His grace toward me did not prove vain; but I labored even more than all of them, yet not I, but the grace of God with me."

In other words, Paul said that when he understood grace, he didn't get lazy. He didn't adopt a lifestyle of sin. No, when Paul understood all that grace had done for him in spite of him, he wanted to work all the more in gratitude for it.

Grace never makes a person lazy. A true embracing of grace makes us more committed, obedient, generous, and enthusiastic because when we see all that God has already done for us, we want to say thank you.

Not only is grace the channel for God extending His favor and blessings into your life, but it's also the means of delivering us from what we often deserve.

> For while we were still helpless, at the right time Christ died for the ungodly. For one will hardly die for a righteous man; though perhaps for the good man someone would dare even to die. But God demonstrates His own love toward us, in that while we were yet sinners, Christ died for us. *Much more then*, having now been justified by His blood, we shall be saved from the wrath of God through Him (Romans 5:6-9).

What I want you to notice in this passage are the words "much more then." The reason why those words are so important is that they indicate that what is coming after them is even greater than what came before them. Before "much more then," we read that when we were at our worst, God sacrificed His Son Jesus Christ for us so that whoever believed on His name would be saved (justified before Him). That in itself is more grace than anyone could comprehend. But Paul says we can have "much more" confidence that "we shall be *saved* from the wrath of God through Him."

We are often confused about this passage, thinking it means we're being saved from hell. But Paul has already told us that we have been justified and therefore not going to be sent to hell. Rather, Paul is saying that we "shall be saved" from God's wrath. But what is God's wrath if it doesn't mean that we are being saved from hell? Romans 1:18-19 tells us:

> For the wrath of God *is revealed* from heaven against all ungodliness and unrighteousness of men who suppress the truth in unrighteousness, because that which is known about God is evident within them; for God made it evident to them.

Oftentimes, we think that the wrath of God will be revealed in hell, and it will—but there is another wrath that is already revealed. Many of us don't have to go to hell to be in hell. This is because we're living in our own personal hell with fires burning all around us. These flames come as a result of God's wrath against sin. Sin comes complete with God's wrath built right in it.

Another way of saying this is that sin comes with consequences. We've all experienced consequences from our sinful decisions. In fact, many of us have probably lived with some of those consequences for years. This is because the very sin that we committed had the consequence for that sin built right into it. It's not that God in heaven is throwing down lightning bolts of wrath upon you. Rather, God's wrath is an outgrowth of the sin itself.

Some people started out with only one drink, but now the drink is telling them they need to have more. Some people started out by popping a pill, but now the feeling they got when they popped the pill is telling them that they need to inject something stronger into their arms. The only way to get rid of the wrath showing up in your life is by having the power to deal with the sin—to be saved, or sanctified.

When we put on the helmet of salvation, we block the rule of sin's consequences in our lives. When we live in the power of a life that's responsive to God and to His sanctifying work, accessing grace through faith, sin no longer has a foothold in our thoughts, emotions, and decisions.

One day a man was given a special gift—a cruise! He had never been on a cruise before, so he was excited to take his first voyage. The cruise came at no cost to him. The person who gave it to him picked up the entire tab.

Throughout the week on the cruise, one of the crew members noticed that the man frequently ate the free crackers and juice provided on the deck. In fact, he had never seen anyone eat as many crackers as this man did. Curious as to the reason why, the crew member spoke to the man as he was disembarking.

"Sir, how did you enjoy the cruise?"

"It was spectacular," the man replied, "I have never experienced anything like it before."

"Very good, sir," the crew member said, and then he continued. "I noticed that you really liked the crackers and juice on the deck. I was just wondering—why?"

"Well," the man replied, looking down, "I saw all of the lavish meals that were being offered all week long, but I didn't have any money. And since the crackers and juice were free, I let them sustain me during the cruise."

The crew member replied, "Someone didn't give you all of the information. When the price of your ticket was paid, it not only included getting on the boat and going everywhere that the boat goes but also included everything on the boat as well. Your food was covered in the price of the ticket."

The helmet of salvation not only takes us to heaven but also supplies—by grace, through faith—everything we need while we're here on earth. When we fail to understand the truth of salvation and wear it as a helmet, we limit the good works God will do both in us and through us.

9

THE SWORD OF THE SPIRIT

e've now come to our final piece in the armor of God. When you successfully put on, take up, and function with all six pieces of the armor, you will have all you need to experience true and lasting victory in spiritual warfare.

Paul tells us what this final piece is in Ephesians 6:17: "Take...the sword of the Spirit, which is the word of God."

This final piece of armor stands out from all of the others. It's unique because this is the only offensive weapon in the arsenal. Everything else is designed to hold us steady from what the enemy is seeking to bring against us "in the evil day." But after God outfits you for battle in order to stand firm, He gives you an additional weapon with which you can attack and advance.

Roman soldiers had two very different types of swords for battle. The first sword was called a *spatha*. The spatha was generally three feet long. A shorter sword, called the *gladius*, was typically about 18 inches, or a foot and a half. When Paul instructs us to "take...the sword of the Spirit," the Greek term he uses is *macaira*, which refers to the shorter sword, the gladius.

So the first image I want you to remove from your mind when you consider the "sword of the Spirit" is that of Zorro or the swashbuckling pirates you've seen on television or in the movies. The gladius was more similar to a dagger and was used for up-close, in-your-face, hand-to-hand combat, most often with a solitary opponent. The Roman soldier could also use the gladius to deliver an unexpected yet deadly blow to his enemy because the enemy would not see it coming, as in the case of targeted assassinations or combat.

Gladii blades were double-edged and needle sharp at the point, allowing for a greater amount of damage at a quicker rate. Oftentimes, a longer sword simply created a wound that enabled the opponent to continue fighting. But the gladius delivered a deathblow straight to the opponent's heart or midsection. A two-inch deep gouge from a dagger often proved fatal more quickly than any length of a swipe from a longer sword.

When Paul instructs us to take up the sword of the Spirit, he's letting us know that in this battle, we will have times when the enemy is so close that it seems like he's right in our face. In fact, it can be compared to an opponent trying to block a shot in a basketball game. The opposing player will often stick his body, face, or hands in the offensive player's face so that the offensive player will become disoriented and unable to advance. Satan doesn't want you or me to send the ball through the net for two points, so to discourage this, he brings his battle—your particular stronghold—as close to you as possible. Oftentimes, that means your battle is being waged within you—in your mind, will, emotions, and body.

Another thing Paul tells us is that this is the sword of the *Spirit*. It's not your sword. It's not the church's sword. It's not the sword of good works or even religion. It's not the preacher's sword. This is the sword of the Spirit, and in fact, is the only weapon we're told that the Spirit uses in the spiritual realm.

Because it's the Spirit who uses this sword in the heavenly places to deliver a deathblow to our enemy, a very important thing to remember is that you cannot deliver that deathblow yourself. If you try, you will soon discover that God gave the instruction to use the sword of the Spirit for a very good reason. You'll learn what Moses learned when he attempted to deliver Israel in his own strength, or what Peter learned when he tried to deliver Jesus by cutting off the ear of one of the soldiers who had come to arrest him: *Our authority for victory in the spiritual realm is rooted and grounded in God.* God reminded Moses and Peter that their human approach was not needed for this battle.

The same holds true for you and me.

One of the reasons so many of us are losing our battles is that we have turned to human resources, methods, and philosophies to try to do battle against someone who is not human. Paul didn't say "take up *your* sword;" he said, "take…the sword of the *Spirit*" and do battle with it. Even with your best intentions, you cannot compete with an enemy who is fighting in a capacity you or I could never function in. The only way to defeat this enemy and walk in a life of victory is according to God's prescribed means.

When you choose a man-made method to go up against a spiritual battle, you nullify God's power in your fight. Scripture says in James 1:20 that "the anger of man does not achieve the righteousness of God." God says it a different way in Deuteronomy 32:35: "Vengeance is Mine, and retribution, in due time their foot will slip." Knowing this, Paul warns Christians everywhere, "Never take your own revenge, beloved, but leave room for the wrath of God" (Romans 12:19).

"Leaving room" means letting go of your approach to spiritual battles and letting go of your need to respond in your emotions. God doesn't sanction our approach, and our emotions are unreliable. Rather, we are to take God's approach by aligning our emotions underneath His overarching rule and putting on His full armor—the last of which is the sword of the Spirit.

It is simply because we have not believed in the power of the dagger that we don't see the enemy sliced and diced as he ought to be. There is so much power in the sword of the Spirit that God gave it to us as the only piece of offensive weaponry in the entire armor. Maybe this sword is the only offensive piece in the collection because it is the only offensive piece necessary.

The Word of God

Scripture tells us another critical aspect of the sword of the spirit— this sword is the Word of God. We are told to "take…the sword of the Spirit, *which is the word of God.*" In order to fully comprehend what's being referred to as the Word of God, we need to consider the different Greek terms used for God's Word.

Graphe

When Scripture (2 Timothy 3:16; 2 Peter 1:20) uses the Greek word *graphe* to refer to the Word of God, what it's defining are the "writings" of God. Another way to put that is that it is referring to the actual book of God—the Bible. For example, when you attend church and the preacher says to turn in your Bible to a certain passage and you turn there, what you are holding in your hands and what you are turning the pages in is the *graphe*. You are holding 66 books which compose the canon of Scripture.

Whether you have the *graphe* on your shelf, on your coffee table, beside your bed, in your kitchen, on the dashboard of your car, at work, or tucked under your arm when you walk into church, what you have is a book. It is the Word of God in written form: *graphe*. But when Paul tells you to "take...the sword of the Spirit, which is the word of God," the term he uses for "word of God" is not *graphe*.

Unfortunately, many people today think that Paul is referring to the word *graphe*. This is made evident by the choices they make. They look to their Bible like others look to a rabbit's foot, assuming that it alone brings about the power needed to live a life of victory in a fallen world. But placing your Bible in your car, thinking it will somehow stop an accident from happening, is just an expression of superstition. Buying an oversized Bible and putting it on your coffee table, thinking it will somehow ward off everything negative and evil from entering your family's life, is just hocus-pocus.

Don't misunderstand me. I'm not saying the Bible isn't powerful or essential for all people—it is. But in order for it to accomplish its purpose, it needs to be *used*, and not simply in a way that allows you to cross it off your checklist for the day.

The *graphe* is the *graphe* regardless of whether you open it, read it, or use it. For example, when people go to court and are told to put their hand on the Bible and swear that they are telling the truth, the whole truth, and nothing but the truth, they are putting their hand on the *graphe.* The judge, jury, defendant, and plaintiff are not indicating an interest in the message of the Bible; they are just using the book for a specific purpose.

Other people will use the Bible in a similar manner when they try to back up what they're saying by telling you, "I swear on the Bible it's true." They're not showing an interest in what anything in the Bible says, they are just concerned about the written documentation and existence of the Bible because people have associated truth telling with the *graphe.*

Logos

Another Greek term for the Word of God found in Scripture is the word *Logos.* Logos refers to the message of the book, or *graphe*; it's the meaning of the words. When you read your Bible, attend a Bible study, or hear a sermon that explains the meaning of the text being referenced, you are experiencing and interacting with the Logos. You started with the *graphe* and have progressed into the Logos.

Logos is a very powerful word. We read about it in the first chapter of the book of John, where in the very first verse we read, "In the beginning was the Word, and the Word was with God, and the Word was God." Jesus is called the Logos in this passage because He was sent as God's messenger to present God to human beings and to embody His message to us. The *graphe* is the message written, and the Logos is the message given. Logos is the understanding of the written record of stories, events, and letters that we come into contact with in God's written Word.

In Hebrews 4:12, God reveals to us the nature and function of the Logos: "For the word [Logos] of God is living and active and sharper than any two-edged sword, and piercing as far as the division of soul and spirit, of both joints and marrow, and able to judge the thoughts and intentions of the heart."

The Logos is more than just words on paper. According to this passage, the Logos is alive and active. The Logos is a force with energy behind it given to accomplish a specific goal. In order to accomplish this goal, the writer of Hebrews likens it to a sword that's "sharper than any two-edged sword," meaning that it can go deeper and further than anything made in the physical realm. This sword goes as deep so as to pierce between soul and spirit in the invisible realm.

When it reaches deep within you, the Logos goes about the job of dividing what makes up your soul (mind, will, and emotions) and what makes up the new spirit God has placed within you. This is necessary for living a life of victory because more often than not, your soul gets in the way of your spirit. Your personality, the way you were raised, your orientation, your thoughts, your feelings, and your desires often keep God's presence, truth, and power from functioning freely in you. We often point to outside forces behind our struggles, but really, most of the time our solution is right inside us if we will simply allow the spirit to dominate our souls.

Doing that isn't as easy as simply reading the words in this book or telling yourself to allow your spirit to dominate your soul. In fact, God says that He has provided the Logos—sharper than any two-edged sword—to do the job of dividing the soul from the spirit and clarifying truth within you. God uses the understanding of the message to cut through your thoughts, your habits, and your strongholds in order to remove their influence over you so the spirit can have free rein over you.

In fact, the Logos is not only able to penetrate the invisible realm and divide between soul and spirit, it is also able to discern and judge both the thoughts and the intentions of the heart. It doesn't simply address the action, but attends to the heart and mind, which propel the action. It doesn't just say, "Put that drink down," "Forgive that person," or "Turn off what you shouldn't be watching." It goes deeper and focuses on the why behind the what. If you can get the why rightly aligned underneath the truth and message of God, you won't have to tell yourself to put down that drink, forgive that person, or turn off what you shouldn't be watching because you'll be motivated to stop doing those things.

Even more than that, Hebrews 4:13 goes on to tell us, "And there is no creature hidden from His sight, but all things are open and laid bare to the eyes of Him with whom we have to do." Basically, whatever the Logos sees, God sees. The Word of God opens you up to reveal all things within you. It exposes you like a spiritual MRI or X-ray machine, showing the inner truth that outward actions don't always reveal. A person can have great actions but also have a bad heart, simply doing those actions out of fear of getting punished or looking bad. Another person can have bad actions but have a right heart, being fully aware of his or her need for mercy and dependence on God. Jesus told a story about this in Luke 18:9-14.

> And He also told this parable to some people who trusted in themselves that they were righteous, and viewed others with contempt: "Two men went up into the temple to pray, one a Pharisee and the other a tax collector. The Pharisee stood and was praying this to himself: 'God, I thank You that I am not like other people: swindlers, unjust, adulterers, or even like this tax collector. I fast twice a week; I pay tithes of all that I get.' But the tax collector, standing some distance away, was even unwilling to lift up his eyes to heaven, but was beating his breast, saying, 'God, be merciful to me, the sinner!' I tell you, this man went to his house justified rather than the other; for everyone who exalts himself will be humbled, but he who humbles himself will be exalted."

Jesus, the Logos, looked past what could be seen and focused deep into the heart of both the Pharisee and the tax collector in order to judge and discern correctly. Likewise, as we meditate on fully understanding God's truth and allow the Logos of God to penetrate and take root deep within us, it reveals our hearts to such a degree that we're able to discern right from wrong and truth from lie. It penetrates us deeply, creating a powerful impact.

Rhema

There's yet a third term in the Bible for the word of God—and it's a very important word. When Paul tells us to "take…the sword of the Spirit, which is the word of God," he's not telling us to take up the *graphe* or the Logos. Instead, he uses the Greek term *rhema*.

Rhema simply means utterance, spoken word, or what has been declared. *Graphe* is the written word, Logos is the message of the written word, and *rhema* is the specific declaration concerning the message of the written word.

A person could have a Bible factory and publish thousands of Bibles every day but never have the power of the sword of the Spirit. A person could have great understanding of the message in the Scripture but still not utilize the power of the sword against the enemy. The sword of the Spirit specifically refers to the *rhema* of God. The *rhema* of God is our one offensive weapon, which is able to plunge quickly into the enemy and draw blood.

The reason so many Christians are living defeated lives is that they haven't graduated from *graphe* to *logos* to *rhema*. Some Christians haven't moved past *graphe*. Bringing your Bible to church isn't the same thing as using the sword of the Spirit. It's just a book to you until you open it, read it, and hear God's Spirit teach you and speak to you through it.

Other Christians live defeated lives because they have gotten stuck in Logos-land. They seek to understand the sermon, they attend the Bible studies, and they take notes on the knowledge, but haven't used what they've learned in spiritual warfare against the enemy. Coming to church and hearing a good sermon, even though the message may penetrate within you, is not enough when you're in close-up battle with the enemy and all hell has broken loose in your life. At times like that, you need the *rhema*. You need the specific utterance of God for your situation. You need to hear God speaking to *you* and to take that truth straight into the heart of Satan and his demons.

Most of us have had a *rhema* experience with the Word of God but didn't realize what it was. Have you ever read some passages in the Bible so many times over the years that you feel as if you know all there is to know about them? And then one day, as you turn to one of these familiar passages, it's like God has marked it with a yellow highlighter. One verse, word, principle, or truth leaps off of the page and speaks directly to the situation you're facing. That is what is called a *rhema*—a word God speaks to you out of His written Word.

God's spoken word was powerful enough to completely change things in the beginning, bringing things into existence out of nothing.

We read in Genesis 1:3, "Then God said, 'Let there be light'; and there was light." On and on in the beginning of Genesis, we read that God said that something was so, and it came to be so. All God had to do was speak the word, and whatever He spoke came about. In other words, the spoken word (*rhema*) had the power within it to accomplish God's desire. The *rhema* was the Spirit's dagger that God used to bring things into being.

How do we know that the Holy Spirit had something to do with God speaking things into existence? Because we read in Genesis 1:2 that when God got ready to create something, the Holy Spirit was hovering over it. It says, "The earth was formless and void, and darkness was over the surface of the deep, and the Spirit of God was moving over the surface of the waters." The Spirit was positioned and ready to move just as soon as God said to move—just waiting for the word.

That's why it's so important to study God's Word, learn it, and engage it as you abide with it. Since it's so powerful, Satan knows that all he has to do is twist God's Word and it will become a dull sword, unable to carry out its purpose both as an internal sword (*logos*) and as an offensive weapon (*rhema*).

When Adam and Eve sinned in the garden, that's exactly what Satan did to them. Satan twisted God's word by questioning Eve: "Did God really say…?" (Genesis 3:1 NIV). He did this because he knew that if he could mix up the word, he would reduce its power to defeat him.

In fact, Satan loves it when you say things like, "Well, I think…" or "Well, my opinion is…" He relishes every time you say, "Well, my dad said…" or "My mom said…" or "My friends say…" Satan loves to hear these words because he knows there is no power in what you think or feel or in what your family or friends say. He'll leave you alone and let you collect that type of information through popular television talk shows, the radio, or phone calls and e-mails to your friends. He's not afraid of that at all.

But as soon as you start saying, "Well, God says…" and jabbing that directly into his midsection, that's when he starts running. Satan is unable to stand against the powerful force of the utterance of God. A perfect example of this is found in Matthew 4:1. "Jesus was led up by the Spirit into the wilderness to be tempted by the devil." What's interesting to note about this verse is that it tells us that God Himself led Jesus straight into the face of the devil. That's a critical point to recognize because later on we discover that Jesus used the *rhema* (the utterance of God) to defeat the devil. God had gone on the advance against Satan by leading Jesus to him, and Jesus responded by using the offensive tool, the sword of the Spirit, to overcome him.

In verse 3 of this passage we read that Satan tempted Christ at His weakest point. Jesus had been fasting for 40 days, so by the time this encounter occurred, He was hungry. In Luke 4:13 we read that Satan looks for "opportune" times to work his deception. He tried to capitalize on Christ's legitimate need for food by saying, "Command that these stones become bread."

Jesus, however, responded by saying, "It is written, 'Man shall not live on bread alone, but on every word that proceeds out of the mouth of God.'"

What Jesus *didn't* do in this situation is just as important as what He *did* do. By saying, "It is written," and then using the full force of the Word of God, Jesus didn't enter into a long debate, meeting, conversation, or dialogue with Satan about the subject. He simply said, "It is written," followed up with what God had said.

Satan came at Jesus two more times, tempting Him in a moment of physical weakness, but each time Jesus responded in the same way—"It is written"—followed by what the Word said about the matter. Now, if the Living Word, Jesus, needed to use the *rhema* to deal with the enemy, how much more must we rely on the *rhema* of God? Jesus embodied perfection in His thoughts and reasoning, but even He didn't approach Satan based on His thoughts. He overcame Satan with the Word of God.

The issue Jesus faced was a legitimate one. He was hungry. He had a legitimate physical need. Satan didn't twist Christ's need. Instead, he tried to twist the way Jesus went about meeting that need, tempting Jesus to find fulfillment apart from God. However, when he did that, Jesus responded in a way we might describe today as Googling God's feeding program. He accessed Deuteronomy 8 and then told Satan what God says about bread and hunger.

After only three times of "It is written," Satan left. He couldn't handle more than three strikes, so he was out of there as quickly as he had come. If you are asking, "Tony, why won't the devil leave me alone? Why is he always up in my face?" my answer to you is a question as well: Are you using the Word of God to make him leave you alone? Satan can hang out with you all day and all night long if he knows you will never read the *graphe*, which will help you understand the *logos*, which in turn will help you hear and use the *rhema* God has given to you for your specific situation. The sword of the Spirit is your offensive weapon to advance against the enemy in the trials and battles he has brought upon you. It's time to take back the ground and restore what has been lost to the deceptive strategies of Satan. After having put on the full armor of God, use the sword of the Spirit to move forward against the enemy and tell him he has to get out of your way. As Paul writes in Romans 8:37, "In all these things we overwhelmingly conquer through Him who loved us."

Go on the Offensive

One day, an elderly man walked into a local lumber mill and told the owner of the company that he wanted to come and work for him chopping down trees. The owner took one look at the wrinkled, old man and laughed. "You're as old as dirt," he said. "What makes you think you have what it takes to work for me?"

"Just give me a chance," the old man replied, "I know I can do this job."

The owner was in a pleasant mood, so he decided to humor the old man by taking him out to the forest where a number of younger men were chopping down trees. In a matter of hours—and to everyone's surprise, the old man had chopped down more trees than all of the younger men. The owner's mouth fell open in amazement.

He asked him, "Sir, where did you learn to chop down trees like that?"

The old man replied, "Have you ever heard of the Sahara Forest?"

"You mean the Sahara Desert?" asked the owner.

"No," the old man said, "I mean the Sahara Forest. That's what they called it before I got there."

When you learn how to use the sword of the Spirit, which is the word of God, as you go on the offensive against the enemy seeking to destroy you, it doesn't matter how old you are or how weak you seem. All you need to know is that the sword in your hand is capable of doing more than you will ever need. As we saw with Jesus in the wilderness, that sword will make the devil flee. I guarantee it. Better yet, God guarantees it. So grab it and use it on your path to living in ultimate spiritual victory.

Part 3

THE VICTORY

10

THE POWER OF PRAYER

A world champion body builder went to Africa on a tour to promote good health and physical fitness. He visited some large metropolitan cities as well as some nearby villages, where the people did not have access to electricity, television, or running water.

One day as this body builder was holding a fitness awareness seminar in a small, remote village, he had an interesting interruption. He had just finished demonstrating all of the different ways he could cause his muscles to bulge and contract all over his body when the local tribal chief stopped him. Slowly making his way up to where the body builder was standing, the tribal chief spoke to him through a translator.

"What you have shown us is impressive. I have never seen that many muscles on one man before."

The body builder, used to hearing such flattering remarks, smiled smugly and gave the crowd another look at his physique. But the tribal chief continued talking. He said, "I only have one question. What do you use those muscles for?"

The body builder answered, "Body building is my profession. This is my job."

"You don't use those muscles for anything else?"

"No," replied the body builder.

"What a waste," said the chief, shaking his head slowly. "What a waste to have all of those muscles and not use them."

The same could be said for any Christian who has access to the full armor of God but doesn't use it to walk in victory. If you read this book but fail to apply the truth of God's Word to your life as an intentional, active approach to spiritual warfare, you will be no closer to living a life of victory than before you began the first chapter.

These next two chapters are critical not only for bringing to fruition all that we have talked about so far but also for setting the stage to launch you into the final portion of this book. Parts 3 and 4 are designed to offer you what you need to experience true victory. In these parts, I've chosen some specific biblical truths that you need not only to know but also to own, apply, and use in spiritual warfare. They are laid out in an easily accessible manner so there will literally be no excuse for a life of defeat. If you will simply use the armor on a daily basis, you *will* walk in victory.

But before we go any further, I want to remind you of the first principle of spiritual warfare one more time: *Whatever is plaguing you today in the physical realm is emanating from the spiritual realm.* If we do not address the cause, we will never get to the cure. The enemy wants you to forget that. He wants you to continue to believe that your spouse, your boss, your friend, that drink, that drug, that emotion, or even you yourself are the problem. All of these (and more) can be manifestations of the problem, but none are the root cause. The battle begins in the spiritual realm. And because you are a believer, you are already victorious in that realm even when everything around you in the visible, physical realm is telling you you're defeated.

If you want to access and walk in the victory that is already yours, you *must* address the physical *spiritually*. If you do not address the physical spiritually, you will continue to experience the effects of the physical realm's domination.

Paul gives us the secret for how we can do this. After instructing us to put on the full armor of God, he goes to the next step in the process of battling in spiritual warfare when he says in Ephesians 6:18, "With all prayer and petition pray at all times in the Spirit, and with this in view, be on the alert with all perseverance and petition for all the saints."

Notice how many times the word "pray" or a synonym for prayer is used in that short statement. We see it as "all prayer," "petition," and "pray." Paul has purposefully chosen to emphasize prayer immediately following his instructions on taking up the armor of God.

The topic of prayer has been studied, written about, talked about, and preached on by millions of people for thousands of years. But in my interactions with believers in nearly four decades of full-time ministry, I've discovered that very few of us actually understand prayer. When people truly understand prayer, that understanding changes how they live, what they pray, whether they pray, and the expectations they have from prayer.

For many people, even some Christians, prayer is like the national anthem before a sporting event. It gets the game started but has absolutely no relevance to what's happening on the field. Prayer is merely a habit. For example, when most of us pray before we eat, we don't really utilize our minds as we're praying; we just say the same general thing each time. Or when many of us pray before we go to bed at night, we simply recite a call for blessing and protection with a little bit of gratitude thrown in for good measure. Prayer has become a routine. Another way to look at it is that prayer has become like a spare tire—we want it there in case we really need it, but if we don't feel as if we need it, we want it out of the way where we don't have to deal with it or see it.

Simply defined, *prayer is earthly permission for heavenly interference.* It's earth giving heaven permission to intervene in the manifestation down here of the spiritual reality up there. Now, I know you might be asking, "Tony, why does heaven need permission? Why do I have to give heaven permission to do anything down here?"

The nature and the topic of this book won't allow us to go into all of the theology behind the answer to that question, but it can be summarized by looking at how God designed the world to function. When God created the heavens and the earth and placed mankind on it, He said, "Let them rule." For whatever reason, God chose to give mankind rulership over the earth. In doing so, He has done two things. First, He has given mankind the option of leaving Him out. The first chapter of Romans summarizes the results of what happens when God is left out.

The second thing He's done is given mankind the option of calling on Him to join in on the rulership He has willingly given us.

There are many things God *can* do but *doesn't* do simply because He has not been requested to do them. But when you go to God and ask for His divine intervention based on His Word, His truth, His promises, and His character, He intervenes in response to your faith, your desire for Him, your submission to Him, and your acknowledgment of your need for Him.

You can leave God out. He's given you that option. You can act independently of God all day long. But you can also bring Him into your situation and watch Him show up in ways you've never even imagined. That's done through prayer.

Now, keep in mind, prayer can never force God to do anything. You can never make God do something He didn't intend to do or plan to do. Even if you prayed all day long, every day, God is not a puppet on your prayer-string. But what prayer does is call on God to intervene in ways that He has already declared that He wants to intervene. He's just waiting for you to ask Him.

This biblical truth is illustrated in James 5:16: "Therefore, confess your sins to one another, and pray for one another so that you may be healed. The effective prayer of a righteous man can accomplish much."

James begins by giving a condition for healing to occur, and that condition is prayer. Following that condition, James makes a general statement that much will be accomplished through the fervent prayer of a righteous person. He doesn't say that only a little will be accomplished. He doesn't even say that some things will be accomplished. James clearly says that *much* will be accomplished through the effective prayer of a righteous person.

You say, "But Tony, I'm dealing with strongholds in my life. I'm struggling. I'm not what most people would consider a righteous person." I hear you. None of us can claim to be perfect. But I want to remind you that when we discussed the breastplate of righteousness, we said that Jesus Christ is the righteousness that God sees in you when you, by faith, access, receive, and walk in His grace. Beyond that, we also read further in this same passage in James that "Elijah was a man *with a nature like ours*, and he prayed earnestly that it would not rain, and it did not rain on the earth for three years and six months."

In other words, I don't want you to throw in the towel and believe that God only worked with the holy prophets back in the Old Testament. James is telling us that Elijah was just like you and me. He had a human nature just like any man, but Elijah earnestly prayed that it would not rain, and it did not rain on the earth for three years and six months. Then, after three years and six months, "he prayed again, and the sky poured rain and the earth produced its fruit" (verse 18).

In this passage we clearly see that an ordinary man with a nature just like yours and mine had the power to both stop the rain and start it again simply through prayer. Elijah got heaven to move on earth by calling the will of God in heaven down to earth. He saw a problem on earth and called on heaven to solve it. Heaven heard and responded.

Look at this scenario a little more closely before we move on. In 1 Kings 18:1, we read, "Now it happened after many days that the word of the LORD came to Elijah in the third year, saying, 'Go, show yourself to Ahab, and I will send rain on the face of the earth.'" Elijah had a *rhema* word from God. God told Elijah that He would send the rain.

The end of chapter 18 gives us greater insight into this.

> Now Elijah said to Ahab, "Go up, eat and drink; for there is the sound of the roar of a heavy shower." So Ahab went up to eat and drink. But Elijah went up to the top of Carmel; and he crouched down on the earth and put his face between his knees. He said to his servant, "Go up now, look toward the sea." So he went up and looked and said, "There is nothing." And he said, "Go back" seven times. It came about at the seventh time, that he said, "Behold, a cloud as small as a man's hand is coming up from the sea." And he said, "Go up, say to Ahab, 'Prepare your chariot and go down, so that the heavy shower does not stop you.'" In a little while the sky grew black with clouds and wind, and there was a heavy shower (verses 41-45).

Once again, there is so much theology packed into this one passage that for the purposes of this book, I'm going to need to give you the Cliff Notes version. Here it is: God said it would rain. Elijah prayed about what God had already said. Elijah didn't make stuff up and attribute it to God. But what God had said—that it would rain—did not come to pass until *after* Elijah had prayed. Even though God had already declared it in the heavenly realm, not a single raindrop hit the earth until it got called down by Elijah on the earth. In other words, prayer called down what God had already intended to do; but what God had already intended to do did not happen until prayer drew it down.

Elijah's prayer didn't make God do something He hadn't intended to do, but it did reach into heaven, grab and draw down what God had already told Elijah He would do.

Another thing to notice about Elijah's prayer is the form in which he prayed. We read that he "crouched down on the earth and put his face between his knees." That may not mean much to you or me reading it in the twenty-first century, but it meant something very powerful in the time period and the culture in which Elijah lived. When a woman gave birth in Elijah's day, she didn't have the luxury of modern hospital beds. What she would often do is position herself by crouching down and placing her face between her knees. This put her in a position of travail. In doing so, she wasn't creating the life of the child within her. She was simply providing the best possible avenue for the life that already existed to be brought into its new realm.

Elijah didn't merely bow his head, close his eyes, hum a hymn, and ask for rain. Scripture tells us that Elijah positioned himself in a posture of travail. Prayer is the work done in faith that accesses all that God has already planned to do. It's earthly participation in a heavenly delivery, and as we see from Elijah, who has been given to us in the book of James as an example of effective prayer, prayer can involve travailing.

God's Secrets

As we see from Elijah, prayer should be predicated on what God has already declared He will do. In order to do this effectively, we need to study His Word (*graphe*), understand His message (*logos*), and become intimate with His utterance (*rhema*) so that when we pray, we will know what we are to pray for in line with His will. The Bible tells us that God has secrets that He's willing to share with you and me. Secrets are special things you tell only those people who are closest to you. God wants you to be so close to Him that He can lean over and whisper His secrets in your ear. We read in Psalm 25:14, "The secret of the LORD is for those who fear Him, and He will make them know His covenant."

When God reveals to you His secrets—His promises in His Word— that is when you are able to take God's Word and send it right back to Him. That is when you can say, "God, You said in your Word..." Prayer is holding God accountable to what He has already said He will do.

Prayer is not simply seeing something you want and claiming it. If God didn't tell you He's going to give you that nice new job with a corner office, then you can pray until you're blue in the face and that nice new job will still belong to someone else. *The foundation of prayer is knowing what God has already said.* God has given us literally thousands of promises in His Word. I encourage you to start there.

We do ourselves a disservice when we don't take the time to learn and know God's Word. Our prayers become vague and empty, or they become full of things God never intended to do. Either way, we end up tossing our armor into the back of the closet and saying, "It didn't work for me." Then we often call someone or meet up with our friends and try to find a human solution, or at least someone who can give us sympathy for what we're battling.

Friend, you need answers much more than you need sympathy. You need heaven to invade earth, and the only way to access heaven's authority on earth is through prayer. It's like the television you have at your home. There are television signals floating around in the air all the time. But you won't be able to use those signals until you turn your television on. When you do, what was invisible becomes visible. You can see the image on your television because you have received the signal that's being broadcast.

God has provided us—His children—with everything we need to broadcast His glory not only within our own lives but also to a world in need of seeing Him. What's available to us in the invisible realm is accessed through prayer. God is present all around us. His angels are moving all around in the physical realm, surrounding us. In fact, there are demons surrounding us as well. We just can't see the spiritual realm until we draw it down into the physical reality.

The Opportune Time

Paul's instruction in Ephesians 6:18 includes a very important term. He directs us to "pray at all times in the Spirit." The English word "times" in this passage is often misattributed to the Greek word *kronos*, which simply refers to time in general—seconds, minutes, hours, and so on. So you'll often hear a believer saying this passage means that we're to be praying all of the time. That's something we do see in 1 Thessalonians 5:17, where we're told to "pray without ceasing." But that's different from what Paul is telling us to do in this particular passage.

When Paul wrote, "pray at all times," he specifically chose the much more distinctly defined Greek word *kairos*. *Kairos* has to do with a specific time. If I were to say to you that I will meet you for lunch at 12:15, you know that I'm going to meet you at 12:15. That's different from saying, "Let's do lunch sometime (*kronos*)" and leaving it at that. This specific time (*kairos*) of 12:15 has been chosen as an opportune, appointed time.

So when Paul tells us in Ephesians 6:18 to "pray at all times," he's specifically pointing out that we're to pray at opportune, appointed times in relation to the "evil day" that he's just written about. Remember, the evil day is the day when spiritual warfare is in your face and all hell is breaking loose. At those times, Paul says, *pray*. It's at those times that the day demands the power of the armor connected with concentrated, specific prayer.

In Romans 8:22-23 we read about those times. "For we know that the whole creation groans and suffers the pains of childbirth together until now. And not only this, but also we ourselves, having the first fruits of the Spirit, even we ourselves groan within ourselves."

Does that sound familiar? Has the battle ever made you so weary that you actually *groan*? Has life hurt you so badly that you find yourself unable to do much more than wait eagerly for the redemption of the body? It's especially at times like these that you must suit up and pray.

What happens when you pray at this time—not according to the flesh, with random, vague prayers out of habit, but rather according to the Spirit, by connecting with and focusing on what God has to say on the matter? Continuing in Romans 8, we read that in those times, the Holy Spirit intercedes for us according to the will of God.

> In the same way the Spirit also helps our weakness; for we do not know how to pray as we should, but the Spirit Himself intercedes for us with groanings too deep for words; and He who searches the hearts knows what the mind of the Spirit is, because He intercedes for the saints according to the will of God (verses 26-27).

It's then that the Spirit groans with you—travails with you—because He knows how deep the problem, hurt, need, or attack really is. He comes alongside of you in those *kairos* moments, when you don't think you can make it one more day. It's then that He ushers you into the very presence of God while He calls on God to do His will in your situation.

Realizing all that's actually going on during prayer ought to invigorate your prayer life. For many people, prayer can seem boring, but that's only because they don't understand what's happening in the invisible realm as the result of their prayers. If we could truly grasp all that happens in the invisible realm in response to our prayers, prayer would be the top priority in all of our lives, and we would do what Paul urges—"pray at all times in the Spirit."

Battle in the Heavenlies

In the book of Daniel, we find one of the greatest illustrations of prayer. We begin by seeing that Daniel is studying God's Word and then responding to God in prayer based on what he has discovered.

> In the first year of [Darius'] reign, I, Daniel, observed in the books the number of the years which was revealed as the word of the LORD to Jeremiah the prophet for the

completion of the desolations of Jerusalem, namely, seventy years. So I gave my attention to the Lord God to seek Him by prayer and supplications, with fasting, sackcloth and ashes (Daniel 9:2-3).

First, Daniel discovered what God had said. Then he talked to God about it. Anytime you take God's Word and talk to Him about it, you are praying in the Spirit. Let's see what happens next.

Now while I was speaking and praying, and confessing my sin and the sin of my people Israel, and presenting my supplication before the LORD my God in behalf of the holy mountain of my God, while I was still speaking in prayer, then the man Gabriel, whom I had seen in the vision previously, came to me in my extreme weariness about the time of the evening offering. He gave me instruction and talked with me and said, "O Daniel, I have now come forth to give you insight with understanding" (Daniel 9:20-22).

Notice that while Daniel was praying, God sent an angel to help him understand even more than he previously had known. However, God did not send the angel to give Daniel understanding until Daniel prayed in response to what God had already said. We see this in the next verse: "At the beginning of your supplications the command was issued, and I have come to tell you, for you are highly esteemed; so give heed to the message and gain understanding of the vision" (verse 23). As soon as Daniel began praying, God gave the directive to Gabriel to go to Daniel to give him more understanding.

Daniel 10 gives us greater insight into this occasion.

Then behold, a hand touched me and set me trembling on my hands and knees. He said to me, "O Daniel, man of high esteem, understand the words that I am about to tell you and stand upright, for I have now been sent to you." And when he had spoken this word to me, I stood up trembling. Then he said to me, "Do not be afraid, Daniel, for from the first day that you set your heart on understanding this and on humbling yourself before your God, your words were heard, and I have come in response to your words. But the prince of the kingdom of Persia was withstanding me for twenty-one days; then behold, Michael, one of the chief princes, came to help me, for I had been left there with the kings of Persia. Now I have come to give you an understanding of what will happen to your people in the latter days, for the vision pertains to the days yet future."

When he had spoken to me according to these words, I turned my face toward the ground and became speechless (Daniel 10:10-15).

When Daniel prayed to God in response to God's words revealed through Jeremiah, God sent a messenger to help him. Twice we read in these two chapters that God sent the angel on the day that Daniel prayed to God in accordance with God's already revealed word. When you or I are praying according to God's own word, He hears us and responds. The delay in receiving that response was caused by spiritual warfare in the heavenly realm. Gabriel had been dispatched to go to Daniel with a message of understanding from God, but the prince of Persia—a demon—blocked Gabriel from reaching his destination for three weeks.

When we fail to realize that our battles are being waged in the spiritual realm, we may make the false assumption that God hasn't heard us or that He doesn't care about our situation. But as we have seen in Daniel's case, God not only heard Daniel's prayer when he first offered it but also responded immediately to Daniel's prayer. Yet because there is a battle taking place in the invisible, spiritual realm, there was a delay in God's response reaching its intended destination. In fact, another angel—Michael—was needed in order to eventually remove the demon from acting as an obstacle for Gabriel. Ultimately, the prince of Persia got double-teamed in order for God to deliver His message to Daniel.

No battle or war has ever lasted for only a minute. Yet sometimes it seems that's what we must believe when we say our prayer and then go our way, disappointed when God doesn't respond immediately. But there are more reasons to keep praying than simply to ask again for the thing you're seeking. If what you're praying is in line with God's Word, you don't need to continue to ask God over and over again. After you ask Him, the remainder of your prayers should be focused on thanking God for His promised response. And since there are demons attempting to block the delivery of that answer in your life, your prayers should also focus on asking God to intervene in the situation to remove Satan from causing a delay in your answer.

Paul urges us to pray in a like manner in the passage we looked at in the opening of this chapter. After detailing the different pieces of the armor, Paul wrote in Ephesians 6:18 that we are to pray at all times in the Spirit, "and with this in view, be on the alert with all perseverance and petition for all the saints." Being on the alert means that we are to pray with our eyes wide open. Peter tells us in 1 Peter 5:8 the reason we are to be on the alert with our spiritual eyes open: "Your adversary, the devil, prowls around like a roaring lion, seeking someone to devour."

We must be on the alert as we pray because prayers prayed in response to God's Word summon the will of God down from heaven to earth and are a dangerous threat to Satan. Hell wants to block heaven from reaching earth, and it will do anything it can to stop us from praying. Have you ever noticed that sometimes when you pray, a number of distractions show up? Or maybe you get sleepy even though you weren't sleepy before you began. Satan and his demons will try everything they can to stop you from praying because prayer is the tool through which the armor of God manifests its greatest potential for victory.

There's a story told about two hunters who had heard that a bounty of $5000 had been put up for every wolf they could kill. So these two hunters decided that they would go wolf hunting and strike it rich. It was a dangerous job that took them deep into the heart of the forest. One night, one of the men was awakened to the sound of growling. Looking outside his small window, he saw more than 50 snarling wolves surrounding them with their teeth glittering in the moonlight.

The man turned to his friend and woke him up saying, "John, we're rich!"

Perspective is everything. If the enemy is trying to distract you from praying, that's a good sign. That means your prayers are causing him to be concerned. But don't let Satan intimidate you or keep you from praying fervently in the Spirit. When you have suited up for battle in the heavenlies, prayer is your ticket to take you straight into the heart of it.

Many of the things you have asked God for in prayer, He has already answered. He has already approved them. It is only that Satan is now attempting to block your answer from reaching you. So don't give up, and don't spend your time focusing on what has already been done. Instead, thank God for what He has promised and persevere in prayer until the *kairos* moment arrives when you will receive your victory.

11

THE SUFFICIENCY OF CHRIST

Not long ago I was walking in New York City when it began to rain. I had seen the weather report, so I had my umbrella ready. Several other people must have seen the report as well because they had their umbrellas too. But a good number of people didn't have umbrellas, causing them to rush around, looking for someplace to find cover. Needless to say, they became miserable as the cold rain drenched them.

Being underneath an umbrella doesn't stop the rain—it simply stops the rain from stopping you. The umbrella doesn't still the storm. What the umbrella does is change the way in which the storm affects you.

Standing firm in the armor of God doesn't stop the spiritual warfare from raging. It stops it from defeating you. That's why one scheme of the devil is to get you to step out from underneath the protective covering God has given you in the six pieces of armor. Once you step out from underneath God's protection, you expose yourself to everything Satan brings your way.

One of Satan's tactics is to get you to believe that God's covering isn't adequate for the tsunami-sized disaster he's going to throw at you. He tries to get you to run. He wants you to drop your umbrella—your armor—and run someplace where you think you might be more safe. But as we've seen, the key to victory in spiritual warfare comes in recognizing the truth that Jesus Christ has already secured the victory we seek, and our proper response is to stand firm in that victory. *There is no safer place you or I could ever be than fully armed in our identity with Christ.*

The Victory of Christ

When Jesus Christ died on the cross, He made it possible for us to be complete in Him and in His rule, which extends over everything—every event, every enemy, every threat—literally *everything*. As we read in Colossians 2:10, "In Him you have been made complete, and He is the head over all rule and authority." In Him, we discover our victory—there is nothing lacking in His headship and rulership over all else.

When you trusted in Christ for your salvation, you were transferred from the dominion of darkness into the kingdom of light. As we saw in chapter 3, "He rescued us from the domain of darkness, and transferred us to the kingdom of His beloved Son, in whom we have redemption, the forgiveness of sins" (Colossians 1:13-14). When you and I believed in Jesus Christ, God changed our location. We have been transferred to a new kingdom with its own kingdom agenda, which is the comprehensive rule of God over every area of life.

The book of Hebrews tells us that Jesus' death rendered Satan powerless.

> Therefore, since the children share in flesh and blood, He Himself likewise also partook of the same, that through death He might render powerless him who had the power of death, that is, the devil, and might free those who through fear of death were subject to slavery all their lives (Hebrews 2:14-15).

In Jesus Christ, you have been set free. You no longer have to cower in fear of anything. Your victory is rooted in the reality that everything is under the rule of the One who has made us complete in Him. "And He put all things in subjection under His feet, and gave Him as head over all things to the church, which is His body, the fullness of Him who fills all in all" (Ephesians 1:22-23).

These are just a few defining truths regarding the victory of Christ we are to live in. Knowing and living by these realities ought to change the way we walk, talk, think, and respond. Jesus Christ has already defeated Satan once and for all. Satan can no longer overcome us with his power. If Satan defeats us at all, he must do so with permission that has been given to him. This is a truth that Satan does not want us to know or own because once we walk in this truth, we will treat him differently, look at him differently, and respond to him differently.

If you were to come to my house during football season, you would see that the NFL Network is perpetually on my television. Anyone who knows me at all knows that I love football. The great thing about the NFL Network is that it shows you the scores of every game of all 32 teams in the NFL each week. This is so you can know how everything ended. But there is something else that the NFL Network does. It also replays the games. So if you didn't happen to see the score, you wouldn't know how the game ended. But if you did see the score, even though you would already know how the game ended, you wouldn't know how it got to that point.

And the NFL Network not only shows games from this season but also replays games from previous seasons. They will show games from the past even though the viewer already knows how the game will turn out.

When I'm watching a football game and I already know the outcome, it changes the entire experience. There's something about knowing how the game ends that alters the way I view it. I might see my team fumble, but I don't get upset because I know where the game is going. I might see my quarterback throw an interception, but I don't get nervous because I know how the game has ended. I might see my team go four and out, but it doesn't matter because I know where the game is headed. At halftime, my team might even be losing, but it doesn't matter. Sure, I may get a little frustrated, but I don't lose my composure. I don't stress. And the reason I don't is that I have already seen the final score. Discovering ahead of time where the victory lies changes everything. Now I'm viewing the game from the vantage point of victory, not in order to determine victory.

Friend, Jesus Christ has already secured your victory over anything that Satan brings at you. When you view your life through that lens, it takes the pressure off and frees you to walk confidently in the strength of the One who has already won. It even changes the way you talk. Instead of speaking in uncertainties, you can now talk with authority and hope. You can speak words of life.

Words are powerful, after all. Proverbs 18:21 tells us, "Death and life are in the power of the tongue." Every time you repeat a negative, defeating statement or speak a hopeless thought, you are handing Satan a stick with which to beat you down. Every time you say, "*If* things get better," or "*If* God comes through," or "I just don't know *if* I'm going to make it," you are giving Satan permission to defeat you. You are loading the bullets into his empty gun.

God tells us to use His Word and the strength found in it to speak life into our situation. Uncover and discover God's perspective on whatever it is you're facing, and speak these truths to God, yourself, others, Satan, and his demons. Speaking something has great significance. Christ said in Luke 4:18 that God sent Him to "proclaim release to the captives." Paul explained in 1 Corinthians 11:26 that when we receive communion, we "proclaim the Lord's death until He comes."

To proclaim something is to speak it, whether in words or in actions. For example, at the church I pastor in Dallas, we offer communion every Sunday. We do it every week because communion is a foundational part of the Christian life. It brings us back to the cross before we ever get into worship or the sermon by reminding us of the mercy, power, and authority in the new covenant we are now under.

However, more than that is taking place during communion. Even if no words are spoken by anyone, a loud message is proclaimed each and every Sunday to the demonic forces in the spiritual realm. The act of communion sends a shout-out to Satan that Jesus Christ has already secured the victory. By proclaiming Christ's death, we serve notice to hell that heaven has already won this battle. We affirm to Satan that even though we may still have problems, fears, and frustrations, through Christ these things no longer rule over us. They no longer have the final say.

But if, as Paul clearly teaches in 1 Corinthians 11:26, the act of taking communion is also the act of proclaiming a critical truth, we are left with a question: Proclaiming it to *whom*? And for what reason?

To proclaim something is similar to preaching it. So Paul is telling us that when we participate in communion, we are preaching a sermon to Satan and his demons about the totality of Christ's death. It's the time in the service when we get to preach to the spiritual realm that victory has been secured. Part of what we're preaching is found in Colossians 2:13-15.

> When you were dead in your transgressions and the uncircumcision of your flesh, He made you alive together with Him, having forgiven us all our transgressions, having canceled out the certificate of debt consisting of decrees against us, which was hostile to us; and He has taken it out of the way, having nailed it to the cross. When He had disarmed the rulers and authorities, He made a public display of them, having triumphed over them through Him.

Communion reminds us that on the cross, Jesus defeated and disarmed the devil. Satan may still have more power than you and I do in our humanity, but the key to understanding spiritual victory in any arena—your marriage, your career, your health, or elsewhere—is to recognize that Satan's power means nothing when you understand he has no authority. On the cross, the devil lost his authority. Jesus "disarmed the rulers and authorities."

Not only that, but this passage tells us that Jesus put them on "display." He held a victory parade. Satan and his demons were put on public exhibition in the spiritual realm as having been defeated. When we operate in our position in Christ in the spiritual realm, we are to look at Satan the same way Jesus sees him. We are to look at him as the loser he truly is, displayed for all to see.

Communion offers still more than a proclamation of Satan's defeat, though. It not only separates us from demonic involvement and influence (see 1 Corinthians 10:20-21) but also draws down covenantal blessings from the heavenly realm. As Paul writes in 1 Corinthians 10:16, "Is not the cup of blessing which we bless a sharing in the blood of Christ?"

Communion is the act of reaching into heaven and grabbing the blessings attached to Christ's covenantal death and resurrection while also reaching into hell to let the enemy know he no longer holds authority over us. Victory in spiritual warfare isn't solely about defeating Satan; it's also about drawing down from heaven all the good things God has in store for us on earth.

Remember Jesus

We're not in the same room together right now, but I can imagine what you may be saying. "Tony, this is a lot to remember, especially when I'm under attack. I can't remember all six pieces of the armor, prayer, and communion—I'm having enough trouble as it is. Give me something simple."

I hear you, so let me break it down from the overview we just studied. If you're in a crunch—the "evil day" is upon you, and Satan and his demons are all up in your face—and you need help immediately, remember this one thing: *remember Christ*. Jesus Christ Himself is the fulfillment of each piece of the armor. He is the embodiment of abiding through prayer. He is the manifestation of the bread and blood in communion. Remember Jesus.

The belt of truth
"I am the way, and the truth, and the life" (John 14:6).
Remember Jesus.

The breastplate of righteousness
"He made Him who knew no sin to be sin on our behalf, so that we might become the righteousness of God in Him" (2 Corinthians 5:21).
Remember Jesus.

The shoes of the gospel of peace
"Therefore, having been justified by faith, we have peace with God through our Lord Jesus Christ" (Romans 5:1).
Remember Jesus.

The shield of faith

"…fixing our eyes on Jesus, the author and perfecter of
faith, who for the joy set before Him endured the cross,
despising the shame, and has sat down at the right
hand of the throne of God" (Hebrews 12:2).
Remember Jesus.

The helmet of salvation

"There is salvation in no one else; for there is no other
name under heaven that has been given among men by
which we must be saved" (Acts 4:12).
Remember Jesus.

The sword of the Spirit, which is the word of God

"In the beginning was the Word, and the Word was
with God, and the Word was God. He was in the
beginning with God…And the Word became flesh,
and dwelt among us, and we saw His glory, glory as
of the only begotten from the Father, full of grace and
truth…No one has seen God at any time; the only
begotten God who is in the bosom of the Father, He
has explained Him" (John 1:1-2,14,18).
Remember Jesus.

In other words, if you can't remember anything else about the
armor, *remember Jesus.*

In Jesus, you have truth, righteousness, peace, faith, salvation, and
the sword of the Spirit, which is the word of God. That's why Paul tells
us in Romans 13:14, "Put on the Lord Jesus Christ." Suit up with Jesus
because when you arm yourself by putting on Him, you'll discover that
you have all the armor you need to live in victory. Jesus secured everything you need when He died on the cross. He took on the penalty so
that He could love the sinner, pay for the sin, satisfy God's just wrath
against sin, and express God's love without compromising divine justice.

The book of Revelation emphasizes the totality and sufficiency of
Christ.

Then I heard a loud voice in heaven, saying,

> "Now the salvation, and the power, and the kingdom of
> our God and the authority of His Christ have come, for
> the accuser of our brethren has been thrown down, he who
> accuses them before our God day and night. And they over-
> came him because of the blood of the Lamb and because of
> the word of their testimony, and they did not love their life
> even when faced with death" (Revelation 12:10-11).

We have already seen that hell is after you day and night. Satan
and his demons have made it their mission to accuse you twenty-four
hours a day and seven days a week. But three principles in this passage from Revelation remind us how we're to respond while armed in
the full armor of God. Before we look at them, we need to remember
that what you and I need to overcome is often not what we think it is.
The circumstances, the problems, the health issues, or the addictions
are not defeating you. Instead, this passage makes it clear that "they
overcame *him*." "Him" is a pronoun for Satan. We wrestle not against
circumstances, problems, health issues, or addictions, but against principalities, powers, and world forces in the heavenly realm. In order to
overcome anything in our physical world, we need to first overcome
Satan because he is the one who is causing the chaos in our life.

The Blood of Christ

The devil is overcome by three things. First, he is overcome by the
blood of the Lamb. The Lamb referred to in this passage is Christ, who
was slain from the foundation of the world (Revelation 13:8). Unfortunately, a number of Christians don't understand the blood. We sing
that there is power in the blood or that the blood will never lose its
power, but the power of the blood has nothing to do with its molecular
construction. In other words, Jesus was a man who had human blood
running through His veins. There was nothing about His blood that
made it different from the blood of any other person.

What carries the power is that He is the Lamb. God told Israel in the
Old Testament that they were to kill a lamb and put its blood on the

doorposts of their houses. He said, "The blood shall be a sign for you on the houses where you live; and when I see the blood I will pass over you, and no plague will befall you to destroy you when I strike the land of Egypt" (Exodus 12:13). When God saw the blood on a doorpost, He passed over the home, not because the lamb's blood had anything special in it, but rather because the blood represented something greater.

In the sacrificial system of the old covenant, the shedding of blood represented atonement for sin. Back then, it was atonement on the layaway plan. Under the new covenant with Jesus Christ, the atonement is immediate. So by referring to the blood of the Lamb, we're not talking about the substance, but rather about the One who died, why He died, and what His death accomplished by bringing us into a right relationship with God.

All of this came to a head on what we now call Easter weekend. On Friday, Jesus Christ hung between heaven and earth—bleeding profusely from His head, hands, side, feet, and everywhere He had been beaten and scourged. Near the end, He looked up to heaven and cried, "*Tetelestai,*" meaning "it is finished" or "paid in full" (John 19:30). At the cross, Jesus completely satisfied the demands of God against you and me. Every accusation that can be made against us, even if it's legitimate, was paid in full by the blood of the Lamb. However, to this day, Satan continues to bring up to God our deficiencies and sins even though the bill was settled long ago.

But the cross didn't end on Friday. You might not have heard a sermon preached about Easter *Saturday*, but a lot happened on that day. Jesus wasn't just laying still and cold in the tomb doing nothing on Saturday. According to the Scripture, between the time He died and the time He rose again, He went down to hell and delivered two sermons Himself right there in hell. Jesus was preaching on Easter Saturday (see 1 Peter 3:19; 2 Peter 2:4).

The first of these two sermons was directed at Satan and his demons. It was a short sermon. Essentially He said, "You lose; go to hell." But Jesus' second sermon was directed at all the saints who were on the other side of Sheol in Abraham's bosom. In this sermon, He told them that because of His payment on the cross, they no longer needed to stay there. Paul tells us in the book of Ephesians, "'When He ascended on high, He led captive a host of captives, and He gave gifts to men.' (Now this expression, 'He ascended,' what does it mean except that He also had descended into the lower parts of the earth?)" (Ephesians 4:8-9). Jesus gathered the Old Testament saints and delivered them up into glory so they could be in the presence of God. Jesus was busy on Saturday.

Then on Sunday, Jesus accomplished the final third in a three-part plan—He rose again.

> So Peter and the other disciple went forth, and they were going to the tomb. The two were running together; and the other disciple ran ahead faster than Peter and came to the tomb first; and stooping and looking in, he saw the linen wrappings lying there; but he did not go in. And so Simon Peter also came, following him, and entered the tomb; and he saw the linen wrappings lying there, and the face-cloth which had been on His head, not lying with the linen wrappings, but rolled up in a place by itself. So the other disciple who had first come to the tomb then also entered, and he saw and believed (John 20:3-8).

The grave was and is empty, positioning Jesus Christ at the right hand of the Father, not only having died to save you and me but also living to do the same (see Romans 5:10). As Satan goes about his business of accusing you day and night, Jesus goes about His business of setting the record straight by the power of His death, burial and resurrection.

> Who will bring a charge against God's elect? God is the one who justifies; who is the one who condemns? Christ Jesus is He who died, yes, rather who was raised, who is at the right hand of God, who also intercedes for us (Romans 8:33-34).

Satan stands there to accuse you in the heavenly realm, but Jesus stands there delivering you, setting you free, releasing you, defending you, and empowering you with His strength. Christ's atonement is a saving work not only for eternity, but for every day.

The Testimony of Christ

The second way Satan is overcome, according to Revelation 12:11, is by "the word of their testimony." Tucked away in the word "testimony" is a key element to having one: *Test*. You don't really have a testimony until you have come through a test. A testimony testifies as to what God has done to bring you through something that no one else could have brought you through. So if God has never brought you through something, your testimony is going to be vague and general—something like "God is good all the time, and all the time God is good."

Sayings like that are nice, and they sound very Christian, but you gain a much more powerful testimony when you know that if God doesn't do something, you are going to lose everything—including your mind. This is when you don't know how you're going to pay your rent, buy your food, get a job, find a spouse, mend your relationship with your spouse, stop the habit, or even believe again. This is when all hope seems to be gone, but then you see Jesus Christ tell your particular manifestation of hell to back off. It's at these times, when God wants us to know that He is the only one who can rescue us, that we get a testimony. But a testimony should never stop at simply receiving a testimony. The Scripture says Satan was overcome by the *word* of their testimony. They spoke, proclaimed, confessed, and declared their victory by telling their testimony.

Jesus is not interested in delivering secret-agent Christians. He is not interested in setting free the Christian equivalent of CIA agents—those who serve only in Christian covert operations. When Christ gives you a testimony, it is to be a tool in your hand to overcome the enemy yet again. In fact, Jesus tells us that when we proclaim Him and the things He has done in our lives—the word of our testimony—He speaks about us all the more. He says, "Everyone who confesses Me before men, I will also confess him before My Father who is in heaven. But whoever denies Me before men, I will also deny him before My Father who is in heaven" (Matthew 10:32-33). This denial or confession shows up in His rejection or endorsement of our requests before the throne of God.

A number of years ago I was asked to pray before the city council in

Dallas. The only stipulation they gave me was that they wanted me to be general and pray to God while not mentioning Jesus. I couldn't do that. Rather, I prayed, "Lord, I first want to thank You for the members of the city council because according to Colossians chapter one, everything that You made, You made through Jesus Christ. Lord, I also want to thank You for creating the government because Paul tells us that the government is to be a ministry of God—this is the same apostle Paul who met Jesus Christ on the road to Damascus. And Lord, I want to ask You to help the city council in their decision-making today so that their decisions will reflect Jesus in all that they do. And if there are any city council members who do not know Jesus, I pray that today they will come to know Him as their Lord and Savior because Your Word tells us that no one can come to You but through Jesus. In Jesus' name. Amen."

You cannot ask me to pray and have me keep quiet about Jesus Christ, who died for my sins, rose from the dead, gave me eternal life, makes intercession for me at the right hand of the Father, and is my righteousness. Without Jesus Christ, I am nothing. Without Jesus Christ, I have no power to overcome Satan and his influence in my own life. The "word of their testimony" that overcomes Satan is the testimony concerning Jesus Christ—who He is, what He has done in the past, and what He is doing in the present.

When you put on the armor of God in order to walk in the victory He has secured for you, your advancement in this victory will be specifically tied to the word of your testimony. And that doesn't just mean the word of your testimony given at your church. It's easy to tell people at church what Christ has done. In addition to that, you can overcome Satan in your workplace, in your home, and anywhere else you can proclaim the testimony of His name and your identification with Him.

Loving Christ

The third way Satan is overcome is found at the end of Revelation 12:11, where we read, "And they did not love their life even when faced with death." This love was so strong, it even trumped their own lives. This committed love is so essential that Jesus rebuked the church at Ephesus for having left their first love (Revelation 2:4). They had their programs, policies, procedures, and even their Bible studies all in place, but they didn't have a love relationship. Without a love relationship, you end up with religion. You end up with something that has no power or authority in the heavenly realm. You end up with a performance, trying to gain God's acceptance or favor while negating the truth that you are *already* accepted in the Beloved because of your saving faith in Jesus Christ. You don't do good works to gain God's acceptance. You do good works to thank Him for having already accepted you. The works we do should always be responses to God's grace; otherwise, they are expressions of religion. Religion will tire you out, make you dread coming to church on Sunday, and even leave you physically weary.

But when you think about the cross, about all that Jesus has done for you, and about all that He has promised He will do for you, anything He asks you, you can do out of a spirit of gratitude. Your attitude of gratitude will often determine your altitude. And remember, we're fighting this battle up high in the heavenly realm. Our gratitude should stem from the truth that God did not judge us the way our sin said He should. That He showed us mercy when He didn't have to. That there is nothing anyone can do—in the spiritual realm or in the physical—to separate us from Him and His love.

When you operate in these truths, nothing can intimidate you. When Paul was told that he was going to be put to death, he said (in effect), "No problem—to die is gain. I'll be better off that way." When he was told that he would be allowed to live, he said (in so many words), "No problem—to live is Christ. I'll just get to serve Christ more before I die" (see Philippians 1:21). And when Paul was told that he would suffer, he said something like this: "No problem—the suffering of this present time is not worth even comparing to the glory that will be revealed in the future" (Romans 8:18).

In other words, "If you kill me, I'm going to be with Christ. If you let me live, I'm going to stay here and serve Christ. If you make me suffer, I'm going to get more reward from Christ. So bring it on, because it's all about Christ!"

When you proclaim these things before Satan—the blood of Christ, your testimony of Christ, and your relationship with Christ—there is *nothing* he can do to defeat you. He is the defeated one, not you. The only thing Satan can do is deceive you into thinking you're on your own. But when you know that Jesus is your advocate and defender, all you need to say is this: "Step aside, Satan, because it is time for Jesus Christ. He has me covered. He has my back."

So even if you can't remember every piece of the armor, *remember Christ*. Without Him, the armor won't do you any good anyhow. But with Him, you are victorious. When you live in the truth of His atoning blood, proclaim the word of your testimony, and abide in an authentic relationship with Him, even the demons will flee.

But as we see in this next example, Jesus' name is not a magic word. The authority comes through the relationship.

> Some of the Jewish exorcists, who went from place to place, attempted to name over those who had the evil spirits the name of the Lord Jesus, saying, "I adjure you by Jesus whom Paul preaches." Seven sons of one Sceva, a Jewish chief priest, were doing this. And the evil spirit answered and said to them, "I recognize Jesus, and I know about Paul, but who are you?" And the man, in whom was the evil spirit, leaped on them and subdued all of them and overpowered them, so that they fled out of that house naked and wounded (Acts 19:13-16).

Without a relationship with Jesus Christ through the atoning work on the cross, you will be overpowered by the demons even if you cry "Jesus, Jesus, Jesus" all day long. The authority comes in the relationship. When that's in place, you can cross over into the heavenly places and watch God do exceeding, abundantly above all that you can ask or think, for His glory. The blood of Jesus Christ is a passport that gives believers legal access and authority in the spiritual realm.

Putting on Christ

If you're tired of being overcome in the physical realm, your solution lies in the spiritual realm. Your point of reference must be in knowing, standing firm in, and utilizing what God has provided for your victory. If Satan is running your life, passions, and emotions, and if he's influencing your decisions, you have taken off your armor. It's time to put it on again. With the armor of God firmly in place, you will be able to handle in the physical realm whatever Satan throws at you in the spiritual.

Remember, though, that God does not dress you in the armor. In grace, He has simply given you everything you need to put it on in faith. Faith is reaching into grace and grabbing what God has graciously supplied through Christ. It's reaching into the spiritual in order that it can be made manifest in the physical. If you do not put on grace by way of faith, you will not benefit from the things God has provided you in grace. For example, if I bought you something nice to wear but you didn't wear it, it wouldn't do you any good, even though it was completely supplied.

The armor of God has been completely supplied. Your victory has been completely provided. But until you grab them in faith, they do you no good. The good news is that when you do grab them in faith, you will know that it was God who secured these things for you because your life will change in such a way that only God can get the credit. Strongholds and problems that you've struggled with for years and even decades can be changed overnight when things are done God's way. Such was the case when Jesus healed the woman who had been bent over for almost two decades. Doctors had undoubtedly tried to heal her during that time, most likely thinking that what she was suffering from was a bad spine. But when Jesus showed up, what couldn't get fixed for eighteen years was fixed immediately.

> On a Sabbath Jesus was teaching in one of the synagogues, and a woman was there who had been crippled by a spirit for eighteen years. She was bent over and could not straighten up at all. When Jesus saw her, he called her forward and said to her, "Woman, you are set free from your infirmity." Then he put his hands on her, and immediately she straightened up and praised God (Luke 13:10-13 NIV).

You know God has intervened when something you have been struggling with for years immediately changes. You know it's the power of God when immediately your taste buds change, or you can turn off that computer, or you can deal with that sin, temptation, or temper. When God shows up, you discover that you only needed two of the twelve steps of that self-help program because by step two you have already been delivered through a supernatural invasion of God in the spiritual realm.

This reminds me of the character Thomas Anderson in the movie *Matrix.* Thomas was a part-time computer programmer and part-time computer hacker living an ordinary life. One day Thomas discovered another realm called the Matrix. Thomas was told that behind the physical realm in which he lived was another realm that actually dictated what went on in his. When Thomas was taken to this other realm, he learned he had powers he had never even dreamed of having in the physical realm. He discovered his mind could think at a level it never could have done in the physical realm. He found out he had capacities he never even knew he possessed. Beyond that, he got a new name (Neo) in the new realm because his old name from the physical realm did not define who he was in the new. He also fell in love in the new realm (with a woman named Trinity) in a way that he had never experienced in the physical realm. He discovered that he had a purpose—something much more than simply punching the keyboards on computers all day long, something with significance and the potential to make a substantial impact on the physical realm.

While Neo was in the new realm, he also got a new set of clothes. Neo's old clothes from the physical realm weren't going to work for his new placement and assignment. He had to dress for the location in order to defeat the enemies who attacked him in the new realm. And he did defeat them, dressed in the clothes given to him for the new realm.

My friend, you can defeat your enemy as well. You can live in the victory Christ has secured for you because when you trusted in Him, He crossed you over into a whole new realm. You have a new name— son or daughter of the living God. You have a new love—the Trinity of God the Father, God the Son, and God the Holy Spirit. You have a purpose and a destiny—to glorify God in all that you do while significantly impacting others and the world around you. And you have new clothes—a belt, a breastplate, shoes, a shield, a helmet, and a sword. Wear them and win. Satan is coming at you in this new realm. But when you operate according to the authority given you in the heavenly realm, you overcome him because "greater is He who is in you than he who is in the world" (1 John 4:4).

Hell no longer has the final say in your life. In fact, hell has no say at all when you are armed for victory God's way.

Part 4

VICTORY OVER STRONGHOLDS

We overcome strongholds in our lives as a result of Christ's power within us as we apply His truths to our situations and use the different pieces of spiritual armor. A stronghold can be defined as a pattern of unrighteousness that holds you hostage outside of the will of God. Strongholds result from something invisible in the spiritual realm cooperating with something visible in the physical realm, keeping a person trapped in an addiction or negative life pattern. Overcoming a stronghold always involves a spiritual solution because the stronghold is rooted in a spiritual cause.

In this final part of the book, we'll address seven prominent strongholds that frequently keep people in bondage today, but the principles for victory can be applied to any stronghold you may be facing. In each chapter, I've offered an overview of the stronghold, God's viewpoint on the stronghold, as well as the biblical solution to the stronghold. I also included a six-day meditation and prayer guide to help you replace the lies that have kept you bound for so long with God's truths for victory. The daily guides include four sections:

- *Wear it.* This introduces the spiritual truth behind the victory through a specific verse related to the piece of armor chosen for that day, as well as a verse reflecting Christ's sufficiency to overcome this stronghold.

- *Stand in it.* This positions the truth into language that will enable you to personally apply these principles to your life.

- *Use it.* Here we communicate the truth to Satan and his demonic realm.

- *Draw it down.* In this part, we reach into heaven with the truth to access God's response to this particular situation.

We have been instructed in Romans 13:14 to do more than wear the armor of God. We are also to "put on the Lord Jesus Christ, and make no provision for the flesh in regard to its lusts." That's why I've called these daily meditations "Putting on the Armor of Christ."

I encourage you to think on these truths, memorize them, repeat them, speak them to yourself, speak them to Satan, pray them to God, copy them, and place them in areas where you will be reminded of them all day long. Let them become the dominant thought patterns governing your life. As you operate with the full armor of God, you will discover both the freedom and the victory that are rightfully yours as a child of the King.

Here's to your victory!

12

VICTORY OVER MARITAL STRONGHOLDS

The Stronghold

Many couples have a marriage that looks as if it was performed not by a justice of the peace, but by the secretary of war. Their relationship isn't a mutual admiration society; it's become a mutual extermination society. As a result, divorce rates soar, not only in the secular society but also in the body of Christ. Our nation is caught in a divorce epidemic as more and more couples decide to call it quits.

We know that marriage strongholds exist when married couples return home every day to miserable homes. It's a stronghold when you argue from the time you wake up until the time you fall back to sleep at night. It's a stronghold when after so many years or decades have passed, you look at your spouse and see a stranger looking back at you. It's a stronghold when two people who have committed their lives to one another cannot even stand each other. This goes much deeper than personality differences. Differences existed when the two first met. They didn't simply appear after the wedding. These differences were just addressed and overcome beforehand because the goal—marriage—made it important enough to do so.

Divorces frequently occur as a result of a stronghold in the way marriage is viewed. Most people look at marriage as a way of finding love, happiness, and companionship. Those things are good, but they are actually secondary to the primary purpose of marriage. We begin to overcome marriage strongholds when we understand the purpose of marriage. God didn't simply institute marriage because He was looking for another thing to do. God created marriage as one of the primary tools through which He fulfills His destiny for you and also advances His kingdom.

Satan was the cause of the first marital conflict in history when he enticed Adam and Eve to rebel against God's word, as we see in Genesis 3:1-6. This led to blame, pain, the battle between the sexes, and sibling rivalry between the children. Marital conflict is indeed a spiritual issue.

God's Viewpoint

Marriage is a covenantal union designed to enhance and strengthen the capacity of both partners to carry out God's plan in their lives. We read about this covenant in the book of Malachi.

> This is another thing you do: you cover the altar of the LORD with tears, with weeping and with groaning, because He no longer regards the offering or accepts it with favor from your hand. Yet you say, "For what reason?" Because the LORD has been a witness between you and the wife of your youth, against whom you have dealt treacherously, though she is your companion and your wife *by covenant* (Malachi 2:13-14).

Strongholds show up in our marriages when we no longer realize that marriage is a *covenant* or don't even understand what a covenant is. In order to break marital strongholds, we need to realign our thoughts in keeping with God's viewpoint of a covenantal marriage.

God's Solution

Biblical covenants are spiritually binding legal arrangements that God makes between Himself and His people. Each covenant involves five facets: transcendence (the rulership of God), hierarchy (the alignment established by God), ethics (the rules that God has set in place for the covenant to operate by), sanctions (the blessings and curses that are attached to the rules), and continuity (the long-term inheritance of the covenant).

This being so, covenants can never function as they were intended without the overarching governance of God. When God's viewpoint and authority is dismissed from the marital covenantal relationship, the door is open for Satan to bring destruction into the home. Marriage is a sacred covenant, not just a social contract.

One of the rules for understanding the Bible is called "the law of first mention." This means that if you want to know what God says about something, study the first time He brings it up. Everything else will build on or expand this original mention. So to go deeper into God's viewpoint on marriage as well as His solution for overcoming marital strongholds, we need to look at the book of Genesis, where God initiated the idea of marriage.

First, God created mankind in His image, and then He said, "Let them rule." In that declaration, God released the exercise of dominion and authority to humanity on earth so that mankind could manage His creation. That doesn't mean that God has relinquished His sovereignty. He has maintained a base of sovereign boundaries across which humanity cannot tread, but He has likewise opened up an arena where you and I get to call the plays and then live by the consequences of either the wisdom or foolishness of those plays.

You can have a satisfying or an unsatisfying marriage based on whether your rule reflects the image of God that you were made in. The health of the home is determined by whether the husband is reflecting God and His character accurately in his role, or whether the wife is reflecting God and His character accurately in her role. Every time there is a marital breakdown, one or both partners are no longer living a life that reflects the rulership of God through them.

What Satan attempts to get us to do is turn our rule over to him or to rule poorly based on our own viewpoints. One reason he does this is that the breakdown of the home leads to the breakdown of society. Most of the negative realities present in our society today can be directly tied to the failure of marriages and families to authentically reflect God's rule. The rebellion that was first introduced in the garden has led to chaos replacing calm, death replacing life, and pressure replacing peace—not only in our homes but also in our communities.

The purpose of marriage extends much further than simply a relationship between two people.

In a covenantal marriage, the first truth to recognize is that there are more than just two individuals entering the covenant. A husband and a wife enter into a covenant when they get married, but they enter into it along with God. The key to overcoming marital strongholds is recognizing the presence of God in the union and functioning in light of His presence. It's the connection of spirit to spirit through the abiding presence of the Holy Spirit that enables couples to gain victory in their marriage.

As we have seen, we are made up of body, soul, and spirit. The physical attraction—our bodies—may have been the initial element in drawing two people together, but it will fade. Our souls, due to their distortion from sin and circumstance, often lead to conflict or attempts to manage the relationship, not to unity. Victory over marital strongholds is thus located in the spirit first. As the Holy Spirit unites with our spirits and we individually draw closer to God, He brings us together as one. You cannot leave God at the altar and expect to have a healthy marriage.

Many people are married today in the body (attraction), or they are married in the soul (companionship), but few are married in the spirit (oneness). When you live in your marriage as spirit mates, you will be able to tackle any problem that comes at you in the body or the soul.

One reason so many strongholds show up in marriages today and so many people want to divorce is that they never got married correctly—in spiritual oneness—to begin with. They have failed to understand a foundational truth found in Genesis 2:24: "For this reason a man shall leave his father and his mother, and be joined to his wife; and they shall become *one flesh*." The problem arises when two people do not want to become one flesh. Instead, they want to remain as two flesh in one home.

In fact, when asked about the issue of divorce, Jesus referenced this "one flesh" principle in His response. The interesting point is that His answer didn't directly connect with the question on the surface. This is because the question had been whether or not it was okay to get a divorce. We read in Mark 10:2, "Some Pharisees came up to Jesus, testing Him, and began to question Him whether it was lawful for a man to divorce a wife." In other words, if people think they have reason enough to divorce, Jesus, do they then have a reason? If they want to call it quits, can they?

Jesus didn't give a yes-or-no answer. Rather, He simply said that they were asking the wrong question. If you understand the nature, purpose, and covenant of marriage—and if you function accordingly—that question will have no need for discussion. In becoming "one flesh," the two are to complement each other so deeply and intimately that they become one without losing their personal identities.

I want to give you one word that can restore life to your marriage *if* you both take it to heart. When you simply live out this one word, I guarantee you by the authority of God's Word that you will overcome your marital strongholds. That word is *grace*. Most marriages today operate by law—you are supposed to do this, or you are supposed to do that. But the law kills. For a marriage to flourish, it must live by grace. Ephesians 5 gives us this truth:

> Husbands, love your wives, just as Christ also loved the church and gave Himself up for her...So husbands ought also to love their own wives as their own bodies. He who loves his own wife loves himself; for no one ever hated his own flesh, but nourishes and cherishes it, just as Christ also does the church, because we are members of His body... Nevertheless, each individual among you also is to love his own wife even as himself, and the wife must see to it that she respects her husband (Ephesians 5:25,28,33).

This truth will change everything. Are you a husband? You are to die for your wife in a spirit of grace. Are you a wife? You are to live for your husband in the same spirit. When this principle is carried out, there will be a dynamic experience in your marriage. It won't be a perfect, problem-free experience, but it will be an authentic, progressive, and complete union.

To the Husband

So what does it mean to die for your wife as Christ gave Himself up for the church? It means allowing your dreams, will, desires, and choices to come second to a true love for your wife. Biblical love can be defined as seeking the well-being of another, even at your own expense. This kind of love places the well-being of your wife above your own well-being. It means viewing her through the same lens of love that God views her.

If you see your wife only as someone to raise your kids, wash your clothes, organize your life, and cook your meals, then what you're seeing is a maid. God has uniquely designed a woman with skills and abilities that are to be utilized to complete and enhance your own masculine skills and abilities. When she trusts and experiences that you value her, she will respond to your needs without the necessity of a law or requirement to do so. Women have been fashioned to *respond*—it is up to the man to set the tone of the home through leadership that demonstrates sacrificial love in order for her to do so.

Now, I know that you know how to do this, because you did it when you were dating. The problem is that most men date to marry rather than marry to date. That's called "Backward, Christian Soldiers." When was the last time you took your wife in your arms and simply told her, "The best thing I did in life was marry you"? When was the last time you cupped her face in your hands and said, "You are my life"? When was the last time you sent a Valentine's card and it wasn't Valentine's Day? Or you watched the kids, listened when she talked, took on her pain, or validated her skills, her dreams, her hurts, and her life?

When was the last time you truly sacrificed something for her? A man once told me, "Tony, my wife is killing me." I replied, "Well, you said you wanted to be more like Jesus, didn't you?" Loving your wife as Christ loved the church is a man's key to overcoming marital strongholds.

To the Wife

Your part as a wife is just as powerful. Keep in mind that nowhere in the Bible is a woman commanded to love her husband. God expects you to love your husband, but it's never commanded the way a man is commanded to love his wife. Why? Because that's not what your husband needs the most. What your husband needs the most is respect.

Your husband ought to feel like a king around you, on top of the world. He should hear you call him your strong tower. He is your head, and your role is to submit to him as your head. That doesn't mean that you are to be walked on or that you have to agree with everything he does. Submission means that even if you disagree with his point, you will respect his position.

And of course, you are never to submit to something that contradicts God's revealed will in His Word, but that's seldom the case. Regardless of differences in education, abilities, and preferences, when your husband seeks to align himself under God and His rulership, he is your head and should be the recipient of your highest respect.

Love and respect, offered in grace. When both parties abide by these principles, the marriage will no longer be under the influence of a stronghold because the two will hold up each other in mutual strength.

Putting on the Armor of Christ

Day One

Wear It

The belt of truth. "Therefore a man shall leave his father and his mother and hold fast to his wife, and they shall become one flesh" (Genesis 2:24 esv).

Putting on Christ. "For where two or three have gathered together in My name, I am there in their midst" (Matthew 18:20).

Stand in It

The Word of God says that now that I am married, I no longer should consider myself as solely on my own. Instead, I have now joined with my mate, and the two of us have become one flesh together. As a result, Jesus Christ is present in the midst of us when we operate and function out of one flesh together in His name.

Use It

Satan, I have left my father and my mother, and I hold fast to my spouse. I am no longer functioning as an individual; instead, I am one flesh with my spouse. We are together in Christ's name. When you attack us, you are attacking Him because He is in the midst of us. He has already defeated you, so we stand secure in His victory over you.

Draw It Down

Father in heaven, You say that when we became married, we were no longer two individuals, but are now one flesh. Let the power of our one flesh abiding together in the name of Jesus Christ manifest itself in how we think, behave, and treat each other so that You may be glorified in this union.

Day Two

Wear It

The breastplate of righteousness. "Likewise, wives, be subject to your own husbands, so that even if some do not obey the word, they may be won without a word by the conduct of their wives—when they see your respectful and pure conduct" (1 Peter 3:1-2 ESV). "Husbands, love your wives, as Christ loved the church...In the same way husbands should love their wives as their own bodies. He who loves his wife loves himself. For no one ever hated his own flesh, but nourishes and cherishes it, just as Christ does the church, because we are members of his body" (Ephesians 5:25,28-30 ESV).

Putting on Christ. "Christ also loved the church and gave Himself up for her, so that He might sanctify her, having cleansed her by the washing of water with the word, that He might present to Himself the church in all her glory, having no spot or wrinkle or any such thing; but that she would be holy and blameless" (Ephesians 5:25-27).

Stand in It

As a wife, I am to be subject to my own husband, so that

even if he does not obey the Word, he may be won without a word by my conduct, when he sees my respectful and pure conduct.

As a husband, I am to love my wife as Christ loved the church and even as I love my own body. I am to nourish and cherish her, just as Christ does the church so that she might be sanctified, having been cleansed by the washing of water with the word, having no spot or wrinkle or any such thing, but that she would be holy and blameless.

Use It

Satan, you do not have the authority to influence my decisions because as a wife, I am to be subject to my own husband, so that even if he does not obey the Word, he may be won without a word by my conduct, when he sees my respectful and pure conduct.

Satan, you do not have the authority to distract me from my role as a husband to love my wife as Christ loved the church and even as I love my own body. In God's strength, I will nourish and cherish her, just as Christ does the church so that she might be sanctified, having been cleansed by the washing of water with the word, having no spot or wrinkle or any such thing, but that she would be holy and blameless.

Draw It Down

Father in heaven, help me as a wife to be subject to my own husband, so that even if he does not obey the Word, he may be won without a word by my conduct, when he sees my respectful and pure conduct.

And Father, help me as a husband to love my wife as Christ loved the church and even as I love my own body. Help me to nourish and cherish her, just as Christ does the church so that she might be sanctified, having been cleansed by the washing of water with the word, having no spot or

wrinkle or any such thing, but that she would be holy and
blameless.

Day Three

Wear It

The shoes of peace. "Enjoy life with the wife whom you love,
all the days of your vain life that he has given you under the
sun, because that is your portion in life and in your toil at
which you toil under the sun" (Ecclesiastes 9:9 ESV).

Putting on Christ. "Let your gentleness be evident to all.
The Lord is near" (Philippians 4:5 NIV).

Stand in It

I will enjoy life with my spouse, whom I love, all the days
of my life under the sun because that is my portion in life.
And I will let my gentleness be evident to all because the
Lord is near.

Use It

Satan, you have no authority to distract me from enjoying
life with my spouse, whom I love, all the days of my life
under the sun because that is my portion in life. I rebuke
any attempts you make to do so in Jesus' name. My gentleness will be evident to all because the Lord is near.

Draw It Down

Father in heaven, give me wisdom on how I can enjoy
life with my spouse, whom I love, to the fullest potential
because You say that this is my portion in life. Show us how
to maximize that enjoyment in ways we have not yet even
considered. Let gentleness be the standard by which we
relate to each other because You are near to us.

Day Four

Wear It

The shield of faith. "For in this way in former times the holy women also, who hoped in God, used to adorn themselves, being submissive to their own husbands; just as Sarah obeyed Abraham, calling him lord, and you have become her children if you do what is right without being frightened by any fear.

"You husbands in the same way, live with your wives in an understanding way, as with someone weaker, since she is a woman; and show her honor as a fellow heir of the grace of life, so that your prayers will not be hindered" (1 Peter 3:5-7).

Putting on Christ. "He has brought me to his banquet hall, and his banner over me is love" (Song of Solomon 2:4).

Stand in It

As a wife, I will hope in God and adorn myself by being submissive to my husband, just as Sarah obeyed Abraham, calling him lord. I have become her child when I do what is right without being afraid.

As a husband, I will make every effort to live with my wife in an understanding way, as with someone weaker, because she is a woman. I will show her honor as a fellow heir of the grace of life, and in this way my prayers will not be hindered. Jesus Christ has brought us to His banquet hall, and His banner over our marriage is one of love.

Use It

Satan, in Jesus Christ we have a banner of love over us. In this love, I choose as a wife to hope in God rather than listen to you, and I choose to submit to my husband without fear, as Sarah obeyed Abraham, calling him lord.

Satan, I choose as a husband to show my wife patience and understanding because she is weaker as a woman. Your attempts to get me to dishonor my wife in my thoughts or actions will not work because in Christ, I will honor my wife as a fellow heir of the grace of life. And because of that, my prayers will not be hindered.

Draw It Down

Father in heaven, as a couple we ask that You will reveal to us the abundance of Your love, which You have given us in Your banquet hall. Let the love found in Your banner over us flow from one to the other.

As a wife, I ask that You will remove any fear that I have in submitting to my husband so that I will be like Sarah, who obeyed Abraham without fear, calling him lord.

And as a husband, I thank You for giving me the wisdom to live with my wife in an understanding way. Help me to see her as You see her, that I might show her honor in Your name.

Day Five

Wear It

The helmet of salvation. "An excellent wife is the crown of her husband" (Proverbs 12:4). "All of you be harmonious, sympathetic, brotherly, kindhearted, and humble in spirit; not returning evil for evil or insult for insult, but giving a blessing instead; for you were called for the very purpose that you might inherit a blessing" (1 Peter 3:8-9).

Putting on Christ. "Greater love has no one than this, that one lay down his life for his friends" (John 15:13).

Stand in It

In my marriage I am to be harmonious, sympathetic, brotherly, kindhearted, and humble in spirit; not returning evil for evil or insult for insult, but giving a blessing instead; for I am called for the very purpose that I might inherit a blessing. Because greater love has no one than this, that he lay down his life for his spouse.

Use It

Satan, an excellent wife is the crown of her husband. And, I am to be harmonious, sympathetic, brotherly, kindhearted, and humble in spirit; not returning evil for evil or insult for insult, but giving a blessing instead; for I am called for the very purpose that I might inherit a blessing.

Greater love has no one than this, that he lay down his life for his friends.

Draw It Down

Father in heaven, Your Word tells me that an excellent wife is the crown of her husband. And that we are to be harmonious, sympathetic, brotherly, kindhearted, and humble in spirit; not returning evil for evil or insult for insult, but giving a blessing instead in our marriage; for we were called for the very purpose that we might inherit a blessing. Help me to show this greater love that no one has than this, that he lay down his life for his spouse.

Day Six/Weekend

Wear It

The sword of the Spirit. "God blessed them. And God said to them, 'Be fruitful and multiply and fill the earth and subdue it and have dominion over the fish of the sea and over the birds of the heavens and over every living thing that moves on the earth'" (Genesis 1:28).

Putting on Christ. "But their minds were made dull, for to this day the same veil remains when the old covenant is read. It has not been removed, because only in Christ is it taken away" (2 Corinthians 3:14).

Stand in It

God has blessed our marriage, instructing us to be fruitful and multiply and fill the earth and subdue it and have dominion over the fish of the sea and over the birds of the heavens and over every living thing that moves on the earth. Through whatever means He will provide, we trust that He will supply an increase to our family, giving us wisdom on how to exercise the dominion He has given to us in this realm—not with minds that have been made dull, but with minds that have been made alive in Christ.

Use It

Satan, we resist any attempts you make to bring brokenness into our marriage, because God has declared that He has blessed our marriage, instructing us to be fruitful and multiply and fill the earth and subdue it and have dominion over the fish of the sea and over the birds of the heavens and over every living thing that moves on the earth. Jesus Christ has removed the dominion from your hands and will now give us wisdom on how to exercise the dominion He has given to us to use in this realm—not with minds that have been made dull, but with minds that have been made alive in Him.

Draw It Down

Father in heaven, thank You for blessing our marriage. Thank You for the assurance that because You have given the command to be fruitful and multiply and fill the earth and subdue it and have dominion over it, You will supply the wisdom and capacity to do that. We praise You that You have not allowed our minds to remain dull, but have renewed and restored them in Christ Jesus our Lord.

13

VICTORY OVER CHEMICAL STRONGHOLDS

The Stronghold

Like me, you probably came into contact with the story of Popeye—either on television or in a comic book—as you were growing up. If so, you remember that Popeye was constantly being brutalized by an overgrown bully (sometimes called Bluto, sometimes called Brutus) who regularly sought to wreak havoc on Popeye.

But every time it looked as if Popeye couldn't last a minute longer, he reached for a can of spinach. After popping open the can and downing its contents, a new Popeye emerged, strong and victorious.

Sadly, today many of us have developed a Popeye syndrome. When circumstances or the people around us bring us pain and anguish, causing us to feel beaten down, burdened, lonely, or stressed, we reach for a can. We reach for a quick fix to provide relief to a long-term problem. Unlike Popeye and his spinach, though, a bottle of Jack Daniels, a cigarette, a pill, or any other chemical infused into our body during a time of need doesn't provide the strength or victory we so desperately seek. Rather than defeating whatever difficulty we are facing, it masks or even compounds it.

A chemical stronghold can be defined as a dependency on chemicals to address, escape, cope with, or find relief from the struggles and stresses of life. People with chemical strongholds often reveal themselves easily. They will say things like, "I just need a drink to unwind," or "I just need a smoke to reduce the stress," or even "I'm ugly until I get my first cup of coffee." All three have said the same thing: I cannot be what I was meant to be without ingesting these chemicals. Sure, coffee is not similar to cocaine in terms of its effects, but it stems from the same root—looking to chemicals to address a spiritual need.

The problem comes in the attempt to get the physical world to provide the fix for the spiritual pain, lack, or emptiness. It would be like a guy who wrapped himself in Band-aids across his chest because his girlfriend had broken his heart. Or someone who drank a lot of milk because she desired to grow spiritually. Neither would do any good at all. A spiritual problem can only be addressed spiritually.

God's Viewpoint

Our bodies are temples of the living God, and anything that controls us makes us slaves to something other than God.

> Therefore do not let sin reign in your mortal body so that you obey its lusts, and do not go on presenting the members of your body to sin as instruments of unrighteousness; but present yourselves to God as those alive from the dead, and your members as instruments of righteousness to God. For sin shall not be master over you, for you are not under law but under grace (Romans 6:12-14).

That drink, cigarette, pill, cup of coffee, drug—whatever it is you struggle with—is not to be the master over you. Because of God's grace, you have been made alive in Him, and that life now has the ability to dominate your responses—if you will align yourself with the truth of God's solution to your stronghold. The key to overcoming chemical strongholds is in knowing who you really are in Christ.

God's Solution

Tad Walgreen died of a drug overdose in 1996 in the midst of a bitter custody battle for his two small children. His widow, Loren Walgreen, died three years later of a drug overdose as well. Both were in their thirties and died while high on cheap stimulants in seedy locations. And yet these two were from the family of Charles Walgreen, the founder and owner of the giant Walgreens pharmacy chain. They allowed the temporary relief of a cheap fix to cause them to forget who their father was and what he could do for them. The same holds true for anyone suffering from a chemical stronghold. When believers in Christ lose sight of who their Father is and that He holds in His hands all of the power they will ever need, they turn to cheap substitutes.

Now, I can hear what you are saying. "Tony, it's not as simple as that. You don't know how deep my problem is. My people [or my boss, my situation, my past, my regrets…] drive me to do what I do in order to cope." Friend, I *do* understand. I understand that your problems are what drives you. But what I'm saying is that it's driving you in the wrong direction. Where it ought to drive you is found in Ephesians. We read, "And do not get drunk with wine, for that is dissipation, but be filled with the Spirit" (Ephesians 5:18). When life crashes in on you, don't turn to the bottle because that will be dissipation—a waste. Be filled instead with the Spirit and let Him satisfy your need.

To be filled with something involves having more than a desire for it. It's an ongoing action. People who depend on alcohol to get them through the day will have a bottle at home, a bottle at work, a bottle in the car…and even with all of that, they may be walking around with something in their hand as well. They know that in order to sustain the feeling that the alcohol brings, they have to keep putting more and more alcohol into their body.

A similar thing happens when you drive your car. As you do, you're continually in the process of depleting your gas tank. You don't have to do anything wrong to deplete your tank. It's simply a result of using the gas you need to get where you want to go. However, if you wish to keep driving, you will have to go to the gas station and fill your tank back up. Blaming your car for not taking you where you need to go when you have not taken it where it needs to go for refueling is much like blaming the Holy Spirit for not giving you victory when you haven't done what He has said in order to be filled with Him.

The next two verses expand on how this filling remains in us: "[Speak] to one another in psalms and hymns and spiritual songs, singing and making melody with your heart to the Lord; always giving thanks for all things in the name of our Lord Jesus Christ to God, even the Father" (Ephesians 5:19-20).

Simply stated, the Holy Spirit's presence involves *worship*. But if the only time you worship and experience God is on Sunday, you're going to run on empty throughout the rest of the week. Worship—being in God's presence—includes several things:

> speaking His truth ("speaking to one another in psalms")
>
> singing ("hymns and spiritual songs")
>
> meditation ("making melody with your heart")
>
> gratitude ("always giving thanks")

Being filled with the Holy Spirit means making worship a lifestyle.

When the Holy Spirit's presence fills you, you will discover that even your cravings change. This is because it is Him working in you both "to will and to work for" (Philippians 2:13) the things God has designed for you. You don't have to live as a slave to what you crave; the Holy Spirit will set you free to be all that you were created to be and to enjoy. We read this in the book of Romans:

> Therefore there is now no condemnation for those who are in Christ Jesus. For the law of the Spirit of life in Christ Jesus has set you free from the law of sin and death. For what the Law could not do, weak as it was through the flesh, God did: sending His own Son in the likeness of sinful flesh and as an offering for sin, He condemned sin in the flesh, so that the requirements of the Law might be fulfilled in us, who do not walk according to the flesh but according to the Spirit (Romans 8:1-4).

What Paul is saying is that the law pulls you down into sin and death, just as the law of gravity pulls you down to the ground. If you make a habit of jumping off tall buildings, the law of gravity will win every single time. It doesn't matter if you like the law or even believe in the reality of the law; either way, it will pull you straight down to the ground. The same is true with sin's hold on your life. It leads to death. But through Jesus Christ, the Holy Spirit has set you free from the power of sin.

For example, if you were to jump off a tall building but were strapped into a hang glider, you would not be pulled down. In fact, depending on the air currents, you may soar two or three times higher than the top of the building. This isn't because the law of gravity no longer exists. Rather, it is because another law—a higher law, the law of aerodynamics—has trumped the law of gravity.

The Greek word used for "Spirit" in the New Testament is *pneuma* and can be translated "breath" or "wind." It's the Spirit's job to set you free from the law of sin by lifting you higher whenever Satan attempts to drag you down. The Spirit can make you soar because He is the wind that carries you during tough times. But in order for Him to do that, you need to hang out with Him. You need to abide in His presence, meditate on His Word, speak His thoughts, sing His songs, and show gratitude in faith for all that God has done and will do for you.

Whenever I'm counseling people with a drug addiction, I try to find a way to get them to a Christian rehab center in New Jersey. The reason is that I appreciate the philosophy at this center. When people arrive there, they're told that they're not drug addicts; they are blood-bought children of the living God, and they have already been given victory over drugs. That's who they are. When they introduce themselves, they say, "Hi, my name is so-and-so, and I am a blood-bought child of the living God, and I have already been given victory over drugs."

Not only that, but their primary form of breaking the addiction is through memorizing, meditating on, repeating, rehearsing, and sharing Scripture verses. That's what they do all day long, all week long, and all month long. It's a simple solution, really, and it works. The success rate for those who stay at the center for six months is higher than 75 percent, no matter how long they have been addicted to drugs. This happens because the action of taking drugs is not the problem. The action is simply a manifestation of the problem. The problem is in the mind. And when we allow God's thoughts—His Spirit—to be the dominating force in our lives, He changes everything.

I was physically trapped once—in an elevator. Being trapped is an uncomfortable feeling, especially in a high-rise with the elevator stuck between two floors. When it happened, the immediate reaction of those around me was to panic. Some cried, some yelled out for help, and some started banging hard on the door.

I stood there for a minute, watching the reactions of the others around me, until the elevator phone caught my eye. When I saw it, I simply made my way to the other side of the elevator, picked up the telephone, and waited. A voice on the other end said, "Is there a problem?"

I answered, "Yes, sir, we are trapped. Can we get some help?"

"We'll be right there, sir," the man replied.

It was as simple as that.

When you feel trapped in an addiction or by a habit, it's easy to forget that God has put a lifeline in each of our lives. He's just waiting for us to pick up the phone and give Him a call. Yet because we forget about it, we go about trying to free ourselves through our own human efforts—we cry, scream, bang on doors, grunt, groan, and try to force our bodies to overcome a stronghold that's rooted in the spiritual realm. But God says that instead of trying to do all of that on your own, you simply need to pick up the phone. He is there. In fact, you don't even have to yell. He can hear you—a whisper will do. Once you connect with the Spirit and remain connected to Him—*filled* with Him—He will deliver you.

Putting on the Armor of Christ

Day One

WEAR IT

> *The belt of truth.* "You were bought with a price; do not become slaves of men" (1 Corinthians 7:23).

> *Putting on Christ.* "Therefore there is now no condemnation for those who are in Christ Jesus. For the law of the

Spirit of life in Christ Jesus has set you free from the law of sin and of death" (Romans 8:1-2).

STAND IN IT

I have been bought with a very high price. I am valuable and have been set free. I no longer need to be a slave to anyone or anything. Likewise, I am not condemned for anything I have done or that has controlled me, because I am forgiven in Christ Jesus. His law of the Spirit of life has given me total freedom from the law of sin and death.

USE IT

Satan, you do not own me. I have been bought with a very high price, higher than you could ever pay. I am valuable and have been set free from your influence over my life. I am not your slave. Neither am I a slave to any substance or chemical addiction you might try to bring my way. I am a blood-bought child of the King. And I am not condemned for anything I have ever done, no matter how terrible it may have been, or anything that has ever controlled me in the past, because I am completely forgiven in Christ Jesus. His law of the Spirit of life has given me total freedom from you.

DRAW IT DOWN

Father in heaven, thank You for the price You paid to buy me, redeem me, and set me free from the law of sin and death to a life of victory in the Spirit. I praise You because when You look at me, You do not see my sin or condemn me, because I have been completely forgiven in Jesus Christ.

Day Two

WEAR IT

The breastplate of righteousness. "Therefore, I urge you, brethren, by the mercies of God, to present your bodies a living and holy sacrifice, acceptable to God, which is your spiritual service of worship. And do not be conformed to this world, but be transformed by the renewing of your mind, so that you may prove what the will of God is, that which is good and acceptable and perfect" (Romans 12:1-2).

Putting on Christ. "If Christ is in you, though the body is dead because of sin, yet the spirit is alive because of righteousness" (Romans 8:10).

Stand in It

I will present my body a living and holy sacrifice, acceptable to God, which is my spiritual service of worship. I will not be conformed to this world, but I will be transformed by the renewing of my mind, so that I may prove what the will of God is, that which is good and acceptable and perfect. Christ is in me, so even though my body is dead because of sin, my spirit is alive because of righteousness.

Use It

Satan, my body is not yours. You cannot tell me what to do. I have presented my body as a living and holy sacrifice, acceptable to God, as a spiritual service of worship. I will not be conformed to what you have to say or what this world dictates; instead, I am transformed by the renewing of my mind and proving what the will of God is, that which is good and acceptable and perfect. Christ is in me, and He has defeated you, so even though my body is dead because of sin, my spirit is alive because of righteousness.

Draw It Down

Father in heaven, I present my body to You as a living and holy sacrifice, which is my spiritual service of worship. Through Your power in me, I will not be conformed to this world, but I will be transformed by the renewing of my mind, so that I may prove what Your will for me is, that which is good and acceptable and perfect. Because of

You, though my body is dead because of sin, my spirit is alive because of righteousness. I am in Christ, so I ask You to manifest in me all the fullness of His righteous life.

Day Three

WEAR IT

The shoes of peace. "I pray that the eyes of your heart may be enlightened, so that you will know what is the hope of His calling, what are the riches of the glory of His inheritance in the saints" (Ephesians 1:18).

Putting on Christ. "Therefore, since we have been justified through faith, we have peace with God through our Lord Jesus Christ, through whom we have gained access by faith into this grace in which we now stand" (Romans 5:1 NIV).

STAND IN IT

God has called me to a hope that includes all the riches of His glorious inheritance in His holy people. Because I have been justified through faith, I can enjoy that inheritance and have peace with God through my Lord Jesus Christ, through whom I have gained access by faith into this grace in which I now stand.

USE IT

Satan, I have hope. The hope I have is rooted in the riches of God's glorious inheritance in His holy people. Not only that, but I have been justified through faith so that I have total peace with God through my Lord Jesus Christ, through whom I have gained access by faith into this grace in which I now stand. You cannot remove or diminish this peace because it has been given to me through Jesus Christ.

DRAW IT DOWN

Father in heaven, I pray that the eyes of my heart may be enlightened in order that I can fully know the hope to which You have called me and the riches of Your glorious inheritance in Your holy people. Show me everything that I can see about this hope and these riches, God. I am justified before You through faith in Jesus Christ, and it is in this truth that I access the peace and grace I need to stand today and every day.

Day Four

WEAR IT

The shield of faith. "Hope does not put us to shame, because God's love has been poured out into our hearts through the Holy Spirit who has been given to us" (Romans 5:5 ESV).

Putting on Christ. "You see, at just the right time, when we were still powerless, Christ died for the ungodly. Very rarely will anyone die for a righteous person, though for a good person someone might possibly dare to die. But God demonstrates his own love for us in this: While we were still sinners, Christ died for us" (Romans 5:6-8 TNIV).

STAND IN IT

Hope will not put me to shame, because God's love has been poured out into my heart through the Holy Spirit, who has been given to me. This is because when I was still powerless, Christ died for me. God demonstrated His own love for me in this: While I was still a sinner, Christ died for me.

USE IT

Satan, I am filled with hope because when I was still powerless, Christ died for me. God demonstrated His own love for me in this: While I was still a sinner, Christ died for me. If you accuse me of my sin, I will point you to Jesus Christ because my hope in Him will not put me to shame. God's love has been poured out into my heart through the Holy Spirit, who has been given to me.

Draw It Down

Father in heaven, thank You for the hope that comes in knowing that when I was still powerless, Christ died for me. You demonstrated Your own love for me in this: While I was still a sinner, Christ died for me. Let me realize Your full love, which has been poured out into my heart through the Holy Spirit, who has been given to me, so my hope will be rooted in Your reality. In that truth, I will not suffer shame.

Day Five

Wear It

The helmet of salvation. "For it is by grace you have been saved, through faith—and this not from yourselves, it is the gift of God—not by works, so that no one can boast. For we are God's handiwork, created in Christ Jesus to do good works, which God prepared in advance for us to do" (Ephesians 2:8-10 TNIV).

Putting on Christ. "But because of his great love for us, God, who is rich in mercy, made us alive with Christ even when we were dead in transgressions—it is by grace you have been saved" (Ephesians 2:4-5 NIV).

Stand in It

I have been saved by grace through faith—and this is not from myself, it is the gift of God, not by anything that I have done. I cannot boast. I am God's handiwork, His masterpiece, created in Christ Jesus to do good works, which God prepared in advance for me to do. He already knows my destiny. He already has it mapped out for me. Because of His great love and mercy for me, He made me alive with Christ even when I was dead in my transgressions. By grace I have been saved.

Use It

Satan, I have been saved by grace through faith. This isn't

from myself; it is the gift of God, not based on anything I have done. I cannot boast. I did not earn it. I am God's handiwork, His masterpiece, created in Christ Jesus to do good works, which God prepared in advance for me to do. He already knows my destiny. He has a plan for me that is both good and full of hope. Because of His great love and mercy for me, He made me alive with Christ even when I was dead in my transgressions. By grace I have been saved. Your accusations carry no authority over me.

DRAW IT DOWN

Father in heaven, You have saved me in Your grace through faith. This is a gift from You. God, I know that it is not a result of anything I have done. I take no credit for it in any way. I am one of Your "good works"—Your handiwork, Your masterpiece—created in Christ Jesus to do the things You want me to do. You have already prepared these things for me, so all I need to do in following You is to follow where You lead and walk into the purpose that You have for me. Because of Your great love and mercy for me, You have made me alive with Christ even when I was dead in my transgressions. By grace I have been saved, and I ask for the fullness of that grace to be made so real to me today that I actually see Your hand in my life.

Day Six/Weekend

WEAR IT

The sword of the Spirit. "Those who sow to please their sinful nature will reap destruction; those who sow to please the Spirit, from the Spirit will reap eternal life" (Galatians 6:8 TNIV).

Putting on Christ. "Remember that at that time you were separate from Christ, excluded from citizenship in Israel and foreigners to the covenants of the promise, without hope and without God in the world. But now in Christ

Jesus you who once were far away have been brought near through the blood of Christ" (Ephesians 2:12-13 NIV).

Stand in It

When I sow to please my flesh, I will reap destruction. When I sow to please the Spirit, I will reap productivity and eternal life. In Christ Jesus, I have been brought near so that I can have hope that God will produce a return on whatever I do in His name.

Use It

Satan, you tell me that pleasing my flesh will satisfy me, but the Word of God says that sowing to please my flesh will reap destruction. Sowing to please the Spirit is what will reap productivity and eternal life. You tried to separate me from God, but in Christ Jesus, I have been brought near. I know that He will produce a return on whatever I do in His name.

Draw It Down

Father in heaven, You say that sowing to please my flesh will reap destruction, but sowing to please the Spirit will reap productivity and eternal life. Lord, give me wisdom on how to sow to please the Spirit. Reveal to me anything and everything I can do to sow to the Spirit, and convict me anytime I am sowing to please my flesh. In Christ Jesus, I have been brought near, so I am confident You will produce a return on whatever I do in Your name. I am trusting You for this return and asking that You will make it known to me as it happens, to encourage me in You.

14

VICTORY OVER
SEXUAL STRONGHOLDS

The Stronghold

The Puritans may have lived as though there was no such thing as sex, but many Americans live as though there is *nothing but* sex! We have all been affected in some form or another by the increase in sexual awareness in our culture. Things that would have shocked moviegoers 15 or 20 years ago now regularly show up on our televisions. Magazines routinely display images of scantily clad models or celebrities posed in sexually alluring positions. Cable television and the Internet have delivered every conceivable form of pornography, not only to televisions and home computers but often to phones as well.

What makes a sexual stronghold more difficult to overcome than many other strongholds is that a sexual stronghold doesn't always show up in the physical world. For instance, people can have a sexual stronghold and never actually engage in sex. Instead, their sexual stronghold may manifest itself through an addiction to pornography, fantasizing, or achieving personal gratification through illegitimate means contrary to God's plan for sex. If people think about alcohol, it won't get them drunk. Or if people think about cocaine, it won't make them high. But thinking about sex is often its own fulfillment. People who would never do anything wrong sexually often find as much satisfaction in the thought as they would in the action. Jesus says, "But I tell you that anyone who looks at a woman lustfully has already committed adultery with her in his heart" (Matthew 5:28 NIV). When God views a sexual stronghold, He doesn't just view the physical.

Scripture talks about sexual strongholds in the book of Romans.

> Therefore God gave them over in the lusts of their hearts to impurity, so that their bodies would be dishonored among them. For they exchanged the truth of God for a lie, and worshiped and served the creature rather than the Creator, who is blessed forever. Amen.

> For this reason God gave them over to degrading passions; for their women exchanged the natural function for that which is unnatural, and in the same way also the men abandoned the natural function of the woman and burned in their desire toward one another, men with men committing indecent acts and receiving in their own persons the due penalty of their error (Romans 1:24-27).

Paul tells us in this passage that the devolution of man in the area of sexuality is directly tied to idolatry. The stronghold of illegitimate sex on any level is not first and foremost a problem with sex itself. After all, God designed each of us with a natural and healthy desire for sex within the confines of the covenant of marriage, which gives us one of the greatest pleasures we're able to experience on earth. However, sexual activity outside of the confines of the covenant of marriage—fantasizing, pornography, or the act itself—produces within the person "the due penalty" of the action.

People often think that when God gets ready to hand down His wrath, He's sitting up in heaven about to send a lightning bolt or some other overt form of destruction. But Romans reveals that the wrath of God comes infused within the sin itself. Commit the sin, and the wrath comes with it. In the verses leading up to Paul's discussion on sex, he writes, "For the wrath of God is revealed from heaven against all ungodliness and unrighteousness" (Romans 1:18).

Essentially, God's wrath came when He "gave them over in the lusts of their hearts to impurity." He did so because at the core of sexual strongholds is the sin of idolatry, and God will not tolerate idolatry.

To exchange "the truth of God for a lie" is to place something or someone above God's rightful position in your life.

The Bible tells us that everything God created was good. God created sex. So the issue is not whether sex is good or bad. Sex is good. This is the real issue: Is sex being enjoyed according to God's intentions and within His boundaries (which keeps it right), or is it being misused outside of God's purposes (which makes it wrong)?

The purpose of sex as God designed it was both to inaugurate a covenant and to renew it. So critical was the act of sex in terms of God's covenantal purposes that He attached blood to it. When a man marries a virgin, there is blood on their honeymoon night as the hymen has been designed to break and produce the shedding of blood.

God often attached blood to covenantal or sacrificial actions that He ordained in Scripture to signify the seriousness of the covenant. For example, the men of Israel were circumcised in order to differentiate them from all of the other people of the world as God's covenant people. Jesus shed His blood on the cross to initiate the new covenant. So the blood as confirming a covenant agreement is something we see repeatedly in Scripture and also in the covenant between a man and a woman in marriage.

However, Satan twists sex to fit his purposes, and in so doing, he seeks to diminish its power both in inaugurating and in renewing the covenantal purposes of the marital union. As we see in Genesis 6, where demonically possessed men had sexual relations with the women of earth producing a group of people called the Nephilim, illegitimate sexual relations led to total depravity. "The LORD saw that the wickedness of man was great on the earth, and that every intent of the thoughts of his heart was only evil continually. The LORD was sorry that He had made man on the earth, and He was grieved in His heart" (Genesis 6:5-6). Satan's purpose in twisting our sexuality is to produce an anti-God covenant where people's thoughts are bent toward evil. This evil way of thinking then produces an evil way of living that can be transferred generationally to our children, destroying not only our homes but also our communities.

There is nothing wrong with having sexual desires. In fact, if you don't have sexual desires, that may be an indication that something *is* wrong. God designed us to *enjoy* sexual passion. Your prayer should never be for God to remove your passion. Rather, it should be for you to manage your legitimate passion and to satisfy it within the context He has provided.*

God's Viewpoint

God's will regarding sexual strongholds is unmistakably clear. We read this in Paul's letter to the church at Thessalonica:

> For this is the will of God, your sanctification; that is, that you abstain from sexual immorality; that each of you know how to possess his own vessel in sanctification and honor, not in lustful passion, like the Gentiles who do not know God (1 Thessalonians 4:3-5).

In this passage, Paul directly ties sexual morality with sanctification and knowing God. Not only that, but he writes elsewhere, "Do you not know that your body is a temple of the Holy Spirit who is in you, whom you have from God, and that you are not your own? For you have been bought with a price: therefore glorify God in your body" (1 Corinthians 6:19-20). This passage takes it a step further than simply abstaining from sexual immorality. God tells us that since we have been purchased through the death of His Son, we are to use our bodies in such a way as to bring Him glory.

God's Solution

Easier said than done, right? To be victorious over this stronghold, it's going to take more than taking a cold shower, turning off the television or Internet, or keeping yourself away from any tempting situation, person, or location. This is because the key to victory over this stronghold is found in how you view yourself. Paul tells us that the first step to overcoming a sexual stronghold is to recognize your identity in Christ.

---

* To find out how this works for singles, see my booklet *Tony Evans Speaks Out on Being Single and Satisfied* (Moody Publishers, 2002).

> Do not be deceived; neither fornicators, nor idolaters, nor adulterers, nor effeminate, nor homosexuals, nor thieves, nor the covetous, nor drunkards, nor revilers, nor swindlers, will inherit the kingdom of God. Such were some of you; but you were washed, but you were sanctified, but you were justified in the name of the Lord Jesus Christ and in the Spirit of our God (1 Corinthians 6:9-11).

The natural reaction when people read this passage is to think, "Oh no. I'm in big-time trouble. Because with God—just thinking the wrong thought about sex is the same as adultery." But what you need to keep in mind is what Paul actually wrote: "Such *were* some of you; but you *were* washed, but you *were* sanctified, but you *were* justified in the name of the Lord Jesus Christ and in the Spirit of our God." Paul is writing this to the membership of the church at Corinth. The Corinthians were mixed up in all kinds of messes. This church had every manner of scandal and sexual activity going on right within it. They were sleeping around on Saturday and singing in the choir on Sunday. But Paul tells them, "Such *were* some of you."

He is saying to each one: "As a believer in Jesus Christ, you are no longer a homosexual. As a believer in Jesus Christ, you are no longer an adulterer. As a believer in Jesus Christ, you are no longer a fornicator. Rather, you are a saint exhibiting homosexual behavior. You are a saint who views pornography. You are a saint committing fornication."

The first step in the process of overcoming sexual strongholds as a believer in Jesus Christ is to recognize who you are. You are a saint—washed, sanctified, and justified. You have a new identity now. When you keep that truth at the forefront of your mind, eventually the craving for whatever behavior you were doing will begin to have less and less control over you because it does not line up with who you are. You will be functioning first and foremost out of your identity in Christ.

Along with recognizing and living in your *position* in Christ, Paul wants you to remember your *perspective*.

> All things are lawful for me, but not all things are profitable. All things are lawful for me, but I will not be mastered

by anything. Food is for the stomach and the stomach is
for food, but God will do away with both of them. Yet the
body is not for immorality, but for the Lord, and the Lord
is for the body (1 Corinthians 6:12-13).

What Paul wants us to remember is that while parts of our physical
bodies were made for physical things—such as the stomach and food—
God did not design the body in its entirety for a physical reason. Our
bodies were made for Him and not for immorality. When we view our
bodies through God's perspective—that He made them for Him and
that He is also there for us—then whatever we do sexually needs to
reflect His will and design. We are not our own.

Because of the often strong influences and desires of the body,
though, the power to carry this off comes only in the presence of the
Holy Spirit through an abiding fellowship with Jesus Christ.

Now God has not only raised the Lord, but will also raise us
up through His power. Do you not know that your bodies
are members of Christ? Shall I then take away the members
of Christ and make them members of a prostitute? May it
never be! Or do you not know that the one who joins himself to a prostitute is one body with her? For He says, "The
two shall become one flesh." But the one who joins himself to the Lord is one spirit with Him. Flee immorality.
Every other sin that a man commits is outside the body, but
the immoral man sins against his own body (1 Corinthians
6:14-18).

If God has enough power to raise Jesus Christ from the dead, friend,
He has enough power to give you the strength to resist and flee from
sexual temptation. The solution is found by turning to Him, replacing your own thoughts on who you are in Christ with His thoughts,
and trusting Him to deliver you. When you live and operate under the
truth of being "one spirit with Him," the craving within you for an illegitimate expression of your sexuality will diminish, and you will find
His strength to redirect your passions and desires toward the manifestation of a pure pleasure and satisfaction.

Putting on the Armor of Christ

Day One

WEAR IT

The belt of truth. "Flee from sexual immorality. All other sins people commit are outside their bodies, but those who sin sexually, sin against their own bodies. Do you not know that your bodies are temples of the Holy Spirit, who is in you, whom you have received from God? You are not your own; you were bought at a price. Therefore honor God with your bodies" (1 Corinthians 6:18-20 TNIV).

Putting on Christ. "Consider yourselves to be dead to sin, but alive to God in Christ Jesus" (Romans 6:11).

STAND IN IT

When I sin sexually, I sin against my own body, which God has bought with a price. My body is a temple of the Holy Spirit and just as the Holy Spirit would not hang around sexual immorality, I am to flee from anything related to sexual sins so I can honor God with my body. I do this in Christ's strength because in Him I am now dead to sin and alive to God.

USE IT

Satan, God has already paid the high price of the blood of Jesus Christ for my body. I resist your attempts to lure me into sexual immorality, and in the power of the Holy Spirit, who has made my body His temple, I flee from sexual sins. In Christ, I will honor God with my body because I am dead to sin and your temptations. I am alive to God and His righteousness in Christ Jesus.

DRAW IT DOWN

Father in heaven, thank You for the Holy Spirit, who has made my body His temple. Give me wisdom on how to flee from sexual immorality so that I will not sin against the body You have purchased with a great price. Because I am not my own and I belong to You, I ask You to show me how to honor You each and every day with my body. By faith, I believe that You have made me dead to sin and alive to righteousness in You, and it is in that truth that I seek to please You.

Day Two

Wear It

The breastplate of righteousness. "For this is the will of God, your sanctification; that is, that you abstain from sexual immorality; that each of you know how to possess his own vessel in sanctification and honor, not in lustful passion, like the Gentiles who do not know God" (1 Thessalonians 4:3-5).

Putting on Christ. "He made Him who knew no sin to be sin on our behalf, so that we might become the righteousness of God in Him" (2 Corinthians 5:21).

Stand in It

God's will is that I abstain from sexual immorality and that I live a life that is sanctified and set apart to Him. I am to know how to manage and possess myself in a way that honors who I am in Christ, and not in lustful passion that dishonors God. It is in Jesus Christ, who became sin on my behalf, that I have become the righteousness of God, and I am fully accepted in His love.

Use It

Satan, I renounce my past sexual immorality by the power of Jesus' name. Jesus has taken on my sin even though He had never sinned, and it is by His sacrifice that I now walk in righteousness before God. Because of this, God says I am to abstain from sexual immorality and live a life of honor. I resist any attempt by you to lure me into anything that will dishonor God through lustful passion.

Draw It Down

Father in heaven, I thank You that as I have confessed any past sexual immorality I have participated in, You have completely forgiven me by the power of Jesus' name. Jesus has taken on my sin even though He never sinned Himself, and it is by His sacrifice that I now walk in righteousness before You. Father, give me wisdom on how to abstain from sexual immorality and live a life that honors You and others with my body.

Day Three

Wear It

The shoes of peace. "How blessed are those whose way is blameless, who walk in the law of the LORD" (Psalm 119:1). "How can a young man keep his way pure? By keeping it according to Your word" (Psalm 119:9).

Putting on Christ. "Therefore, since we have a great high priest who has passed through the heavens, Jesus the Son of God, let us hold fast our confession. For we do not have a high priest who cannot sympathize with our weaknesses, but One who has been tempted in all things as we are, yet without sin. Therefore let us draw near with confidence to the throne of grace, so that we may receive mercy and find grace to help in time of need" (Hebrews 4:14-16).

Stand in It

When I walk according to God's Word and let His law be my guide, I will be pure and blameless. I have a great high priest who has passed through the heavens, Jesus the Son of God. I do not have a high priest who cannot sympathize with my weaknesses, but One who has been tempted in all things as I am, yet without sin. Because of this, I draw near with confidence to the throne of grace, so that I may receive mercy and find grace to help in time of need.

Use It

Satan, God's Word and His law is the truth and the standard by which I will live my life. I renounce any attempt by you to twist His commandments in my mind. When His Word is my guide, I am pure and blameless. I have a great high priest who has passed through the heavens, Jesus the Son of God. I do not have a high priest who cannot sympathize with my weaknesses, but One who has been tempted in all things as I am, yet without sin. Jesus Christ resisted you in the desert, and by His strength in me, I resist your attempts to keep me bound by sexual sin. Because of what Jesus Christ has secured for me, I draw near with confidence to the throne of grace, and it is there that I have found mercy and grace to defeat you.

Draw It Down

Father in heaven, Your Word is perfect. It guides, protects, and instructs me. Help me to know Your Word and meditate on Your truths as my guide so that I will be pure and blameless. In Jesus, You have given me a great high priest who has passed through the heavens. Jesus can sympathize with my weaknesses because He has been tempted in all things as I am, yet without sin. Lord, in Christ, I ask You to give me all the grace and mercy that You say is mine to use to live a life of victory this day and each day.

Day Four

Wear It

The shield of faith. "No temptation has overtaken you but such as is common to man; and God is faithful, who will not allow you to be tempted beyond what you are able, but with the temptation will provide the way of escape also, so that you will be able to endure it" (1 Corinthians 10:13).

Putting on Christ. "Set your mind on the things above, not on the things that are on earth. For you have died and your life is hidden with Christ in God. When Christ, who is our life, is revealed, then you also will be revealed with Him in glory" (Colossians 3:2-4).

STAND IN IT

No temptation has overtaken me that He hasn't already empowered other people to overcome. And God is faithful—He will not allow me to be tempted beyond what I am able, but with the temptation will provide a way for me to escape so that I will be able to endure it. He has instructed me to set my mind on the things above, not on the things that are on earth. For I have died, and my life is hidden with Christ in God. When Christ, who is my life, is revealed, then I also will be revealed with Him in glory.

USE IT

Satan, no temptation you can use against me can overtake me because God is faithful, and He won't allow me to be tempted beyond what I am able. With every temptation, He will provide a way for me to escape so that I will be able to endure it. My mind is set on the things above, not on the things that you tempt me with on earth. What is on the earth is passing away. For I have died, and my life is hidden with Christ in God. When Christ, who is my life, is revealed, then I also will be revealed with Him in glory, and your defeat will be made visible to all.

DRAW IT DOWN

Father in heaven, thank You for Your faithfulness! You promise me that my temptations are no harder than what people have already overcome, and You will not allow me to suffer more temptation than I can handle. Instead, with the temptation, You will provide a way for me to escape so that I will be able to endure it. Bring things into my life each hour and every day to remind me to set my mind on the things above, not on the things that are on earth. For I have died, and my life is hidden with Christ in You. When Christ, who is my life, is revealed, then I also will be revealed with Him in glory in Your presence. Remind me of this throughout my day, Lord, and help me to make my decisions with this in mind.

Day Five

WEAR IT

The helmet of salvation. "God has not called us for the purpose of impurity, but in sanctification" (1 Thessalonians 4:7).

Putting on Christ. "By this will we have been sanctified through the offering of the body of Jesus Christ once for all" (Hebrews 10:10).

STAND IN IT

God has not called me for the purpose of impurity, but in sanctification. By this will I have been sanctified through the offering of the body of Jesus Christ once for all.

USE IT

Satan, God has a different plan for my life than you do. He has not called me for the purpose of impurity and sexual sin, but in sanctification—to be set apart for Him. By this will I have been sanctified through the offering of the body of Jesus Christ once for all. Jesus has defeated and disarmed you on the cross.

DRAW IT DOWN

Father in heaven, You have not called me for the purpose of impurity, but in sanctification. Show me how to walk in the sanctification You have given me through the offering of the body of Jesus Christ.

Day Six/Weekend

WEAR IT

> *The sword of the Spirit.* "...Things which eye has not seen and ear has not heard, and which have not entered the heart of man, all that God has prepared for those who love Him" (1 Corinthians 2:9).
>
> *Putting on Christ.* "You are a chosen race, a royal priesthood, a holy nation, a people for God's own possession, so that you may proclaim the excellencies of Him who has called you out of darkness into His marvelous light; for you once were not a people, but now you are the people of God; you had not received mercy, but now you have received mercy. Beloved, I urge you as aliens and strangers to abstain from fleshly lusts which wage war against the soul. Keep your behavior excellent among the Gentiles, so that in the thing in which they slander you as evildoers, they may because of your good deeds, as they observe them, glorify God in the day of visitation" (1 Peter 2:9-12).

STAND IN IT

> I have neither seen nor heard nor received into my heart all that God has prepared for me because I love Him. I am a member of a chosen race, a royal priesthood, a holy nation, a people for God's own possession, so that I may proclaim His excellencies. He has called me out of darkness into His marvelous light. I once was an outsider, but now I am included in the people of God. I once had not received mercy, but now I have received mercy. I will abstain from fleshly lusts, which seek to destroy my soul, and I will keep my behavior excellent so that no one will have cause to slander me in anything. If anyone is to speak of me, let him only speak of the good works that God Himself has done through me, thus giving God the glory that He deserves.

USE IT

> Satan, you tell me that I do not have a future and that

tomorrow will be filled with pain and loss and emptiness, but God tells me that I have neither seen nor heard nor received into my heart all that He has prepared for me because I love Him. You tell me that I am worthless, a nobody, and that I don't belong. But God tells me that I am included in a chosen race, a royal priesthood, a holy nation, a people for His own possession, so that I may proclaim His excellencies. You want me to stay in darkness, but God has called me out of darkness into His marvelous light. I once was an outsider, but now I am included in the people of God. I once had not received mercy, but now I have received mercy. Rather than listen to you, I will abstain from fleshly lusts because you are using them to destroy my soul. I will keep my behavior excellent so that no one will have cause to slander me in anything. If anyone speaks of me, he will only speak of the good works God Himself has done through me, thus giving God the glory He deserves for defeating you.

Draw It Down

Father in heaven, I have neither seen nor heard nor received into my heart all that You have prepared for me because I love You. I am a member of a chosen race, a royal priesthood, a holy nation, a people for Your own possession, so that I may proclaim Your excellencies. You have called me out of darkness into Your marvelous light. I once was excluded, but now I am included in Your people. I once had not received mercy, but now I have received mercy. Because of all of these blessings, Lord, I ask You to enable me to abstain from fleshly lusts. I ask You to give me power through the Holy Spirit and the indwelling Christ to keep my behavior excellent so that no one will have cause to slander me in anything. If anyone speaks of me, he will speak only of the good works You have done through me, thus giving You the glory that You deserve.

15

VICTORY OVER GAMBLING STRONGHOLDS

The Stronghold

All of us gamble to some degree if we define gambling as simply taking a risk. The last time you got into your car, you gambled. The last time you boarded an airplane, you gambled. The last time you ate out at a restaurant, you gambled. Your last investment in the stock market was a big gamble. Taking a risk is not wrong in and of itself. In fact, in Matthew 25:14-30 we read that Jesus condemned the unjust servant for his unwillingness to take a risk. He buried his master's money in the ground instead of investing it in hopes of a return.

The question is not whether it's okay to take a risk; the question is what kind of risk is okay to take. Gambling becomes a stronghold when illegitimate risk replaces God's revealed approach in whatever area of life we're facing. One of the ways a gambling stronghold is manifested is when the motivation is greed. Jesus tells us in Luke 12:15, "Be on your guard against every form of greed." Scripture says that get-rich-quick schemes fall into this category and lead to ruin.

- "The plans of the diligent lead surely to advantage, but everyone who is hasty comes surely to poverty" (Proverbs 21:5).

- "A faithful man will abound with blessings, but he who makes haste to be rich will not go unpunished" (Proverbs 28:20).

- "A man with an evil eye hastens after wealth and does not know that want will come upon him" (Proverbs 28:22).

These are just a few of the biblical warnings that making haste to be rich is an illegitimate attempt to get what God has planned for us. There is no other way to describe the lottery or the casinos available to us today other than as opportunities to get rich quick. This places them in the category of illegitimate risk. By illegitimate I simply mean they aren't sanctioned or provided by God.

Having money is not wrong. Seeking wealth becomes wrong when the motivation is greed and the approach to acquiring it is illegitimate. Neither is prosperity wrong. God Himself declares that He wants to prosper us (Jeremiah 29:11). It only becomes wrong when God is no longer sought after as God but rather as a means to the end of becoming prosperous.

When my children were younger, I tried to pick them up a gift at the airport on my way home from a trip. Looking forward to the gift, on their part, was not wrong. But after a while, I started hearing, "Hey, Dad, when are you going on a trip?" When the focus shifted from my return to what was I bringing for them, I got lost in the process. God doesn't want us to lose Him in the process of seeking His provision, and one way we can easily lose Him is by using what He has given us in a way that He has not sanctioned through illegitimate risk-taking.

Gambling is a stronghold not only when it's based on greed but also when it's not tied to productivity. We read in Proverbs 10:4, "Poor is he who works with a negligent hand, but the hand of the diligent makes rich." We also read in 2 Thessalonians 3:10 that "if anyone is not willing to work, then he is not to eat, either." Throughout the Bible, God links personal responsibility and productivity with His provision. Even when the rich were instructed to leave portions of their fields available to the poor for gleaning, the poor were required to make the effort of doing the physical act of gleaning. If that effort was not made, the leftovers in the field would have remained there.

I was recently in South Carolina when there was legislation pending regarding the lottery. As a result, several reporters wanted to interview me on the subject. My answer was simple. "When a government must sponsor a lottery in order to have a tax base to produce a service for its citizenry, it is saying that we have so little faith in our community's ability to be productive that we have to give them a game to play in order that we might have enough money to keep our programs running." Rather than encourage personal responsibility and productivity, illegitimate risk-taking through get-rich-quick gambling schemes promotes an atmosphere of dependency rather than an atmosphere of empowerment and productivity.

Not only that, but it also fosters poor stewardship. For example, financial planners are professional stewards of other people's money. If you were to give your financial advisor $10,000 for him to manage in your portfolio, and he told you he was going to give it to his wife because she had been wanting her kitchen remodeled for a number of years, you would demand your money back. Or if your bank told you they were going to take the money you had in your account and buy lottery tickets with it because they were feeling lucky that day, you would pull your money out of that bank immediately.

God is the owner of everything, as we read in Psalm 24:1: "The earth is the LORD's, and all it contains, the world, and those who dwell in it." Therefore, we are stewards—financial planners—of anything He allows us to have. Our money is not our money. It's God's money entrusted to our care. God says we should never use the money He has given us without Him in mind because ultimately it is His anyhow.

Perhaps you have read everything so far and you are saying, "Tony, I don't gamble for those reasons. I just gamble because it's fun." God is not opposed to you having fun (see 1 Timothy 6:17). He is just against unrighteous fun. He doesn't want you to have the wrong kind of fun with His money, just as you wouldn't want your financial planner to have a weekend of fun with his wife using your money.

God's Viewpoint

God compares illegitimate risk-taking through gambling to idolatry when He addresses the Israelites' rebellion: "But you who forsake the LORD, who forget My holy mountain, who set a table for Fortune, and who fill cups with mixed wine for Destiny, I will destine you for the sword, and all of you will bow down to the slaughter" (Isaiah 65:11).

To gamble illegitimately is to trust luck rather than the sovereignty of God. It's telling God that you have more faith in the numbers on the ticket than in His ability to provide you with everything you need. God says you are proving that you have forsaken Him when you spin your own wheel of fortune in order to create your own destiny. Forsaking God means turning from Him as your Source and placing your hopes in something else as your source. It is a form of idolatry. *Anything that eclipses God's rightful place in your life is idolatry.*

God's Solution

The stronghold of gambling exists because God has been replaced as the ultimate source, so the way to overcome a gambling stronghold is to return to God. As I referenced earlier, God "richly supplies us with all things to enjoy" (1 Timothy 6:17). Likewise, "Every good thing given and every perfect gift is from above, coming down from the Father of lights, with whom there is no variation or shifting shadow" (James 1:17). Not only that, but God's provision comes without a price tag. We read, "It is the blessing of the LORD that makes rich, and He adds no sorrow to it" (Proverbs 10:22). That is a key principle to understand when you have received a blessing from God. When you get that new car, new house, new job, or whatever it is, you need to see that as a blessing from God. There is great inner satisfaction and peace that comes with acknowledging God alone as your source. Many of us are paying for things we can't afford, and as a result, these things are not blessings to us because a blessing is always infused with the contentment with which to enjoy it.

Overcoming a gambling stronghold comes purely through adopting a mind-set of trusting God to take care of your needs and honoring Him with what He has given you as your first priority. It also includes trusting God to both empower you to be productive as well as cover areas where you are lacking in your capacity to work. You won't need to spend your money on a get-rich-quick scheme once you realize that you know the One who owns it all and that He has given you "every spiritual blessing" in the heavenly places through His grace. Instead, your time, effort, and attention ought to go toward responding to whatever God would have you do in faith in your walk with Him.

Let me give you a tip about a very important conjunction. The conjunction is "but." How you use that conjunction can make all of the difference in the world in freeing you from the stronghold of gambling. It can go one of two ways. Here's the first way:

> God is good, *but* I'm in a problem.
>
> God owns the cattle on a thousand hills, *but* I am buried under a mound of debt.
>
> God is able, *but* I'm in a mess.

The second way changes everything:

> I'm in a problem, *but* God is good.
>
> I'm buried under a mound of debt, *but* God owns the cattle on a thousand hills.
>
> I'm in a mess, *but* God is able.

The way you use the conjunction "but" determines whether you will fret or rest. For example, Joseph said, "You meant evil against me, *but* God meant it for good" (Genesis 50:20).

One of my most enjoyable ministry opportunities has been to serve the NBA Dallas Mavericks as their chaplain for the past three decades. Basketball is a fast-paced, precision sport, filling every minute with adrenaline and feats of skill. When someone is an excellent shot from the three-point line, he will often earn the nickname "Money." If he is really self-confident before he takes the shot, he'll even say his name to himself—"Money"—before he sends it up. However, the best three-point shooters in the league only make the shot 40 percent of the time. That means that 60 percent of the time they are not going to get any points at all and will most likely turn the ball over to the other team on the rebound. And yet they are still called "Money."

Friend, God never misses a shot. Every time He goes up for one and

He wants to score, it's nothing but net. The key to overcoming gambling strongholds is to get close to God, learn from Him, abide with Him, access His grace through faith, and let Him not only call the shots in your life but also make them. Aligning your financial dreams and desires underneath the overarching rule of God is a gamble worth taking simply because He has already guaranteed to "supply all your needs according to His riches in glory in Christ Jesus" (Philippians 4:19). Last I checked, God's jackpot has more than enough for anyone who will follow Jesus' command: "Seek first His kingdom and His righteousness, and all these things will be added to you" (Matthew 6:33).

Putting on the Armor of Christ

Day One

Wear It

> *The belt of truth.* "Seek first His kingdom and His righteousness, and all these things will be added to you."

> *Putting on Christ.* "In everything I showed you that by working hard in this manner you must help the weak and remember the words of the Lord Jesus, that He Himself said, 'It is more blessed to give than to receive'" (Acts 20:35).

Stand in It

> Each and every day, I will seek to find out what God has to say about what I'm facing and how His kingdom can be advanced and glorified through my life. He has promised me that when I make this my priority, all I need will be given to me. I will also strive to work hard so I can help the weak because the Lord Jesus said, "It is more blessed to give than to receive."

Use It

> Satan, seeking to find out what God has to say about what

I'm facing and how His kingdom can be advanced and glorified through my life is my highest priority. I do not need to worry about whether or not I will have enough for everything I need because God promises that "all these things" will be provided for me when I put Him first. It is not more blessed to gamble money on trying to get rich quick because Jesus says, "It is more blessed to give than to receive."

Draw It Down

Father in heaven, show me and reveal to me Your will on what I'm facing and how Your kingdom can be advanced and brought glory through my life so that I will live a life that puts You first. I know You will provide everything I need when I put You first because You have assured me of this in Your Word. Give me opportunities to work hard as well as open doors to help those in need with things that will truly benefit them while maintaining their personal dignity because You value and treasure them as much as You value me. Bless me, Father, by allowing me to give beyond what I ever even imagined I could.

Day Two

Wear It

The breastplate of righteousness. "Wealth obtained by fraud dwindles, but the one who gathers by labor increases it" (Proverbs 13:11).

Putting on Christ. "No one can serve two masters, for either he will hate the one and love the other, or he will be devoted to the one and despise the other. You cannot serve God and wealth" (Matthew 6:24).

Stand in It

Wealth obtained by fraud dwindles, but what I gather by labor increases. I cannot serve two masters, for either I will hate the one and love the other, or I will be devoted to the one and despise the other. I cannot serve God and money.

Use It

Satan, wealth obtained by fraud dwindles, but what I gather by labor increases. I cannot serve two masters, for either I will hate the one and love the other, or I will be devoted to the one and despise the other. I cannot serve God and money.

Draw It Down

Father in heaven, I desire to serve You, but You say that I cannot serve two masters. If I am placing money higher than You and Your principles, then I am serving money instead of You, Father. Wealth obtained by fraud dwindles, but what I gather by labor increases. Help me to labor well. Show me the work You have ordained for me to do, and I ask that You will then grant me the increase that I can enjoy.

Day Three

Wear It

The shoes of peace. "He who loves money will not be satisfied with money, nor he who loves abundance with its income" (Ecclesiastes 5:10).

Putting on Christ. "In Him we have redemption through His blood, the forgiveness of our trespasses, according to the riches of His grace which He lavished on us. In all wisdom and insight He made known to us the mystery of His will, according to His kind intention which He purposed in Him with a view to an administration suitable to the fullness of the times, that is, the summing up of all things in Christ, things in the heavens and things on the earth" (Ephesians 1:7-10).

Stand in It

I will never be satisfied with money if I love money more

than I love God. But when I place Christ as the highest love in my life, I will live in the freedom of the redemption I have through His blood, the forgiveness of my trespasses, according to the riches of His grace, which He lavished on me. In all wisdom and insight He makes known to me the mystery of His will, according to His kind intention, which He purposed in Him with a view to an administration suitable to the fullness of the times, that is, the summing up of all things in Christ, things in the heavens and things on the earth.

Use It

Satan, I rebuke the lure of fast money through gambling. I will never be satisfied with money if I love money more than I love God. Only when I place Christ as the highest love in my life will I live richly in the freedom of the redemption I have through His blood, the forgiveness of my trespasses, according to the riches of His grace, which He lavished on me. In all wisdom and insight He makes known to me the mystery of His will, according to His kind intention, which He purposed in Him with a view to an administration suitable to the fullness of the times, that is, the summing up of all things in Christ, things in the heavens and things on the earth.

Draw It Down

Father in heaven, I will never be satisfied with money if I love money more than I love You. But when I place Christ as the highest love in my life, I will live in the freedom of the redemption I have through His blood, the forgiveness of my trespasses, according to the riches of Your grace, which You lavished on me. Give me all wisdom and insight and make known to me the mystery of Your will, according to Your kind intention, which You purposed in Him with a view to an administration suitable to the fullness of the times, that is, the summing up of all things in Christ, things in the heavens and things on the earth.

Day Four

WEAR IT

The shield of faith. "…Giving thanks to the Father, who has qualified us to share in the inheritance of the saints in light" (Colossians 1:12).

Putting on Christ. "Calling ten of his servants, he gave them ten minas, and said to them, 'Engage in business until I come'" (Luke 19:13 ESV).

STAND IN IT

I give thanks to God, my Father, who has qualified me to share in the inheritance of the saints in light. Because of His great grace, I am to use what He has given me and to maximize it in legitimate means until He returns for me.

USE IT

Satan, the only thing you have ever qualified me for is death and destruction. You do not deliver on your promises because you are a liar, but I thank my Father, who has qualified me to share in the inheritance of the saints in light, and I will wisely use what He has given me, conducting business with it rather than gambling in ways He has not ordained.

DRAW IT DOWN

Father in heaven, thank You for qualifying me to share in the inheritance of the saints in light. Please reveal to me the full manifestation of this inheritance in my life today and each day. Also give me wisdom, Lord, on how to be a good manager of the resources (time, talent, and finances) You have given me to use until Christ returns.

Day Five

WEAR IT

The helmet of salvation. "There was not a needy person

among them, for all who were owners of land or houses would sell them and bring the proceeds of the sales" (Acts 4:34).

Putting on Christ. "The Spirit Himself testifies with our spirit that we are children of God, and if children, heirs also, heirs of God and fellow heirs with Christ, if indeed we suffer with Him so that we may also be glorified with Him. For I consider that the sufferings of this present time are not worthy to be compared with the glory that is to be revealed to us" (Romans 8:16-18).

Stand in It

There was not a needy person among them, for all who were owners of land or houses would sell them and bring the proceeds of the sales. The Spirit Himself testifies with my spirit that I am a child of God, and if I am a child, I am an heir also, an heir of God and a fellow heir with Christ, if indeed I suffer with Him so that I may also be glorified with Him. For I consider that the sufferings of this present time are not worthy to be compared with the glory that is to be revealed.

Use It

Satan, the Holy Spirit testifies against you when you say that I do not belong and that I am not loved. In fact, the Holy Spirit tells my spirit that I am a child of God and also an heir. I am an heir of God and a fellow heir with Christ, if indeed I suffer with Him so that I may also be glorified with Him. For I consider that the sufferings of this present time are not worthy to be compared with the glory that is to be revealed to us.

Draw It Down

Father in heaven, show me how I am to give out of the resources that You have given me to help others in need. In fact, show us as a church how to give in such a way that there will not be a needy person in Your body of Christ. Thank You for letting my spirit know that I am Your child as well as Your heir and a fellow heir with Jesus, if indeed I suffer with Him so that I may also be glorified with Him. For I consider that the sufferings of this present time are not worthy to be compared with the glory that is to be revealed to us.

Day Six/Weekend

Wear It

The sword of the Spirit. "Beware, and be on your guard against every form of greed; for not even when one has an abundance does his life consist of his possessions" (Luke 12:15).

Putting on Christ. "For if by the transgression of the one, death reigned through the one, much more those who receive the abundance of grace and of the gift of righteousness will reign in life through the One, Jesus Christ" (Romans 5:17).

Stand in It

I am to be on guard against every form of greed; for not even when one has an abundance does his life consist of his possessions. Because if by the transgression of Adam, death reigned through Adam into all humanity, much more do I, who have received the abundance of grace and of the gift of righteousness, reign in life through the One, Jesus Christ.

Use It

Greed, envy, coveting...these are all things that I resist in Jesus' name. Because of the power of Christ, they no longer have permission to influence my mind. For not even when one has an abundance does his life consist of his possessions. If by the transgression of Adam, death reigned through Adam into all humanity, much more do I, who have received the abundance of grace and of the gift of righteousness, reign over you, Satan, in life through the One, Jesus Christ.

DRAW IT DOWN

Father in heaven, give me wisdom and open both my eyes and heart to be on guard against every form of greed. If by the transgression of Adam, death reigned through Adam into all humanity, much more do I, who have received the abundance of grace and of the gift of righteousness, reign in life through the One, Jesus Christ. Let that reigning power be manifest fully today in my thoughts and actions.

16

VICTORY OVER FOOD STRONGHOLDS

The Stronghold

One of the most overlooked strongholds today is that of eating. Often, it's not even viewed as a stronghold. In fact, in Christian circles, we will frequently condemn the alcoholic, the drug addict, or the porn addict, all the while excusing the food addict. However, eating strongholds dominate such a large percentage of the population that a majority of our health problems stem from this root.

An eating stronghold doesn't always have to show up through a person eating too much food. An eating stronghold can also show up in someone who either won't eat enough food (anorexia) or eats too much food only to purge themselves afterward (bulimia). An eating stronghold exists when food (its presence or lack) becomes the dominant factor in someone's life. A dependence on food can result in eating as a way to escape from stressful situations, to feel in control, to gain comfort, or even to inflict self-punishment.

Food plays a prominent role throughout the Bible. For starters, the whole world was plunged into sin over food from a fruit tree in the Garden of Eden. We also see that for a bowl of porridge, Esau gave away his future. In 1 Samuel, we read that the priest Eli fell backward and broke his neck because he was a heavy man. The Bible also tells us that his sons were gluttons who took food by force. Scripture declares that

Nabal was a gluttonous fool who died of a heart attack. These are just a few examples.

Food was responsible for a number of deaths in the Bible and is responsible for many deaths today as well. God has explicitly commanded us, "Thou shalt not kill," and yet every year hundreds of thousands of us dig our graves with our teeth and commit suicide with our forks.

In fact, the stronghold of eating leads to such disastrous ends that God even warns us not to hang around those who are entangled with it. In Proverbs 23:20-21 we read, "Do not be with heavy drinkers of wine, or with gluttonous eaters of meat; for the heavy drinker and the glutton will come to poverty, and drowsiness will clothe one with rags." Proverbs 28:7 says, "He who keeps the law is a discerning son, but he who is a companion of gluttons humiliates his father."

Food is the object of eating strongholds, but it is not the cause. Food is merely the symptom. Paul gives greater clarity on this in his letter to the church at Philippi.

> For many walk, of whom I often told you, and now tell you even weeping, that they are enemies of the cross of Christ, whose end is destruction, whose god is their appetite, and whose glory is in their shame, who set their minds on earthly things (Philippians 3:18-19).

The problem is not a food problem. The problem is a God problem. Paul compares the stronghold of an uncontrolled appetite to that of an idol—"whose god is their appetite." Many of us say that we would never bow to an idol, but when we give in to the demands of our appetite or do not permit ourselves to eat, we have essentially bowed to an idol. We have placed food in the position of preeminence in our lives that only God should hold.

God's Viewpoint

Paul directs us to the Old Testament as an example of how God views misplaced desire, or idolatry. We read first about this example in the book of Psalms, where it talks about the Israelites complaining against God in the wilderness after they had been set free from the Egyptians.

Then they spoke against God; they said, "Can God prepare a table in the wilderness? Behold, He struck the rock so that waters gushed out, and streams were overflowing; can He give bread also? Will He provide meat for His people?"

Therefore the LORD heard and was full of wrath; and a fire was kindled against Jacob and anger also mounted against Israel...He sent them food in abundance...When He rained meat upon them like the dust, even winged fowl like the sand of the seas, then He let them fall in the midst of their camp, round about their dwellings. So they ate and were well filled, and their desire He gave to them. Before they had satisfied their desire, while their food was in their mouths, the anger of God rose against them and killed some of their stoutest ones, and subdued the choice men of Israel (Psalm 78:19-21,25,27-31).

Paul elaborates on this in his first letter to the church at Corinth.

Nevertheless, with most of them God was not well-pleased; for they were laid low in the wilderness.

Now these things happened *as examples for us*, so that we would not crave evil things as they also craved. Do not be idolaters, as some of them were; as it is written, "The people sat down to eat and drink, and stood up to play" (1 Corinthians 10:5-7).

We are not to place the desire for food (or the desire to control food) above God. In fact, God tells us how we are to view food. Paul writes, "Whether, then, you eat or drink or whatever you do, do all to the glory of God" (1 Corinthians 10:31). Food must be brought into its proper perspective underneath the purposes and program of God.

God's Solution

Your god, or your idol, is whatever it is that you obey. If food calls to you and you obey it outside of God's will for its natural use in your body, you have made food an idol. The solution to overcoming an eating stronghold can be found in Paul's letter to Titus.

For the grace of God has appeared, bringing salvation to all men, instructing us to deny ungodliness and worldly desires and to live sensibly, righteously and godly in the present age, looking for the blessed hope and the appearing of the glory of our great God and Savior, Christ Jesus (Titus 2:11-13).

Paul says that the solution is *grace*. Remember, grace is what God does for you. A diet is what you do for yourself. Cutting back on this or eating more of that is law. It can last a minute, but it rarely lasts long because law does not lead to life. The first principle of the grace diet is this: *You are uniquely created to bring glory to God through your life.* We read in 1 Corinthians 6:20, "For you have been bought with a price: therefore glorify God in your body."

You wouldn't walk into the New York City Ballet or any other expensive place of architecture and spray graffiti all over the walls. God says that you too have been purchased with a very high price—His Son Jesus Christ. You are not a closeout special or an item on the sale rack. God paid top dollar for you, and He wants you to treat your body in a way that reflects His value of you. Not only that, He has designed you with your individual qualities you can bring Him glory in ways that no one else on earth can. When you view and value your body as a tool for reflecting God's glory, it becomes difficult to surrender it to anything that might bring it damage.

Here's the second principle of the grace diet: *You must move from self-discipline to Spirit-discipline.* Let me explain. Diets are usually tied to willpower. The problem with that is that the human will is limited. Even though you *want* to stop giving in to that piece of cheesecake or that fast-food favorite, you may feel unable to will yourself to do so. Only grace, supplied through the ongoing presence of the Holy Spirit to your spirit, will enable you to have a power that's beyond your own. When the Holy Spirit's power is supplied through grace, He aligns your thinking under the viewpoint of God that says that your body is here in order to glorify God. Food then becomes a means to that end.

Once the first two principles have been put in place—that you are to glorify God in your body and that you need Spirit-discipline instead of self-discipline—the next part of the grace diet can begin. We read about it in Paul's letter to Timothy.

> But the Spirit explicitly says that in later times some will fall away from the faith, paying attention to deceitful spirits and doctrines of demons, by means of the hypocrisy of liars seared in their own conscience as with a branding iron, men who forbid marriage and advocate abstaining from foods which God has created to be gratefully shared in by those who believe and know the truth. For everything created by God is good, and nothing is to be rejected if it is received with gratitude; for it is sanctified by means of the word of God and prayer (1 Timothy 4:1-5).

Something is "sanctified" when it's set apart for a special purpose. Sanctification as it relates to food means turning mealtime into a spiritual time. You receive your food, whether a meal or a snack, in a spirit of thanksgiving. You remember what God's Word reveals as your purpose—to bring Him glory through your body, which He has purchased at a high price. These things change the way you approach that food. Instead of eating to satisfy your flesh, emotions, or desires, you eat to satisfy God's destiny in you. You recognize God in His position over you, because now when you pray, you say something like this:

> Lord, I thank You for this food and also for my body, which You have given to me. I don't want to dishonor You by what I put in it, and I want to bring You as much glory as I can, so will you have the Holy Spirit convict me and let me know when I'm eating too much? Will Your Spirit control my thoughts so that I will feel uncomfortable when I have gone too far with this food or when I turn to food to meet a spiritual need that You want to meet in me Yourself? Your Word says You will give me anything I ask according to Your will, and because I know that this prayer is according to Your will, I am trusting that You will do this, and I am thanking You in advance, in Jesus' name. Amen.

Friend, if you have an eating stronghold, I know exactly what you're facing because I faced one in my life for a number of years too. It wasn't until I put the principles from these passages into place in my own life a few years ago that I was able to overcome my eating stronghold. I now no longer have to respond to its dictates. In fact, I lost ten pounds in the first three weeks that I began to live by these principles. That was more than I had lost in the previous three months on diet after diet. God's Word is truly the way to overcome any stronghold in our life.

Grace simply means that you come to God and say, "God, I can't do this. I can't give this up. This one is bigger than me, but because I am Yours, please let Your Holy Spirit loose in me so that whatever I eat or drink, it is done to bring You greater glory and to maximize this temple that You have given me while I am on earth in order that I may serve and enjoy You the rest of my life."

Putting on the Armor of Christ

Day One

Wear It

The belt of truth. "I can do all things through Him who strengthens me" (Philippians 4:13).

Putting on Christ. "If you have died with Christ to the elementary principles of the world, why, as if you were living in the world, do you submit yourself to decrees, such as 'Do not handle, do not taste, do not touch!' (which all refer to things destined to perish with use)—in accordance with the commandments and teachings of men? These are matters which have, to be sure, the appearance of wisdom in self-made religion and self-abasement and severe treatment of the body, but are of no value against fleshly indulgence" (Colossians 2:20-23).

Stand in It

I can do all things through Him who strengthens me,

including eating only until I'm full or even eating what I need to instead of avoiding food.

Use It

Satan, food does not have the final say over me. I can do all things through Him who strengthens me. If I need to stop eating something, I can stop eating it in Christ's strength. If I need to eat better foods, I can eat them through Christ's strength in me. I have died with Christ to the elementary principles of this world, so I will no longer be controlled by rules of men, but by the Spirit of God.

Draw It Down

Father in heaven, thank You for giving me the promise that I can do all things through Christ who strengthens me. Because of Jesus Christ, I have died to the elementary principles of this world. I no longer have to live in accordance with the commandments and teachings of men. Instead, I trust myself to Your Spirit's power at work in me to give me the self-control I need to eat in a way that glorifies You.

Day Two

Wear It

The breastplate of righteousness. "You shall love the LORD your God with all your heart and with all your soul and with all your might" (Deuteronomy 6:5). "His divine power has granted to us everything pertaining to life and godliness, through the true knowledge of Him who called us by His own glory and excellence" (2 Peter 1:3).

Putting on Christ. "Therefore if you have been raised up with Christ, keep seeking the things above, where Christ is, seated at the right hand of God" (Colossians 3:1).

Stand in It

I am to love the Lord my God with all my heart and with all

my soul and with all my might because His divine power has granted me everything I need to live a full life through the true knowledge of Him who called me by His own glory and excellence. I have been raised up with Christ and am to seek the things above, where Christ is, seated at the right hand of God.

Use It

Satan, I love the Lord my God with all my heart and with all my soul and with all my might because His divine power has granted me everything I need to live a full life through the true knowledge of Him who called me by His own glory and excellence. I have been raised up with Christ and am seeking the things above, where Christ is, seated at the right hand of God.

Draw It Down

Father in heaven, help me to love You with all my heart and with all my soul and with all my might because Your divine power has granted me everything I need to live a full life when I truly know You—the One who called me by Your own glory and excellence. I have been raised up with Christ, so I ask that You empower me to seek the things above, where Christ is, seated at Your right hand.

Day Three

Wear It

The shoes of peace. "Go, eat of the fat, drink of the sweet, and send portions to him who has nothing prepared; for this day is holy to our Lord. Do not be grieved, for the joy of the LORD is your strength" (Nehemiah 8:10).

Putting on Christ. "And the peace of God, which surpasses all comprehension, will guard your hearts and your minds in Christ Jesus" (Philippians 4:7).

Stand in It

God has said that in Him I am to eat of the fat, drink of the sweet, and send portions to him who has nothing prepared, for this day is holy to our Lord. I am not to be grieved, for the joy of the Lord is my strength. While I am enjoying what God has provided, His peace, which surpasses all of my own willpower and understanding, will guard my heart, my appetite, and my mind in Christ Jesus so that I have the self-control to stop before my eating becomes excessive.

Use It

Satan, God has said, "Go, eat of the fat, drink of the sweet, and send portions to him who has nothing prepared; for this day is holy to our Lord. Do not be grieved, for the joy of the LORD is your strength." And it is written, "The peace of God, which surpasses all comprehension, will guard your hearts and your minds in Christ Jesus."

Draw It Down

Father in heaven, because of Your goodness, You have instructed me to eat of the fat, drink of the sweet, and send portions to him who has nothing prepared; for this day is holy to You. In You, I am not grieved, for Your joy is my strength. I ask You to let that joy to show up in my life at this moment and be an ever-present part of my life. Help me to recognize Your joy in my life and to turn to it to find deep satisfaction. And while I am enjoying and celebrating Your goodness and all that You have supplied, guard me with Your peace in Christ so that I do not indulge in excess.

Day Four

Wear It

The shield of faith. "For whatever is born of God overcomes the world; and this is the victory that has overcome the world—our faith" (1 John 5:4).

Putting on Christ. "Who is the one who overcomes the world, but he who believes that Jesus is the Son of God?" (1 John 5:5).

Stand in It

I have overcome the world because I am born of God. My faith in God is the victory that has overcome my eating stronghold. Because I believe in Jesus Christ, the Son of God, I have all that I need to overcome everything in the world that is seeking to defeat or control me.

Use It

Satan, I resist you because it is written that whatever is born of God overcomes the world, and this is the victory that has overcome the world—our faith. Who is the one who overcomes the world, but he who believes that Jesus is the Son of God? I believe in Jesus, the Son of God.

Draw It Down

Father in heaven, I have overcome the world because I am born of You. Show me how to walk in the reality of this victory I already have. When I look at food that I should not be eating, remind me that my faith in You has given me all that I need to overcome the temptation in front of me. Satisfy me with the truth that my belief in Jesus Christ, Your Son, is enough to overcome the world.

Day Five

Wear It

The helmet of salvation. "The grace of God has appeared, bringing salvation to all men, instructing us to deny ungodliness and worldly desires to live sensibly, righteously and godly in the present age" (Titus 2:11-12).

Putting on Christ. "...Looking for the blessed hope and the appearing of the glory of our great God and Savior, Christ Jesus" (Titus 2:13).

Stand in It

The grace of God has appeared, bringing me salvation,

instructing me to deny ungodliness and worldly desires and teaching me to live sensibly, righteously, and godly in the present age. I am looking for the blessed hope and the appearing of the glory of our great God and Savior, Christ Jesus.

Use It

Satan, I resist you because it is written that the grace of God has appeared, bringing salvation to all men, instructing us to deny ungodliness and worldly desires and teaching us to live sensibly, righteously, and godly in the present age. I am looking for the blessed hope and the appearing of the glory of our great God and Savior, Christ Jesus. I have more than enough with which to be content.

Draw It Down

Father in heaven, thank You for Your grace, which has appeared and brought me salvation. Use it to instruct me to deny ungodliness and worldly desires and to teach me to live sensibly, righteously, and godly in the present age. Enable me to respond quickly to Your instruction, Lord. And focus my eyes on the blessed hope and the appearing of the glory of our great God and Savior, Christ Jesus.

Day Six/Weekend

Wear It

The sword of the Spirit. "For everything created by God is good, and nothing is to be rejected if it is received with gratitude; for it is sanctified by means of the word of God and prayer" (1 Timothy 4:4-5).

Putting on Christ. "He has filled the hungry with good things" (Luke 1:53).

Stand in It

For everything created by God is good, and nothing is to

be rejected if it is received with gratitude, for it is sanctified by means of the Word of God and prayer. Jesus has filled and satisfied me with good things.

Use It

Satan, it is written that everything created by God is good, and nothing is to be rejected if it is received with gratitude, for it is sanctified by means of the Word of God and prayer. In the life of Christ, God has filled the hungry with good things.

Draw It Down

Father in heaven, everything You have created is good, and nothing is to be rejected if it is received with gratitude. With gratitude, Lord, I receive the food You give me. Help me to use the food in a way that pleases and honors You. Sanctify this food for Your purposes. And thank You for satisfying me with the life of Christ in me. I look to Him to meet not only the hunger in my body but also the hunger in my soul. For Your gifts to me are sanctified by means of the Word of God and prayer (1 Timothy 4:4-5).

17

VICTORY OVER EMOTIONAL STRONGHOLDS

The Stronghold

Far too many Christians are held hostage by emotional strongholds such as anger, depression, discouragement, frustration, inferiority complexes, fear, and countless other volatile feelings. People dealing with emotional strongholds usually know it. When they wake up in the morning, they don't say, "Good morning, Lord." Rather, they say, "Good Lord, it's morning." They struggle simply to survive, often living in a perpetual state of hopelessness, worry, or despair.

An emotional stronghold isn't the same thing as simply having a bad day. We all have bad days or even bad weeks. An emotional stronghold is an attitude or emotion that stays with you day in and day out. It does more than just show up from time to time. It dictates and often even dominates your thoughts and choices and thus your life itself.

God never ordained for you to wake up every day depressed or to always be paralyzed by fear. He didn't create you to carry anger around for five, fifteen, or fifty years. God has promised you a full life in Christ. Jesus said, "I came that they may have life, and have it abundantly" (John 10:10). If you're not experiencing the abundant life that Christ freely gives, it may be a result of living with an emotional stronghold.

God wants to free you from the endless and fruitless task of denying or suppressing emotional strongholds through distractions, pills, entertainment, or even spending. He wants to reveal to you the root behind what you are experiencing. Just as a doctor will not only listen to how you feel when you go in for an examination but will also probe deeper through X-rays or tests, so too overcoming emotional strongholds involves going deeper than just your feelings to discover the root cause behind them.

Certainly, some emotional strongholds are tied to physiological causes, such as a chemical imbalance. And those need to be addressed physically. However, a large number of emotional strongholds are not physiological. They are rooted in sin. The sin may be your own, or someone else's sin may be affecting you, or your environment may be contaminated by sin. Maybe you were abused as a child, raped, betrayed in a relationship, or unwanted. It wasn't *your* sin that created the stronghold of fear, insecurity, guilt, or shame that you may be facing now, but it was still sin that caused it.

Emotional strongholds often come as a result of what I call *atmospheric sin*—sin that so clouds the atmosphere around us that its results affect us whether we committed the sin or not. It's similar in concept to secondhand smoke and lung cancer. You may not have smoked the cigarettes yourself, but studies show that if you grew up in a home contaminated by cigarette smoke, you have a higher potential for contracting lung cancer. The same holds true for sin. An environment deeply contaminated by sin leads to a greater susceptibility to emotional strongholds.

There are three general categories of emotional strongholds. The first category includes those strongholds rooted in our past. This is when emotional damage happened during a person's developmental years either through trauma, neglect, or any number of negative factors. These situations create emotional grooves in our mind that eventually become part of our normal mode of thinking and perceiving. A biblical example of someone who had past emotional strongholds to overcome would be Joseph in the Old Testament, who was picked on by his brothers and eventually betrayed, left for dead, and then sold into slavery as a youth.

The next category of emotional strongholds are those that are part of your present. This is when the trials and tests you're currently facing result in continual emotional fatigue. Maybe you're in a bad relationship or your work environment is unstable. It could be a health challenge, finances, problems with your kids or your spouse—any number of things. This is when the challenges of each day relentlessly attack your emotional well-being. The best example in the Bible would have to be Paul. Beaten, imprisoned, hungry, facing physical ailments, and often in danger of death, Paul labored through countless emotional trials, boasting only of God's strength evident in his weaknesses (see 2 Corinthians 11:23-33).

The third category of emotional strongholds involves the fear of the future. This is what we call *worry.* Worry can be referred to as interest paid on trouble before it is due. Worry means you're scared about your tomorrow. You ask yourself questions like these: What if I get cancer? What if I have a heart attack? What if one of my children dies? Or we lose our retirement funds? Or we have to foreclose on our mortgage? Or our marriage doesn't make it? What if? The Bible commands us not to be anxious for tomorrow (see Matthew 6:34) because a person bound by an emotional stronghold for the future becomes paralyzed today. Esther was a woman who had every reason to be held hostage to a fear of the future. After all, she was fully aware that the king gave an irreversible decree to completely annihilate not only her but also all of her people in the land. Regardless, Esther did not cower to a fear of the future, so she was able to walk victoriously in the present.

God's Viewpoint

Jesus says that in this world—past, present, and future—we *will* face trials and the effects of sin, but in spite of those trials, we're to "be of good cheer" because He has "overcome the world" (John 16:33 NKJV). Our emotions are based on choices we make, which in turn are based on what we believe. If we truly believe that Jesus has overcome whatever it is that we're facing and that we're fully accepted and made complete in Him, that will alter how our emotions respond to our trials.

That doesn't mean you will "be of good cheer" all day, every day. But it does mean that it will be the normative mode in which you function.

God's Solution

The cure for any emotional stronghold is not to deny that it exists. Just as you can't cure cancer by pretending you don't have it, so too, you can't overcome an emotional stronghold by wishing it away. Neither does the cure come through distracting yourself out of it. Distractions can provide temporary relief at best, but they offer no long-term solution. In fact, oftentimes distractions can eventually develop into their own strongholds (such as eating, spending, drinking, sex, and entertainment), leaving you with more to overcome than when you first began.

You also can't overcome an emotional stronghold by obeying it. If you feel like cutting, cussing, or simply shutting down—doing any of those things will not bring about an end to the stronghold. It will just pacify you until the next time the emotion asks you to repeat the behavior.

The key to overcoming emotional strongholds is—as in the cases we've talked about already—to understand and address their root. This is because emotions have no intellect with which to reason. They are dumb. They don't think. Emotions simply react off of borrowed thoughts. Therefore, whatever or whoever controls your thought life controls your emotions. The root of all emotional strongholds can be found in what you think and believe to be true. If Satan is influencing your thought life, you will feel what he wants you to feel. If God is dominating your thought life, you will feel what God has designed you to feel. "For as he thinks within himself, so he is" (Proverbs 23:7).

Say you go to buy a car, and the salesman tells you the dealership can't offer you a loan even though you have excellent credit. Most likely, you will leave the car lot with your emotions running low. However, let's say the dealership called you on your way home and said they had made a mistake—you do qualify for the loan. In fact, you qualify for a loan with 0 percent interest. Now your emotions are high again. Emotions merely respond to our thoughts. Therefore, we overcome emotional strongholds through our thoughts.

What you believe determines how you respond, which ultimately determines how God responds. For example, with only a few seconds left in the game, a basketball player rushes to the basket to make a shot but gets knocked to the ground by the opponent. As he's laying on the ground, a referee—the man in stripes—blows his whistle, altering the current experience of the game by relocating the basketball player who got knocked to the ground to the free-throw line for an unhindered opportunity to score.

However, if that same basketball player didn't like getting knocked down, and he decided to respond by getting back up and knocking down the opponent who fouled him, that would change what the referee would do. The referee would no longer put him on the free-throw line. In fact, the referee might even throw him out of the game altogether for unsportsmanlike conduct.

How you respond is often a reflection of what you believe. The basketball player on the free throw line believed that the referee was going to handle the situation, so he simply got back up and continued in the game. But if you don't believe that God has your best interest at heart and that He won't do anything about the wrongs that happen to you or the emotional struggles you're facing, you will try to take things into your own hands. This places God in a different position. He now has to respond to you in a different way, based on what you have done.

Friend, God saw what happened to you, and He sees what is happening to you now and your fear about what may happen to you in the future. Oftentimes we inhibit His response and deliverance in our lives by trying to take care of things our own way. This only compounds the problem as we add our sin to the atmospheric sin impacting us. In other words, God is saying through His Word and His promises that *He* is the One with the stripes, and *He* will handle it for us if we will only let Him. Why *don't* we let Him? Because we don't believe Him when He says "vengeance" is His (Deuteronomy 32:35), He has "overcome the world" (John 16:33), "and by His stripes we are healed" (Isaiah 53:5 NKJV).

Intimacy with Christ that offers a perspective on God in all of His fullness, goodness, and power is the key to overcoming emotional strongholds. When you know Christ in a real, abiding way and live according to His truth—whatever is going wrong in your life no longer has the final say. It may have *a* say; it just won't have *the* say. Jeremiah lived life in this way. If anyone had a reason to be bound in an emotional mess, it would be the prophet Jeremiah. His city was destroyed. His people were falling apart. His future looked bleak. Yet, this is what he said in spite of it all:

> This I recall to my mind, therefore I have hope. The LORD's lovingkindnesses indeed never cease, for His compassions never fail. They are new every morning; great is Your faithfulness. "The LORD is my portion," says my soul, "Therefore I have hope in Him" (Lamentations 3:21-24).

Hope can take you a long way. Whenever I counsel people struggling with emotional strongholds, I always want to check their hope meter. Because when you have lost your hope, you have lost everything. Simply defined, hope is the belief that my tomorrow will be better than my today. David knew about the power of hope when life looked hopeless. He said, "My tears have been my food day and night" (Psalm 42:3). When your tears are your food, that means you are no longer eating. You have lost your appetite. You are checking out of life. Yet when David reached this low point, he talked to himself. He encouraged himself. He spoke hope back into his situation.

> These things I remember and I pour out my soul within me...Hope in God, for I shall again praise Him for the help of His presence...The LORD will command His lovingkindness in the daytime; and His song will be with me in the night...Hope in God, for I shall yet praise Him, the help of my countenance and my God (Psalm 42:4,5,8,11).

David said that even though he was in misery at the moment, he would remember what God has done for him in the past. In fact, both David and Jeremiah said that they would "recall" or "remember" some aspect of God's truth. In doing so, David trusted that God would "command His lovingkindness" once again. He hadn't done it yet; things still looked discouraging. But David knew that God would come through in His perfect timing. It was that truth that caused David to change his emotional well-being from that of tears to hope.

Friend, God can turn a mess into a miracle if you put your hope in Him. He promises, "Those who hope in me will not be disappointed" (Isaiah 49:23 NIV). In fact, God is able to turn things around so completely and satisfy you so fully that He will do more than merely bring you out of your emotional bondage. He can even cause you to forget how deep it ever was. He did it for Joseph, and He can do it for you.

When God restored to Joseph all he had lost and more, Joseph gave his sons two very revealing names. The first son he called Manasseh, which means, "The Lord has helped me to forget." The second son was named Ephraim, which means, "The Lord has made me fruitful in my suffering."

I know your emotions may seem overwhelming, and you may even wonder how you could ever overcome them, but if you will hope in God, replace the lies holding you hostage with His truth in your mind, and address any related sin, He can turn emotional suffering into a victorious life.

Putting on the Armor of Christ

Day One

WEAR IT

> *The belt of truth.* "'For I know the plans that I have for you,' declares the LORD, 'plans for welfare and not for calamity to give you a future and a hope" (Jeremiah 29:11).

> *Putting on Christ.* "Who will bring a charge against God's elect? God is the one who justifies; who is the one who condemns? Christ Jesus is He who died, yes, rather who was raised, who is at the right hand of God, who also intercedes for us" (Romans 8:33-34).

STAND IN IT

> God knows the plans He has for me. They are plans for welfare and not for calamity, plans to give me a future and a

hope. Who will bring a charge against me? God is the one who justifies; who is the one who condemns? Christ Jesus is He who died, yes, rather who was raised, who is at the right hand of God, who also intercedes for me.

Use It

Satan, God says that He knows the plans He has for me, and they are plans for welfare and not for calamity, plans to give me a future and a hope. Your accusations carry no weight against me because God is the one who justifies. Christ Jesus is He who died, yes, rather who was raised, who is at the right hand of God, who also intercedes for me.

Draw It Down

Father in heaven, thank You for the plans that You have for me—to give me both a future and a hope. Because of You, I am forgiven of my sins, and regardless of what Satan accuses me of, You have already justified me before You because of Jesus Christ, who died for me and was raised. He is sitting at Your right hand, interceding for me. Let His prayers on my behalf bring about a great result in my life, Lord, as I look to You to fulfill the promise of a future with hope.

Day Two

Wear It

The breastplate of righteousness. "Do not be anxious about anything, but in every situation, by prayer and petition, with thanksgiving, present your requests to God" (Philippians 4:6 NIV).

Putting on Christ. "Who will separate us from the love of Christ? Will tribulation, or distress, or persecution, or famine, or nakedness, or peril, or sword?...But in all these things we overwhelmingly conquer through Him who loved us" (Romans 8:35,37).

STAND IN IT

Instead of being anxious and worrying, I will give God thanks for all He has done and is doing in my life. After that, I will present my requests to Him because He loves me and has my best interest at heart. Nothing can separate me from His love in Christ. Absolutely nothing. Whether it's a trial, or distress, or loss, or abuse, or anything I have done—in all these things I overwhelmingly conquer through Christ, who loves me.

USE IT

Satan, rather than worry or stress about the thoughts you bring my way or the trials and pain that I am facing, I can give God those troubles through prayer and petition, with thanksgiving, and He will hear my requests. Nothing I have ever done or will ever experience can separate me from His love. In all of the things that you use to overwhelm me, I have overwhelmingly conquered through Jesus, who loves me.

DRAW IT DOWN

Father in heaven, thank You for all that You have done for me. Thank You that You never abandon me in my pain and that You promise me You hear me when I present my requests to You. Give me the wisdom and power right at this very moment to walk victoriously in the love of Christ, which enables me to overwhelmingly conquer all I'm facing in my life.

Day Three

WEAR IT

The shoes of peace. "'Comfort, O comfort My people,' says your God" (Isaiah 40:1). "The LORD is near to the brokenhearted and saves those who are crushed in spirit" (Psalm 34:18).

Putting on Christ. "These things I have spoken to you, so that in Me you may have peace. In the world you have tribulation, but take courage; I have overcome the world" (John 16:33).

STAND IN IT

God gives me His comfort because He cares for me. He is near to the brokenhearted and saves me when I feel crushed in spirit. In Christ, I have peace even though I face trials, problems, and pain in the world I live in. But Jesus has overcome the world, and in Him, I will take courage.

USE IT

Satan, when you tell me that God has abandoned me, I remember His word that shows me that He is a God who cares deeply for me and for any of His children who are hurting. He says, "Comfort, O comfort My people." He is near to the brokenhearted and saves me when I am crushed in spirit. In Him I find my peace because He has overcome you.

DRAW IT DOWN

Father in heaven, You have promised me comfort, so I ask for an experience of that comfort right now. You have told me that You are near when my heart is broken. God, my heart is broken. You say that You are near when I feel crushed. God, I feel crushed. I need You to make Yourself known to me right now and each day so I can feel Your presence and turn to You to satisfy and relieve my pain. In You, I have peace. Let that peace overpower me at this moment and throughout this week.

Day Four

WEAR IT

The shield of faith. "This I recall to my mind, therefore I have hope. The LORD's lovingkindnesses indeed never cease, for

His compassions never fail. They are new every morning; great is Your faithfulness. 'The LORD is my portion,' says my soul, 'therefore I have hope in Him.' The LORD is good to those who wait for Him, to the person who seeks Him. It is good that he waits silently" (Lamentations 3:21-26). "Behold, his soul which is lifted up is not upright in him: but the just shall live by his faith" (Habakkuk 2:4 KJV).

Putting on Christ. "I have been crucified with Christ; and it is no longer I who live, but Christ lives in me; and the life which I now live in the flesh I live by faith in the Son of God, who loved me and gave Himself up for me" (Galatians 2:20).

STAND IN IT

This I recall to my mind; therefore I have hope. The Lord's lovingkindnesses indeed never cease, for His compassions never fail. They are new every morning; great is Your faithfulness. The Lord is my portion, therefore I have hope in Him. The Lord is good to those who wait for Him, to the person who seeks Him. It is good that I wait silently. My soul is not lifted up in me, but instead I live by faith. I have been crucified with Christ, and it is no longer I who live, but Christ lives in me. The life that I now live in the flesh, I live by faith in the Son of God, who loved me and gave Himself up for me.

USE IT

Satan, your thoughts of discouragement must leave me because this I recall to my mind, therefore I have hope: The Lord's lovingkindnesses indeed never cease, for His compassions never fail. They are new every morning. (Great is Your faithfulness, Lord!) The Lord is my portion, so I have hope in Him. The Lord is good to those who wait for Him, to the person who seeks Him. It is good that I wait silently. I live by faith. I have been crucified with Christ, and it is no longer I who live, but Christ lives in me. The life that I now live in the flesh, I live by faith in the Son of God, who loved me and gave Himself up for me (Galatians 2:20).

Draw It Down

Father in heaven, You give me hope because Your loving-kindnesses indeed never cease, for Your compassions never fail. They are new every morning—great is Your faithfulness! You are my portion. Be my portion today, Lord. Show Yourself to me as my portion. Reveal Yourself in a way that will satisfy me fully with hope. You are good to those who wait for You, to the person who seeks You. It is good that I wait silently. I have been crucified with Christ, and it is no longer I who live, but Christ lives in me. The life that I now live in the flesh, I live by faith in the Son of God, who loved me and gave Himself up for me.

Day Five

Wear It

The helmet of salvation. "Do not let your heart be troubled; believe in God, believe also in Me. In My Father's house are many dwelling places; if it were not so, I would have told you; for I go to prepare a place for you. If I go and prepare a place for you, I will come again and receive you to Myself, that where I am, there you may be also" (John 14:1-3).

Putting on Christ. "He was pierced through for our transgressions, He was crushed for our iniquities; the chastening for our well-being fell upon Him, and by His scourging we are healed" (Isaiah 53:5).

Stand in It

I will not let my heart be troubled; I believe in God, so I believe also in Christ. In heaven are many dwelling places; if it were not so, Jesus would have told me. He is there now, preparing a place for me. He will come again and receive me to Himself so that I may be where He is. He was pierced through for my transgressions; He was crushed for my iniquities. The chastening for my well-being fell upon Him, and by His scourging I am healed.

Use It

Satan, you are trying to make my heart give up, but my heart will not be troubled. I believe in God, and I believe also in Christ. In heaven are many dwelling places; if it were not so, Jesus would have told me. He is there now, preparing a place for me. He will come again and receive me to Himself, that where He is, there I may be also. Jesus was pierced through for my transgressions; He was crushed for my iniquities. The chastening for my well-being fell upon Him, and by His scourging I am healed.

Draw It Down

Father in heaven, thank You that I do not need to worry or have my heart burdened with troubles. I believe in You and in Christ Jesus. In heaven are many dwelling places; if it were not so, Jesus would have told me. He is there now, preparing a place for me. He will come again and receive me to Himself, that where He is, there I may be also. Thank You that He was pierced through for my transgressions and that He was crushed for my iniquities. The chastening for my well-being fell upon Him, and by His scourging I am healed. Show me how to walk in the realness of that healing this very day.

Day Six/Weekend

Wear It

The sword of the Spirit. "He knows the way I take; when He has tried me, I shall come forth as gold" (Job 23:10). "For this reason I also suffer these things, but I am not ashamed; for I know whom I have believed and I am convinced that He is able to guard what I have entrusted to Him until that day" (2 Timothy 1:12).

Putting on Christ. "I am convinced that neither death, nor life, nor angels, nor principalities, nor things present, nor things to come, nor powers, nor height, nor depth, nor any other created thing, will be able to separate us from the love of God, which is in Christ Jesus our Lord" (Romans 8:38-39).

Stand in It

He knows the way I take; when He has tried me, I shall come forth as gold. For this reason I also suffer these things, but I am not ashamed. For I know whom I have believed, and I am convinced that He is able to guard what I have entrusted to Him until that day. For I am convinced that neither death, nor life, nor angels, nor principalities, nor things present, nor things to come, nor powers, nor height, nor depth, nor any other created thing will be able to separate me from the love of God, which is in Christ Jesus my Lord.

Use It

Satan, God knows about everything you are throwing at me. In fact, He knows the way I take; when He has tried me, I shall come forth as gold. For this reason I also suffer these things, but I am not ashamed. For I know whom I have believed, and I am convinced that He is able to guard what I have entrusted to Him until that day. For I am convinced that neither death, nor life, nor angels, nor principalities, nor things present, nor things to come, nor powers, nor height, nor depth, nor any other created thing will be able to separate me from the love of God, which is in Christ Jesus my Lord.

Draw It Down

Father in heaven, I trust that when You have tried me, I shall come forth as gold. For this reason I also suffer these things, but I am not ashamed. For I know that I have placed my belief in You, and I am convinced that You are able to guard what I have entrusted to You until that day. For I am convinced that neither death, nor life, nor angels, nor principalities, nor things present, nor things to come, nor powers, nor height, nor depth, nor any other created thing will be able to separate me from Your love, which is in Christ Jesus my Lord.

18

VICTORY OVER DEBT STRONGHOLDS

The Stronghold

All of our cars have indicator lights that come on to serve notice when something is wrong. When the light comes on, the problem is not with the light. The light is letting you know that there's a deeper problem.

Not long ago, an indicator light came on in our nation serving notice that we had a problem. This light showed up under several different names: recession, economic downturn, bailout, and others. What this light revealed is that a certain level of financial irresponsibility had caught up with us as a country. Not only that, but it had caught up with—and is still catching up with—many of us as individuals as well.

There is no more poignant way that this stronghold is being revealed today than in the debt level of God's people. Many in the body of Christ are living in economic slavery to the consumer debt that controls their lives. Someone once said there are the haves, the have-nots, and the have-not-paid-for-what-you-haves. Another person said, "Money talks—and it says 'Good-bye!'" Many of us, like the Seven Dwarfs, leave every morning singing, "I owe, I owe, so off to work I go." Americans are drowning in a sea of debt, and until we address the spiritual stronghold behind this destructive financial reality, we will remain in trouble, the indicator light still trying to warn us of impending danger.

To understand what victory over a debt stronghold looks like, we first need a point of reference in our understanding of what living in financial blessing—instead of financial debt—looks like.

A blessing is your capacity to experience, enjoy, and extend the goodness of God in your life. It's not merely having stuff. A blessing is the ability to enjoy the stuff you have. Many people have houses that are not a blessing because their houses are not *homes*. Many people have nice cars that are not a blessing because they hate driving that car to a job where they do not feel satisfied and fulfilled. Others have many nice clothes that are not a blessing because they're miserable on the inside while wearing them.

Blessings involve much more than mere external things. A blessing is your capacity to enjoy what God has given you with a spirit of contentment, ease, and satisfaction while simultaneously being a blessing to others. When people are no longer free to make life choices apart from how they are going to be able to continue to pay 18 percent interest (or more) on credit cards or make their mortgage or car payment while making no progress toward lessening the mountain of debt they're under, that's no longer a blessing—it's a form of slavery. As Proverbs 22:7 says, "The borrower becomes the lender's slave."

God's Viewpoint

Scripture tells us that it's abnormal for a Christian to live in debt. We read in Psalm 37:21, "The wicked borrows and does not pay back, but the righteous is gracious and gives." In Romans 13:8 we read, "Owe nothing to anyone except to love one another; for he who loves his neighbor has fulfilled the law." In fact, God makes a direct connection between spiritual responsibility and financial accountability. In Luke 16:10-11 we read, "He who is faithful in a very little thing is faithful also in much; and he who is unrighteous in a very little thing is unrighteous also in much. Therefore if you have not been faithful in the use of unrighteous wealth, who will entrust the true riches to you?" A refusal to handle money God's way can actually limit God's responsiveness to any requests you make for greater things.

Although the Bible does not condemn legitimate borrowing, it does condemn borrowing in such a way that you're not able to pay it back—or pay it back without incurring a substantial loss.

God's Solution

God's solution to the debt stronghold can be summarized with three simple words: give, save, and spend. Your financial freedom is inextricably tied to these three principles.

Give

The first principle is the initial action that should happen anytime you receive from God—*give* to Him. The average Christian in America gives less than 3 percent of his or her income to God. Roughly 85 percent of Christians do not tithe, and approximately 40 percent of Christians give nothing at all. Essentially, mass larceny is taking place in the kingdom of God, and yet we wonder why the kingdom is failing to advance in our nation and in our world. In light of how much we rob God (see Malachi 3:8), it's no surprise that we often end up as victims rather than victors in spiritual warfare. God delights in and rewards faith (Hebrews 11:6). No greater faith can be revealed with regard to your finances than that of giving to God out of what He has given to you.

Whenever God gives something, He always holds something back. For example, when God created Adam and Eve and placed them in the garden, He gave them everything except what was on one tree— the tree of the knowledge of good and evil. Adam and Eve were free to enjoy all that had been created for them in the garden except what was on that one tree. By holding something back, God reveals two things: our trust in Him and our submission to His sovereignty. The act of giving to God out of our finances and material gains will show our trust and His sovereignty.

Throughout the Bible we're instructed to honor God with the best of the resources that He has provided for us. The principle of giving shows up very early in the Scripture. One important place we see it is in the book of Genesis, where we read that Abraham gave the priest Melchizedek, king of Salem, "a tenth of all" (Genesis 14:20). Proverbs 3:9-10 gives a condition we must fulfill if we are to reap from God: We must sow to God. "Honor the LORD from your wealth and from the first of all your produce; *so* your barns will be filled with plenty and your vats will overflow with new wine." In these verses and others, God connects giving to Him with the state of the economy in which He enables you to live. He says that by trusting Him—coming underneath His authority and returning to Him a portion of what He has given to you—you open the door for Him to return to you.

In fact, God says in Malachi 3:10 that He will open up the floodgates of heaven and pour out so much that you won't even have enough room to put it all. *God longs to bless you.* He just wants to know first that you acknowledge Him as your ultimate source—that you fear Him, delight in Him, and trust Him.

God says when you honor Him with your finances, He will *then* do things for you that you could never do for yourself. God will turn things around that you didn't even know could be turned around. Right now, maybe you're so deep in debt that you can't see the way out. God can show you the way out if you will trust Him by walking in faith through giving to Him. Even more, He will also rebuke Satan and his demons from devouring what you already have (see Malachi 3:11). He will make what you do have stretch further than you thought it could.

Now, I can already hear you saying, "But Tony, didn't the practice of the tithe stop when Jesus fulfilled the Old Testament law?" That's a fair question; however, we need to remember that the tithe was first mentioned in Genesis 14:20, *before* the law was given, as we saw in reference to Melchizedek. Hebrews 7:11 tells us that Jesus came as the high priest "according to the order of Melchizedek," and verse 8 also references the continuation of the tithe. While the law has been fulfilled, both the principles behind the tithe and the priest over the tithe have continued.

The greatest truth I could ever give you regarding your finances is that God is your only source. Everything else is a *re*source. Never treat the resource as if it were the source because then the resource will control you. Not only that, the resource will get the honor, time, and attention that should be going to God. Honor God first and foremost not only through a tithe but also by giving to Him as He leads you. In so doing, you acknowledge Him as your provider. And if you're still hesitant and saying, "Tony, I can't afford to give," my response is simple, "You can't afford *not* to give." God is your Source, and giving is what He asks of you.

Save

The second word we're looking at in overcoming debt strongholds is *save*. An estimated 35 percent of all Americans have absolutely no savings. While debt is paying for yesterday, savings is putting something away for tomorrow. In Proverbs 21:20 we read that only a foolish man spends all that he has, setting aside nothing for savings. In fact, in Proverbs 13:22, Scripture equates goodness with leaving an inheritance for your grandchildren.

One of the greatest examples of savings in the Bible comes through the wisdom of Joseph. When Egypt and the surrounding nations were about to enter into a famine, Joseph advised Pharaoh, "Collect all the food of these good years that are coming and store up the grain under the authority of Pharaoh, to be kept in the cities for food. This food should be held in reserve for the country, to be used during the seven years of famine that will come upon Egypt, so that the country may not be ruined by the famine" (Genesis 41:35-36 NIV).

The story of Joseph illustrates the biblical wisdom of setting aside money now for possible hard times ahead—or for retirement. So, whatever your present income, it's essential that you set aside a portion of every dollar you earn for savings. Start somewhere because you are not only saving for your future but also for the futures of your children and children's children.

Spend

The last word we will look at in overcoming debt strongholds is *spend*. The question with regard to spending is, how do you spend well? If you don't manage your money, it will soon manage you—your emotions, time, and decisions. Proverbs 16:3 tells us that God blesses plans that have been committed to Him. We read in Proverbs 21:5 (NIV), "The plans of the diligent lead to profit." And yet in spite of this truth, many households do not operate on a budget. A budget is simply a plan. Without a plan, our spending may easily exceed what is coming in—and that's how many people accrue debt.

Another thing to consider as you make your financial plan is the difference between what you want and what you need. Philippians 4:19 assures us that "God will meet all your needs according to his glorious riches in Christ Jesus (NIV)." But what we must recognize is what is meant by "needs."

> If we have food and clothing, we will be content with that. People who want to get rich fall into temptation and a trap and into many foolish and harmful desires that plunge men into ruin and destruction. For the love of money is a root of all kinds of evil. Some people, eager for money, have wandered from the faith and pierced themselves with many griefs (1 Timothy 6:8-10).

You may not have what John and Jenny have, but that's not the point. The question is, do you have all that you need? You may want to drive a souped-up Escalade, but what you need is a dependable car. You may want a Gucci bag, but what you need is a purse. You may want a five-bedroom house, but what you need is a roof over your head.

There's nothing wrong with having material blessings if you can pay for them after you have given and after you have saved. But what we can't do is confuse our wants with our needs. We are free to spend what God has given us, but that spending needs to be done with wisdom.

When you align your finances underneath God's overarching principles of giving, saving, and spending, you will see God work in freeing you from the stronghold of debt.

Putting on the Armor of Christ

Day One

WEAR IT

The belt of truth. "The young lions do lack and suffer

hunger; but they who seek the LORD shall not be in want of any good thing" (Psalm 34:10).

Putting on Christ. "And my God will supply all your needs according to His riches in glory in Christ Jesus" (Philippians 4:19).

STAND IN IT

The young lions do lack and suffer hunger, but when I seek the LORD, I will not be in want of any good thing. My God will supply all of my needs according to His riches in glory in Christ Jesus.

USE IT

Satan, the young lions do lack and suffer hunger, but it is written that whoever seeks the Lord will not be in want of any good thing. God says He will supply all of my needs according to His riches in glory in Christ Jesus.

DRAW IT DOWN

Father in heaven, You say that even though the young lions lack and suffer hunger, if I seek You, I will not be in want of any good thing. You say that You will supply all my needs according to Your riches in glory in Christ Jesus. For these things, I thank You in advance.

Day Two

WEAR IT

The breastplate of righteousness. "The wicked borrows and does not pay back, but the righteous is gracious and gives" (Psalm 37:21). "Instruct those who are rich in this present world not to be conceited or to fix their hope on the uncertainty of riches, but on God, who richly supplies us with all things to enjoy" (1 Timothy 6:17).

Putting on Christ. "In everything I showed you that by working hard in this manner you must help the weak and remember the words of the Lord Jesus, that He Himself said, 'It is more blessed to give than to receive'" (Acts 20:35).

STAND IN IT

The wicked borrows and does not pay back, but I will be gracious and give. I will fix my hope on God, who richly supplies me with all things to enjoy. In everything I will work hard so that I can help the weak while remembering the words of the Lord Jesus, who said, "It is more blessed to give than to receive."

USE IT

Satan, God says that the wicked borrows and does not pay back, but I am to be gracious and give. I am to fix my hope on God, who richly supplies me with all things to enjoy. In everything I am to work hard so that I can help the weak because Jesus says that it is more blessed to give than to receive.

DRAW IT DOWN

Father in heaven, please help me to pay back everything I owe and then live in such a way that I am not burdened by debt. Help me not to become what You have called a wicked person, who borrows and does not pay back. Rather, help me to be gracious and give. I have put my hope in You because You are the One who richly supplies me with all things to enjoy. In everything, give me strength to work hard so that I can help the weak.

Day Three

WEAR IT

The shoes of peace. "You shall remember the LORD your God, for it is He who is giving you power to make wealth, that He may confirm His covenant which He swore to your fathers, as it is this day" (Deuteronomy 8:18). "Humble yourselves under the mighty hand of God, that He may exalt you at the proper time, casting all your anxiety on Him, because He cares for you" (1 Peter 5:6-7).

Putting on Christ. "And when the Chief Shepherd appears, you will receive the unfading crown of glory" (1 Peter 5:4).

STAND IN IT

It is God who gives me power to make wealth. I will humble myself underneath His mighty hand so that He may exalt me at the proper time. I will cast all my anxiety on Him because He cares for me. And when the Chief Shepherd appears, I will receive the unfading crown of glory.

USE IT

Satan, it is God, and not you, who gives me the power to make wealth. His mighty hand lifts me when I am humbled beneath Him. He exalts me at the proper time, so I do not need to worry about how things are going to work out because He cares for me. When the Chief Shepherd appears, I will receive the unfading crown of glory.

DRAW IT DOWN

Father in heaven, You give me the power to make wealth. I am asking to access that power in You as I align myself humbly beneath Your mighty hand. I give You all of my fears, worries, and doubts because You care for me. I thank You that when the Chief Shepherd appears, I will receive the unfading crown of glory.

Day Four

WEAR IT

The shield of faith. "Make sure that your character is free from the love of money, being content with what you have; for He Himself has said, 'I will never desert you, nor will I ever forsake you'" (Hebrews 13:5).

Putting on Christ. "Thanks be to God, who always leads us in triumph in Christ, and manifests through us the sweet aroma of the knowledge of Him in every place" (2 Corinthians 2:14).

STAND IN IT

I choose to be free from the love of money, being content with what I have. God Himself has said, "I will never desert you, nor will I ever forsake you." Thanks be to God, who always leads me in triumph in Christ and manifests through me the sweet aroma of the knowledge of Him in every place.

USE IT

Satan, you lure me with money and what money can provide, but God says I am to be free from the love of money, being content with what I have. God Himself has said, "I will never desert you, nor will I ever forsake you." God always leads me in triumph in Christ and manifests through me the sweet aroma of the knowledge of Him in every place.

DRAW IT DOWN

Father in heaven, convict me through Your Holy Spirit and Your Word if I have the stronghold of the love of money, and then set me free through confession, repentance, and forgiveness. For You Yourself have said, "I will never desert you, nor will I ever forsake you." Thank You for leading me in triumph in Christ and manifesting through me the sweet aroma of the knowledge of You in every place.

Day Five

WEAR IT

The helmet of salvation. "Beloved, I pray that in all respects you may prosper and be in good health, just as your soul prospers" (3 John 2).

Putting on Christ. "The thief comes only to steal and kill and destroy; I came that they may have life, and have it abundantly" (John 10:10).

STAND IN IT

In all respects I will prosper and be in good health, just as my soul prospers. The thief comes only to steal and kill and destroy, but Christ came that I may have life and have it abundantly.

USE IT

Satan, the Word of God says that in all respects I will prosper and be in good health, just as my soul prospers. You have come only to steal and kill and destroy. Christ came that I may have life and have it abundantly.

DRAW IT DOWN

Father in heaven, thank You that in all respects I can prosper and be in good health, just as my soul prospers. Even though the thief comes to steal and kill and destroy, You have sent Christ that I may have life and have it abundantly. Let me live in light of this truth today, experiencing all of the abundant life You sent Jesus to secure for me.

Day Six/Weekend

WEAR IT

The sword of the Spirit. "I have been young and now I am old, yet I have not seen the righteous forsaken or his descendants begging bread" (Psalm 37:25).

Putting on Christ. "The book of the prophet Isaiah was handed to Him. And He opened the book and found the place where it was written, 'The Spirit of the Lord is upon me, because He anointed me to preach the gospel to the poor. He has sent me to proclaim release to the captives, and recovery of sight to the blind, to set free those who

are oppressed, to proclaim the favorable year of the Lord'"
(Luke 4:17-19).

STAND IN IT

David has said that he has never seen the righteous forsaken
or his descendants begging bread. When Jesus came, He
proclaimed, "The Spirit of the Lord is upon me, because
He anointed me to preach the gospel to the poor. He has
sent me to proclaim release to the captives, and recovery of
sight to the blind, to set free those who are oppressed, to
proclaim the favorable year of the Lord."

USE IT

Satan, God does not forsake the righteous. Neither do their
descendants beg for bread. Jesus Christ came to preach the
gospel to the poor and to proclaim release to the captives
and recovery of sight to the blind. He has set free those
who are oppressed by you and has proclaimed the favorable year of the Lord.

DRAW IT DOWN

Father in heaven, because of You, the righteous are not forsaken. He who trusts in You will always have enough and
never have to beg. Jesus Christ has come to proclaim my
release and the favorable year of the Lord. Because of Jesus,
I know that I have all that I need. Thank You for giving me
back what Satan has stolen. Help me to walk in Your ways
and to experience what You have in store.

SCRIPTURE INDEX

About Dr. Tony Evans...

Dr. Tony Evans is one of the country's most respected evangelical leaders. The first African-American to graduate with a doctoral degree from Dallas Theological Seminary (DTS), he served as an associate professor in the DTS Pastoral Ministries Department in the areas of evangelism, homiletics, and Black church studies.

Dr. Evans has served as the senior pastor of Oak Cliff Bible Fellowship for more than 35 years, witnessing its growth from ten people in 1976 to now more than 8500 congregants and over 100 ministries.

Dr. Evans also serves as president of The Urban Alternative, a national ministry that seeks to bring about spiritual renewal in America through the church. His daily radio broadcast, *The Alternative with Tony Evans*, can be heard on more than 600 stations throughout the United States and in 40 countries.

Through his local church and national ministry, Dr. Evans has set in motion a Kingdom Agenda philosophy of ministry that teaches God's comprehensive rule over every area of life as demonstrated through the individual, family, church, and society.

Dr. Tony Evans is married to Lois, his wife and ministry partner of over 40 years. They are the proud parents of four (Chrystal, Priscilla, Anthony Jr., and Jonathan) as well as proud grandparents of ten (Kariss, Jessica, Jackson, Jesse Jr., Jerry Jr., Kanaan, Jude, Joel, Kelsey, and Jonathan II).

THE URBAN ALTERNATIVE
The National ministry of Dr. Tony Evans

The Philosophy

Dr. Tony Evans and The Urban Alternative (TUA) equip, empower, and unite Christians to impact individuals, families, churches, and communities for rebuilding lives from the inside out.

We believe the core cause of the problems we face in our personal lives, homes, and societies is a spiritual one; therefore, the only way to address them is spiritually. We've tried political, social, economic, and even religious agendas. It's time for a Kingdom Agenda—God's visible and comprehensive rule over every area of life.

The Purpose

TUA ministers to a world in chaos with the goal of restoring every area of life to its divine order under the rule of God. When each biblical sphere of life functions in accordance with God's Word, the net results are evangelism, discipleship, and community impact. As people learn how to govern themselves under God, they then transform the institutions of family, church, and society from a biblically based kingdom perspective.

The Programs

To achieve our goal we use a variety of strategies, methods, and resources for reaching and equipping as many people as possible.

Broadcast Media

Hundreds of thousands of individuals experience *The Alternative with Tony Evans* through the daily radio broadcast, which plays on more than 600 stations and in more than 40 countries. The broadcast can also be seen on several television networks and is viewable online at TonyEvans.tv.

Leadership Training

THE KINGDOM AGENDA LEADERSHIP CONFERENCE

This conference progressively develops churches to meet the demands of the twenty-first century while maintaining the gospel message and the strategic position of the church. The conference introduces intensive seminars, workshops, and resources, addressing issues affecting...

> community
> family
> leadership
> organizational health and growth
> ministry programs
> theology, Bible, and more

PASTORS' WIVES MINISTRY

Founded by Dr. Lois Evans, this ministry provides counsel, encouragement, and spiritual resources for pastors' wives as they serve with their husbands in the ministry. A primary focus of the ministry is the First Lady Conference, which offers senior pastors' wives a safe place to reflect, renew, relax, and receive training in personal development, spiritual growth, and care for their emotional and physical well-being.

THE KINGDOM AGENDA FELLOWSHIP OF CHURCHES (KAFOC)

This fellowship provides a viable network for like-minded pastors who embrace the Kingdom Agenda philosophy. Pastors have the opportunity to go deeper with Dr. Tony Evans as they are given greater biblical knowledge, practical applications, and resources to impact individuals, families, churches, and communities. KAFOC welcomes senior and associate pastors of churches regardless of size, denominational affiliation, or race.

NATIONAL CHURCH ADOPT-A-SCHOOL INITIATIVE (NCAASI)

This initiative prepares churches across the country to impact communities by using public schools as the primary vehicle for effecting positive social change in urban youth and families. This training is patterned after Dr. Tony Evans' local outreach model, The Turn•Around Agenda. Leaders of churches, school districts, faith-based organizations, and other nonprofit organizations are equipped with the knowledge and tools to forge partnerships and build strong social-service delivery systems.

Resource Development

We are fostering lifelong learning partnerships with the people we serve by providing a variety of published materials. We offer booklets, books, CDs, and DVDs to strengthen people in their walk with God and ministry to others.

Contact us for more information on TUA, a catalog of Dr. Tony Evans' ministry resources, and a complimentary copy of Dr. Evans' devotional newsletter.

TUA
PO Box 4000
Dallas TX 75208
(800) 800-3222
TonyEvans.org

To learn more about Harvest House books and
to read sample chapters, log on to our website:

www.harvesthousepublishers.com

HARVEST HOUSE PUBLISHERS
EUGENE, OREGON